Arthur William Upfield is well known as the creator of Detective Inspector Napoleon Bonaparte (Bony) who features in 29 crime detection novels, most set in the Australian outback. He also wrote more than 220 short stories and articles, based on his experiences in the bush between 1911 and 1931.

Up and Down the Real Australia is the second published collection of Upfield's short works. Kees de Hoog has selected 45 autobiographical articles, ranging from humorous outback anecdotes to personal experiences at Gallipoli and the Somme during the First World War.

Kees has added *The Murchison Murders*, Upfield's account of how the "perfect murder" was developed for his second Bony novel, *The Sands of Windee*; how Snowy Rowles used it to commit at least one, probably three, murders in 1929; how the crime was solved; and what happened at Rowles' trial in 1932.

Up and Down the Real Australia

Arthur Upfield

Edited and Introduced by

Kees de Hoog

ETT Imprint
Exile Bay

This edition published by ETT Imprint, Exile Bay 2016

ETT IMPRINT

PO Box R1906

Royal Exchange NSW 1225

Australia

First published by Lulu Enterprises 2009

ISBN 9781925416640 (pbk)
ISBN 9781925416435 (ebk)

Contents

Introduction

Arthur Upfield is well known to aficionados of crime detection novels as the creator of the Australian Detective Inspector Napoleon Bonaparte (Bony) who appears in twenty-nine novels written over forty-two years from 1924 to 1966. It is not so well known that Upfield also wrote six other published novels, and many short stories and articles published in newspapers and magazines in Australia and other countries.

He was born in 1890 into a family of drapers at Gosport on Portsmouth Bay in England. An avid reader of boys' adventure magazines, at school he did well only in subjects that took his interest. Apprenticed to a firm of estate agents, auctioneers and surveyors just before his sixteenth birthday, he was more interested in writing novels and other, more daring, escapades. He once claimed his father sent him to Australia in despair, saying: "It is so far away that you will never save enough money to return,"[1] but it is more likely he wanted to go.[2]

Soon after arriving in Adelaide in 1911, Upfield went to the outback where he worked in a variety of jobs including fence building, boundary riding, droving and opal digging. He quickly developed a lasting passion for the Australian bush that laid the foundations for the rest of his life,[3] and eventually carried his swag to all the mainland states and the Northern Territory.

On the outbreak of World War I in 1914, he joined the Australian Imperial Forces and served in Egypt, Gallipoli, England and France. Returning to Australia in 1921 with a wife and child, and probably still suffering from shell shock, he "went bush" again soon afterwards as he could not tolerate working in a Melbourne factory and missed the outback lifestyle.

Upfield had continued to write desultorily, and in 1924 was persuaded to "have a go" at writing professionally, drawing on his experiences in the bush.[4] After four novels and a number of short articles and stories had been published, he left the bush in 1931 to

[1] Hetherington J, *Forty-two Faces*, Melbourne: Cheshire, 1962, p21.

[2] See Upfield A W, "The Land of Opportunity, Part 1," *The Wide World Magazine*, Vol 61, No 365, August 1928, pp363-374; and "The Musical Hut."

[3] See "Opal Goughing."

[4] One version of this story is in "The Call of the Wild."

join his family in Perth, and to write full time. Two years later he moved to Melbourne to join *The Herald* newspaper, but resumed freelance writing after about six months.

His production of short stories and articles was most prolific between 1931 and 1940 as he sought to supplement the income from his novels. Of more than 220 of his published short stories and articles I have found, about 170 were published during those nine years.

Upfield joined Australian military intelligence as a censor during World War II. With much less time for writing, he sent some Bony novels to a United States publisher in 1943. Americans had become interested in Australia through their troops visiting and stationed here during the war, and the books were very popular. Within a few years most of the earlier Bony novels were published there, as were those he wrote later. The extra sales allowed Upfield to live comfortably from writing mainly Bony novels until his death in 1964.

For this anthology I have selected forty-five autobiographical articles based on his life experiences during the twenty years after he first arrived in Australia, plus *The Murchison Murders*. Many of the articles are anecdotes, while others reflect fond memories and observations. All but nine were first published in 1934; eight were earlier, and the other in 1935. The previous publication details I have so far uncovered for each article are listed under the heading "Sources"at the end.

My selection of Upfield's short stories, *Up and Down Australia*, was published last year.[5] As a companion volume, this selection has been given a similar title. The words "the Real" were inserted to reflect his view, expressed several times in these articles, that the interior of the Australia – the outback or the bush – is the part of Australia that he cherished. He put it much more eloquently when he wrote:

> "Cities bore me. Farming country leaves me cold. Neither cities nor the farming country is Australia, the real Australia adequately described only by the immortal Lawson. . . There are dozens of Melbournes in the world, a dozen Sydneys. There is only one Australia, a virgin, living Australia unspoiled by brick and cement, axe and plough, the Australia which can reveal a thousand facets of beauty, and never fail to reveal at least one."[6]

[5] Upfield A, de Hoog K (Ed), *Up and Down Australia: Short Stories*, Lulu.com, 2008.
[6] See "Opal Gouging".

With the extra words the title also reflects the autobiographical flavour of the selection.

This anthology does not constitute an autobiography of Upfield. He did, in fact, start writing an autobiography in 1934 with early drafts called *The Tale of a Pommy.*[7] He finished it in 1938, renamed *Beyond the Mirage*,[8] but he could not get it published. It covers roughly the same period as this selection and contains a number of very similar anecdotes. I suspect he wrote the articles first and later incorporated many of them into *Mirage*.

Upfield's official biography, *Follow my Dust*, by his then partner Jessica Hawke, was published in 1957.[9] It also includes many of the same anecdotes and themes but, like *Mirage*, it includes no details of his war service. In addition, it makes only one passing reference to his marriage, and none to his son, and there are many inconsistencies with *Mirage*.

Arthur William Upfield: A Biography by Travis Lindsey was published in 2005. It is an academic thesis that gives a comprehensive account of Upfield's life, works, philosophy and outlook, and positions him "as a writer in the context of the first half of 20th century Australian history . . . who dealt with issues of Aboriginality at a time when this was an under-theorized area of critical knowledge." Lindsey's biography is thoroughly researched and is undoubtedly much more factually accurate than either *Mirage* or *Dust*.[10]

Another biography, *Arthur W. Upfield: Life and Times of Bony's Man* by Andrew Milnor, has been published recently. It is also an academic treatise, and proposes "Australia and Arthur Upfield, both caught between immigration and nationhood, walked parallel routes [during the early 1900s] from beginning stage though to maturity and success, where each arrived at a place coincident with their characters, skills and communities."[11]

The biographies by Lindsey and Milnor refer to and draw on a number of articles in this collection, but do not quote or describe

[7] Upfield A W, *The Tale of a Pommy*, University of Melbourne, Baillieu Library, Sp/C Upfield, TALE/MS.
[8] Upfield A W, *Beyond the Mirage*, National Library of Australia, MS9590.
[9] Hawke J, *Follow My Dust*, Melbourne: Heineman, 1957.
[10] Lindsey T, *Arthur William Upfield: A Biography*, wwwlib.murdoch.edu.au/adt/browse/view/adt-MU20051003.113934, 2005, p1.
[11] Milnor A J, *Arthur W. Upfield: Life and Time of Bony's Man*, Newcastle: Cambridge Scholars, 2008, p2.

them at length. It therefore makes sense to read these articles *before* the biographies. They are much more than simply source material for Upfield's biographers – each stands alone as entertaining and informative in its own right – the reason they were written and published in the first instance. Like the readers of *Up and Down Australia*, readers of this selection will sample life in the Australian outback during the early decades of the twentieth century.

Mirage has never been published; copies of *Dust* are now hard to find and expensive, and it is unlikely to be republished because of gaps and doubts about its accuracy. My reasons for compiling this selection for publication are the same as for *Up and Down Australia* – to make this part of Upfield's life works accessible to enthusiasts, and to entertain and inform other interested readers.

It must be borne in mind, however, that Upfield employed poetic licence quite liberally in most of these articles. Indeed, I had difficulty determining whether some should be included in this selection of autobiographical articles that, by definition, should have at least some factual basis. My solution was to apply the test devised for *Up and Down Australia* in reverse, so if an element of the plot is in *Mirage* or *Dust* it could be included in this selection.

Having said that, I strongly suspect many of the articles are more fiction than fact, and that "Pimple's Elixir," in particular, has only a few drops of truth. I included it because the same unorthodox approach to making wine from grapes is mentioned in *Dust*, and another article with many similarities, "Pinky Dick's Elixir", had already been included in *Up and Down Australia*. Also, I am rather sceptical of the factual basis for "A Real Life Drama", but included it partly because I had heard similar theories while growing up in rural Australia, and because it features in several Upfield novels, such as *The Barrakee Mystery*.[12]

The articles are presented chronologically – as far as possible. Sorting them was complicated because similar stories in *Mirage* and *Dust* are not always in the same sequence, and/or their timeframes do not fit with known facts. It was made even more difficult when the articles themselves suggest different timelines.

[12] Also published as *The Lure of the Bush*.

I have done my best but accept no responsibility for "errors of chronology."

They have been grouped according to four phases of Upfield's life during the twenty years from 1911 to 1931. The first and largest group of nineteen articles covers the shortest period of less than three years before he joined the army. They are mainly amusing anecdotes of his experiences in the bush, and most are also in *Mirage*, *Dust* or both.

The next group contains accounts of his war service – two are sombre descriptions of his experiences at Gallipoli in 1915 and in France in 1917. The five articles go some way to fill the gaps in *Mirage* and *Dust*.

The third group of nine articles spans the last nine years Upfield spent in the bush from 1922 to 1931. His lifestyle during this period would have been more sedate than his pre-war years in the bush. He was more mature and had to address important personal issues such as recovering his health, his responsibilities as husband and father, and becoming a professional writer, so perhaps there were fewer memorable moments he wished to share with his readers.

Next is *The Murchison Murders*, marking the end of the period covered by this selection. While working on the No 1 Rabbit-Proof Fence in Western Australia in 1929, Upfield developed a method to dispose of a body – the perfect murder – for his next Bony novel, *The Sands of Windee*, with the help of friends and acquaintances. Fact and fiction collided when an acquaintance, Snowy Rowles, adopted that method when he murdered at least one person, and probably two more, later that year. As a consequence, Upfield was almost charged with criminal offences, and was summoned to give evidence at Rowles' trial in Perth in 1932. Rowles was found guilty and hanged.

The Murchison Murders is Upfield's account of devising the "perfect murder", of how the murder was detected and the murderer was found, and of the trial proceedings.[13] It was commissioned and first published in 1934 by Bernard Cronin as a sixty-page booklet,[14] and republished by Dennis McMillan in 1987. Copies of both publications are rare and expensive; only a

[13] See also Walker T, *Murder on the Rabbit Proof Fence*, Perth: Hesperian, 1993.
[14] The booklet is undated but 1934 is the accepted date based on other evidence.

few copies of the 1934 booklet can be found in libraries, and McMillan printed only 600 copies.

Upfield's involvement in the case was a major turning point in his life. Exposure in the Australian press boosted sales of his books and demand for his articles.[15] It gave him the confidence to leave the bush and become a full-time professional writer in 1931.

The final group consists of twelve articles in which Upfield looked back on aspects of his life.

Like his short fiction, many of these articles have themes, events and characters in common with his other works. There is drought in "Waiting for Rain" as in *Death of a Lake* and "Why Markham Bought a Radio" in *Up and Down Australia*; there is a sandstorm in "A Dog-proof Fence Job" as in *Wings Above the Diamantina*[16] and "The Dream That Did Not Come True" in *Up and Down Australia*; and the dangers of living alone in the bush are highlighted in "Two Camels and a Goanna" and "The Man Who Lost Count" as in *The Bone is Pointed* and "The Stalker of Lone Men" in *Up and Down Australia.*

The Midnight Mail is mentioned in "The Ration Sheep" and he stars in "The Dream That Did Not Come True" and "Frozen Pumps" in *Up and Down Australia*; Dead March Harry appears out of the night in "The Man Who Thought He Was Dead" and also in *The Body at Madman's Bend*;[17] and Rainbow Harry is a cook in "Tramping by the Darling" and "The Test of Good Cooking" as well as in *The Barakee Mystery* and "The Great Rabbit Lure" in *Up and Down Australia.*

The articles in this selection reflect the attitudes and the ways of talking about women and Australian aborigines in the early 1930s. By selecting them for this anthology I do not endorse those attitudes and opinions.

I am grateful to the late Arthur Upfield for writing the articles in the first instance, and to Bonaparte Holdings Pty Ltd for permission to publish them. I thank the staff of the Battye Library in Perth, the National Library of Australia in Canberra, the State Library of Victoria in Melbourne, and the Mitchell Library in Sydney, who helped me to find them. And last, but not least, I am

[15] For example, *The Sands of Windee* was serialised in a local newspaper during the trial.
[16] Also published as *Winged Mystery* and *Wings above the Claypan*.
[17] Also published as *Madman's Bend*.

grateful to my wife, Margaret Robertson, who advised and encouraged me throughout the search and the publication process.

I hope readers enjoy these articles as much as I did collecting, selecting, editing and introducing them.

Kees de Hoog
Perth Western Australia
January 2009

Going Bush

Australia was extraordinarily blessed when in 1910 a young man landed in Adelaide, his mind filled with allusions of a beautiful farm and a rose-clad cottage easily created from land even more easily obtained from a Government which, figuratively, had gone on its knees to implore him to migrate.

However, that migration was dictated less by immigration propaganda than by a doctor's views on the probable state of my health if I remained in England a further three years – as well as by two considerations of almost equal importance.

To use a war-time expression – I was a dud. During the three years I attended my last school I was kept in the same class. In history and geography I headed it both in term work and in examination; in all other subjects I was not even an "also ran." I never ran at all.

Not a rich man my father nevertheless paid a hundred guineas to article me for three years to an estate agent and surveyor. When serving the articleship I was supposed to pass three examinations which would make me a Fellow of the Auctioneers' Institute of London. But, bless you! despite the expenditure of more money on coaching fees, I wrote a 150,000 word novel on the Yellow Peril and wrote political letters to the editor of the local paper as from two heated gentlemen – which he published.

The doctor was wise in his generation. He pointed a way out. Only fools wrote novels. Only youthful idiots wasted time courting girls. Send this particular idiot to Australia. Australia will make him or break him.

Followed then a short but intensive study of immigration literature, more elaborate, more beautiful than any gold brick prospectus, further money spent on a passage, and lo! the fool arrived one spring morning in Adelaide.

During a short stay in the City of Churches I met several young men who had left my home town a year or so before I did to become Australian farmers. One was a tram conductor; another was a delivery van driver; and a third was preparing for the Methodist ministry. From them I received most peculiar views anent farming in Australia – peculiar because diametrically opposed to all those facts and figures and pictures I had assimilated from Australian literature. My inexperience prompted me to reject such opinions as having been given by men this country had proved to be without backbone.

Those were the years when Australia really and truly was a workingman's Paradise; when there were about two jobs vacant for every man offering. At every station to Pinaroo, farmers waited on the off chance of persuading a new chum to leave the train to work for him instead of going on to his assigned destination. It was all comparatively new land when wheat was selling at 4/2 a bushel, and when machinery, horses and labour were cheap. Another thing which was plentiful was loan money.

My employer was a German, farming five miles out of Pinaroo, and whilst we drove to the farm in a springless buckboard, I failed to see any lush pastures, any fat and glossy cows, and not one sweet little rose-clad cottage of which my girl and I had dreamed in England. The German's house amazed me. It was built of hessian stretched on a bush frame which supported a corrugated iron roof – all delightfully cool for that time of the year.

Even more amazed did I become at my own quarters – an old 2000-gallon rain tank turned upside down, and having an opening cut for a door. Within was a roughly made bush bunk.

"It's pretty hot in here just now," remarked my employer. "But you won't notice it because we don't live indoors much."

He was right. We did not live indoors much. I was aroused at three o'clock every morning. By the first glimmer of daylight the horses had been fed and harnessed, our own breakfast eaten. We carted hay until eight o'clock, and at nine o'clock, or when it was hot enough to strip, took out a second team to strip till noon. It was eight o'clock in the evening before I had washed up the eating utensils, and nine o'clock before I crept to bed.

Alas! like my friends I had no backbone. I determined to be a tram conductor, or a delivery van driver, or a minister. And one of the hardest letters ever I wrote was that bitter disillusioned outpouring to the girl in England. All the way out into and back from the Pinaroo country I saw not one farm which came anywhere near the ideal painted on my brain by that immigration literature.

I secured a job in one of Adelaide's largest hotels as "fourth cook." My, what a job that was! If only I had stuck to it. The chef was drawing £20 a week. He liked me and offered to teach me all he knew – which would not be in five minutes. We worked from seven to one, and from four to seven o'clock. We ate just what we liked, and in less than a fortnight the best was not good enough.

"There will be overtime for all hands," was one day announced. "A Colonel is giving a special dinner to commemorate some battle or other."

"Do you know how to make iced coffee royal?" I was asked by the chef who had called me into his office. "No? Well I'll show you. Go down to the bar and get this order. Bring it here."

On the order were rum and vermouth and brandy, and twelve bottles of beer. It occurred to me that vermouth might possibly go into the coffee royal but I was sure that bottled beer did not.

"The beer? That's all right. Put all the order in my office. The beer, you idiot, is for the staff."

Eight tall Cleopatra needles of iced coffee royal went into the private dining room, and about six came out. Beside us cooks, the waiters had a share in the beer, but they had no share in the iced coffee royal. That night the chef slept on the first back landing to his room, the second cook chose the ice chamber for his resting place, whilst I found the bread table good enough.

Yes, I was mentally deficient to leave that job, but, you see, I was young; I still retained some illusions. I knew that beyond the horizon was adventure and romance. Wheat! Pouf! Gold – opals – cattle – sheep – riding horses – camp fires, and the long, long track awinding.

The door to this alluring world was shown me by an advertisement which read:

Boundary Riders
wanted for Northern Stations.
Apply Younger Jones and Co.

"How long have you been in the country?" asked the poker-faced Secretary of a pastoral company.

"Two months, sir."

"Oh! Can you ride?"

"Yes. I was in the Hampshire Yeomanry."

"Oh! Can you kill a sheep?"

"I think I can manage that all right – even if I have to take an axe."

"Oh! I don't think you have enough experience yet to go north as a boundary rider."

"You give me a chance and see," I pleaded.

"Nothing doing. Good day."

At the same time the next day I again applied.

"I told you yesterday that there's nothing doing."

The next day I applied at the same time – with the same result. The following day I was snarled at and ordered to keep out. At the sixth successive application I won.

"Confound you! I'll send you to get rid of you," the poker-faced man actually howled.

Among pastoral companies there then was a system in vogue to send young men to cattle and sheep stations, paying their fares, which was deducted from their wages, and repaid if they remained twelve months. As a man who had been legally bound to an employer for three years, I discovered in Australia the admirable custom of being sacked on leaving a job at a moment's notice. Oh! Here was democracy! Here was freedom!

The hotel manager smiled and gave me advice with the pay envelope. The French-Australian chef swore, then wept, at losing a pupil, and sent out a coffee royal order which did not contain vermouth and rum – only beer. He gave me a hamper which must have cost the hotel a fiver, and, standing beside the poker-faced secretary, watched me slide out of Adelaide as though I were Sydney Carton riding away to the guillotine.

The jumbled hills of the Barrier Range were my first glimpse of the Australia which was to become the passion of my life. Broken Hill was then in its heyday, but I saw little of it, for I arrived at eight o'clock, and left for Wilcannia, on the Darling, at ten o'clock, on the box of a Cobb and Co.'s coach.

The driver knew and recited every poem written by the immortal Lawson. His father drove coaches stuck up by the Kelly heroes. The coach, the vast, flat saltbush plain, beyond the horizon of which, as the day wore on, the hills sank like blue-black rocks, the immensity of this world of space, all spelt romance. The grooms at the horse changes, set twenty miles apart, were the real thing in Texas gunmen, although their clothes recalled bargees. The Toper Hotel, situated at the edge of the mulga lands, at which we arrived at dusk, was the original saloon at Dead Man's Gulch.

All that night, and until two o'clock the next afternoon, I rode the box of a jolting coach. Without sleep on the train, without sleep on the coach, the people of Wilcannia witnessed the arrival of a stunned youth. Not then did I know that in the Queen City of the West there were nearly twenty hotels, a very fine gaol, and a brewery, and that on Saturday nights one had to elbow one's way along the sidewalks.

Lashed to the seat of a buckboard, I left with the Wanaaring mail at four o'clock. Every time the horses stopped, I slept; every time they started, an iron-hard elbow was dug into my ribs to awaken me.

At midnight I was informed that here "I got off." Together with the Tearle Station mail and my suitcase, I fell off. The buckboard vanished in the darkness of a calm, hot night. The ground beneath my feet was yet warm, soft, sandy. No feathered bed was ever so welcomed.

And then a voice, drawling and compassionate, said:

"Better get up and have some breakfast. If you stops there the sun'll burn the whiskers off you."

I had arrived at the land of my dreams.

One-Spur Dick

To One-Spur Dick I owe a debt never to be repaid. Here on Tearle Station, western New South Wales, set down in the middle of the night by a mail driver, blurred into obscurity by lack of sleep, it had been One-Spur Dick whose drawling injunction to "Get up before the sun burns the whiskers off you," which awoke me to this new world.

Fully dressed, I arose from the soft sand beside the track where I had collapsed like a pricked balloon into unconsciousness on alighting from the buckboard, to observe four men regarding me with amused eyes.

"Another parcel post bloke," one observed as though I were a beetle.

"Yass. English or Orstralian?"

"What are you, young feller?" inquired a one-eyed, thick-set, whiskery, sun-blackened man, dressed in blue shirt and moleskin pants, and wearing but one draggled spur.

"English," was my reply, then to gaze around me at the stone-built bungalow house and the skirting corrugated-iron buildings.

I slept part of the time I ate breakfast, and retained a dim memory of being escorted by the whiskery man to the men's hut in which I slept that day and night. The following morning, with the others, I presented myself to the manager for orders, and was told to assist the tinsmith. He was making two 4,000-gallon iron water tanks, and my job was to hold a hammer-head against which he riveted the curved iron sheets. It was mid-February and the sun was trying.

For two weeks I lived in close contact with Blue Evans, a fourteen-stone Welshman; Mick Conolly, a tall, flashily dressed stockman; Sam, a full blood aboriginal; Sam, No. 2, a half-caste who shot galahs on the wing with a 0.22 bore rifle; the Wandering Burglar, wife of one Charlie Monger, and the mother of eight children, only two of whom were not half-castes; and One-Spur Dick, then the bullock driver.

Never before had I met such people; never have I met their like beyond outer Central Australia. Their language was terrific, saved from crudeness by its artistry. Their leg-pulling was severe;

tempers quick, and fists hard. Their hearts were big, their humour dry, and the standard of general knowledge surprisingly high.

The tanks having been made, I was sent as offsider to One-Spur Dick to fetch in the winter wood supply, with fourteen bullocks drawing an ordinary waggon; and during the morning of the first day, when we were among dense mulga, it occurred to me how I would get back to the homestead were my companion to drop dead.

The one-eyed driver – he had lost an eye in a fight at Mt. Brown – sternly repressed a leering grin and commanded me to use my brain. For half-an-hour I endeavoured to do this, my cursed imagination producing vivid pictures of a lost man dying of thirst. Eventually admitting my failure to use my brain, Dick said with grave deliberateness:

"I like a bloke who arsts questions. I got no time for a bloke, be he new chum English or new chum Australian, wot thinks he knows everything and arsts no questions to hide his ignorance. Now you see them wheel tracks? You go and stand in one of 'em with your back towards the waggon."

Having done as he ordered, he said: "Now shut your eyes. Got 'em shut?"

Receiving my affirmative answer, he said: "Now you keep your eyes shut and walk in that track for twenty minutes, and you'll knock out your mosquito brain against the store wall."

Here is an illustration typifying the character of this great man. When assured that in me he had a willing pupil, nothing was too much trouble to explain, and nothing was ever explained unless accompanied by a lesson which could not be forgotten. He taught me how to bake a damper, how to kill and dress a sheep, how to make horse hobbles, how to ride in the Australian fashion, and how to use my fists. He demonstrated that neither bullocks nor mules nor horses understood pure English or pure Chinese, but would pull like the devil when addressed with a proper mixture of all the oaths of both nations, topped up, as it were, by the worst oaths favoured by the Afghans.

"Here, have a go at 'em," he urged on our first 120-mile trip to Broken Hill with wool.

He stopped the team. I took up the eight-foot whip. He climbed up to the top of the mountain of wool and pretended to go to sleep.

I called to the team of sixteen mules. The leaders looked around with bored curiosity. Twice I almost managed to choke myself to death with the whip. When I managed to lash the shafters, they pulled the waggon forward, but the front part of the team one and all yawned. Three times I fell flat, tipped by the whip. I played on a simple variation of two bad words, but they were seasoned, hackneyed, British oaths, and of no earthly use. The team was enjoying a quiet siesta whilst I became very hot.

And then over them, rushing outward through the quiet bush, roared a flood of language of such artistry as to be unequalled in any other part of the world. The effect was electrical. Sixteen animals, a huge table top waggon and ten tons of wool abruptly sped towards Broken Hill. As the waggon passed, I managed to grab an eye-bolt at its rear, and despite entanglement with the whip, kept with it.

Without using the single near-side rein – Dick scorned such aid excepting when negotiating the steep hills of the Barrier Range – my chief pulled up the astounded mules as easily as he had started them – with his voice.

Eventually, having learned the language, I got on much better.

My memories of Dick are still vivid. I see him trudging beside the team, an old felt hat set back on his head, the one clanking spur, the long-handled whip over his shoulder with the thong trailing along the ground making a snake track. The whip he seldom used; it was seldom necessary. Swags unrolled on the ground, my head towards the fire which he carefully fed to keep a good light, I read aloud for hours Sexton Blakes, and the work of Stanley Weyman and Charles Darwin. Unable to read, his memory was prodigious, his appetite for any quality of food contained between covers insatiable, equalled only by that for beer when that kind of food was available.

Three trips we made to Broken Hill that winter, going south with a mountain of wool, returning north with a mountain of cased rations and fencing wire. The two leaders and the two shafters were allegedly broken in. The twelve body mules we broke in on the track. Twice I saw a pair of hoofs presented one foot beyond my face; once the sleeve of my dungaree jacket was torn away.

Towards the end of the trip the team was settling down, but the end of the third trip dictated a change of employment. It so happened that camping a night on the Wilcannia Common, coming back we failed to find two of the mules the next morning, and were compelled to go on without them. I was sent to the Common Ranger to report the matter, and, having done this, I found the team drawn up outside the Globe Hotel and poor Dick very drunk within.

"Best thing to do is for us to plant him on top of the load, and for you to drive out of town and camp," said the publican. "You can't pull the team out here."

I thought the best thing he could have done was not to permit Dick to become drunk. I was a mule driver. I was a new chum. There were four mules which even then required our united efforts to unharness and harness.

So they shifted the load a little and made a hole in the top of the mountain into which Dick was dumped, and picking up the whip I whistled to the team, uttered some of the Esperanto of the bush, and away we went.

Now we were bound for the Tearle outstation, to reach which it was necessary to cross the dry Parroo River, a few miles out of town. There were two ways of crossing it: over the bridge, or by taking the track twisting down one bank and up the other. Twice before we had come this way, and because Dick feared that the team would be frightened by the bridge rumble, he had chosen twisting river bed track.

Discovering that I was getting along famously, knowing that this part of the Common was as bare of feed as a city street, I determined to push on until Dick regained consciousness. And now there was the white-painted long bridge making me debate which crossing I would take, and before I had made any decision the leaders reached the bridge.

Now they were on it, their hoofs sounding hollowly on the loose flooring. One of the body mules snorted. Now the shafters, now the waggon itself was on the bridge. I clung to the brake handle, praying that if they bolted they would not draw the waggon over the bridge on my side. And then, when halfway across, Dick roared, and the team instantly stopped.

I looked up. I saw his face peering over the edge of the mountain. His frozen eyes were gazing down, down beyond me, down to the river bed fifty feet below the bridge. The team was halted. Several of the mules were snorting like donkeys. The leaders looked likely enough to turn and rush back. Dick's voice was a faint whisper.

"Go on – get 'em off the bridge," he implored, incapable of any other thought, mentally and physically frozen with horror – in a place where angels would fear to tread. Six feet either side of the waggon was a fifty-foot drop.

We would have been across the bridge ere then had he not come to. I was now as windy as poor Dick enduring a nightmare, but with unmeasured luck, although three of the team began to plunge, the leaders pulled straight as did the shafters.

Once clear of the bridge Dick stopped the team and very nearly fell down off the load. In Chinese he described my ancestors back for 500 years, danced with rage, and rushed away to return to the hotel.

Thereabouts was no place to camp even if I did successfully manage to unharness the team, and, even had I done this, it would have been impossible to harness them in the morning, new chum as I was. There was nothing else for it but to accept the gamble and to push on to the outstation singlehanded, despite two bad creeks to cross.

Yet babies, drunken men and new chums seldom come to harm. Taking that team on to the outstation I thought was something heroic, but the fellows could not see it. All they could visualize was Dick looking over the edge of the ration mountain down to the dry bed of the river.

But to One-Spur Dick I owed a thorough breaking in, and the acquisition of a new and up-to-date foreign language.

Opal Gouging

The six months spent under the tutorship of One-Spur Dick did more for me than to remove the rawness of a new chum. The constant travelling over those 120 miles between Tearle Station and Broken Hill banished forever any longing for city life, delayed by twenty years the final and compulsory settling down. After the one terrible period of nostalgia, hastened by the letter from a woman in England in reply to mine describing the falsity of the immigration literature we had studied together, a letter asking to be released from her vows of fidelity, I found a mental peace never to be described with mere words. In me was born a passionate love for the Australian bush which will burn until the end, a love stronger than love of family, so strong that even now it threatens to claim me and pluck me out of a city.

In this respect I am not singular by a long shot. Cities bore me. Farming country leaves me cold. Neither cities nor the farming country is Australia, the real Australia adequately described only by the immortal Lawson. It has been written by literary folk that the great Australian novel will come out of the cities of Australia. Impossible! There are dozens of Melbournes in the world, a dozen Sydneys. There is only one Australia, a virgin, living Australia unspoiled by brick and cement, axe and plough, the Australia which can reveal a thousand facets of beauty, and never fail to reveal at least one.

Lucky the man to be broken in by One-Spur Dick who, when lounging beside the camp fire amidst the mulga or on the horizon-wide saltbush plains around Broken Hill, would recite Lawson's poems, name the glittering store which belonged to us, teach a simple philosophy born of that soft, warm earth and soft, bright sky. And, too, lucky the man to live and to labour with Jack Musgrove from Tasmania, who drank hard, laughed hard, fought hard and worked hard; when one is feeling the old accustomed world of dependence and bodily comforts and habit slipping away far beyond the skyline of a new world of independence, self-reliance, astounding interest, tolerance and content.

"Let's go opal gouging for a spell," urged Jack Musgrove, six feet three inches in his socks – when he wore them, which was seldom – three feet wide, a face like Atlas, and a fist like a ham.

Go! It was impossible to do anything else. We demanded our cheques at five o'clock one afternoon, and could not wait until the morning to start away. Twenty-one miles we tramped that night with our heavy swags, water bags and billies, and Marie Lloyd clinging to Jack's neck.

The real Marie Lloyd would have loved Jack Musgrove as much as did the black and white cat who rode him like Sinbad's Old Man of the Sea. Jack's love affairs provided a mine of doubtful anecdotes, which he would relate with winks and nods and thumb-jerks after the great Marie's inimitable fashion.

And wherever Jack went, the cat was sure to go.

At this time White Cliffs had passed its high water mark of production. Like Mt. Brown and Tibooburra, the goldfields not far distant from it, it was a poor man's show, never being taken over by powerful companies. In the '90s men went to White Cliffs, dug out pockets of opals, sold their stuff to German buyers, rushed to Sydney, Melbourne, or Adelaide, for a space lived at the millionaire rate, and then went back to dig up a second pocket; to repeat the process and find a third, and even a fourth pocket.

Naturally, that was before my time. It would be! £26 an ounce was paid for some of it, and when Queen Victoria declined to wear opals and British fashion slavishly followed suit, the harems of India provided a fresh market.

Save for investment, I see no beauty in diamonds, and but little in rubies and sapphires in comparison with the flickering green and blue and yellow and red fires in the heart of an opal. Neither did Jack Musgrove. He had opals in a shammy hung from his neck which he loved almost as much as he loved Marie Lloyd, stones with which he would not part when years later he tramped for work, the soles of his boots gone, his gunny sack empty, and with not one flake of tobacco to press into a cold and empty pipe. Opals fascinate. Diamonds are to be bought and sold, fought for, and murdered for their money value. Opal lights remind me of sunsets, of flowers, of the hope of paradise. Diamonds recall to mind, ice, hate, and a knife in the back.

At White Cliffs it was as easy to start opal gouging as to pay a

Chinaman £5 for a pack of cards, and receive from him five shillings for every card "got out" in solitaire. From an urbane celestial we hired picks and shovels and windlass gear. For a sheer gamble, opal gouging stands alone. You may strike a pocket just under the surface, or take over an abandoned shaft and strike a pocket after continuing it downward one foot.

We selected a site not far distant from an old partly wrecked hut which we utilised as a camp windbreak. I used to wonder what kind of a man built it and first lived in it, and at night I used to fancy hearing the heavy tread of men going and returning to it; always going away steadily, often returning slowly wearisome, sometimes returning at the double announcing the making of a strike.

The weather was hot, being the month of March, but what cared we for heat and flies and the dust-storms? Were we expected to work for others as we worked for ourselves, Musgrove, I am sure, would have started a revolution. He sank the shaft. I laboured at the windlass. Marie Lloyd lay stretched in a little stone-made sun-shelter erected specially for her, from which at times she would saunter to the shaft edge and look down to be assured that Jack was not asleep, or gone on a journey.

Down went the shaft, foot by foot.

Father Ryan came one morning to ask how we fared. He knew more of geology than all the geologists in Australia. Round-faced, thick-set, bespectacled, he lived among his flock which included every living soul whether he be Christian, or heathen, or had not religion at all.

"Don't be swearin' so down there," he commanded Jack, then in the bowels of the earth. "Don't be sayin' who the, what the! Just say, 'Who is that?' Brevity be the soul of wit, me bhoy. I always fine a man a penny for every swear word I hear him say."

"Oh – is that you, Father Ryan," Musgrove shouted. "Good day to you, Father. Hey! Arthur! slip across to the hut and dig out a fiver from me swag! Give it to the reverend gentleman on account of me swearing fines."

"After, afterwards, me son," Father Ryan requested me. To Jack: "An' how's things down there? Any luck, yet? Come on up and let me have a looksee."

I wound up Jack in the bucket, and Jack lowered Father Ryan

foot by foot whilst he examined every square yard of the four walls.

"Ye might be finding a trifle by going deeper. But its not impressed that I am," he said, when finally he reappeared.

"Well, what the –!" remarked Jack conversationally.

To which Father Ryan chuckled and said: "I think I'll be after reminding you of that fiver, me son. It won't be long before you owe me another, I much fear."

So we laboured sinking a new shaft, and when we had sunk it about ten feet there arrived at our camp two new chums. They were dressed in ready-made suits, starched collars, and cloth caps. They had left their suit cases at one of the hotels, hired a pick and a shovel, wanted to dig somewhere, and would bring out a windlass the next day. Where could they dig?

We were eating morning lunch in the shade of the old hut. They accepted a pannikin of tea, and yet were anxious to get to work. Musgrove suggested the hardest piece of ground within fifty miles – a place but a few feet beyond the hut doorway, beaten and tramped into almost solid rock by countless boots.

They went to it.

"Bet you a quid the bloke takes off his collar within two minutes," implored my companion, referring to the one who began to use the pick.

It was quickly evident that those two were miners. That they hailed from Yorkshire was evident too. That they had arrived at Adelaide on the Orsova they told us.

I won my bet for the pick man did not take off his collar before the expiration of the time limit. He loosened a square of earth and his mate shovelled it away. Still wearing his collar, he began on the second layer of rock-hard earth.

Then his pick crashed through what sounded like a bottle. A roar from Musgrove stopped the pick from descending again into the "bottle". As though we were financially interested, we showed them how to lift a pocket of wonderful opal, for which a German buyer paid £377.

So stunned by their fortune, they left White Cliffs without even thanking us, but they recovered a little in Adelaide, from which city they sent both of us £10; said they were leaving by the Orsova on her return trip, and wished us luck.

"Blast opal gouging!" Musgrove shouted when sure Father Ryan was not within hearing. "Let's get back to the station."

"Do me," I agreed. "I'm wanting a holiday badly."

Camels and a Goanna

Have you ever noticed that the sum total of a man's life may be expressed by one short and simple word? Take the failure – Mr. If. If he had not done this or that, he would have been such and such. Then there is the man, stolid and solid, both physically and financially. Mr. Yes is unable to bow, he is so solid and stolid. He is the antithesis of Mr. No, poor and starving, weak-chinned and watery-eyed. The difference between these two is that Mr. Yes never accepted the negative answer, and Mr. No could never do ought else but accept it.

Success in life depends wholly upon the ability to accept the little word "no," or the ability not to accept it. Were I a normally intelligent person, I would have grasped this profound truth when I got my first bush job because I would not take "no" for an answer. After a further exhibition of this gift of stubbornness which, of course, was rewarded with success, I deserve flogging every Monday morning for not making the refusal to accept "no" an unbreakable habit.

When Strike-a-Light! George told me there was a vacancy on the vermin fence surrounding a pastoral company's holdings of about 1½ million acres, I said that the job was mine. And because I said it, it was so.

The manager was short and plump and fiery, but kindly enough he pointed out that my bush experience was far short of that necessary for the work for which I asked.

The next day when I applied he said: "I told you yesterday why I won't give you the job."

The third day, he said: "It is no use bothering me."

The seventh day he yelled: "Oh curse and doubly curse the fools who permit new chums to enter the country! You'll go and get bushed or the camels will roll on you, and I'll have to send out search parties, and waste my time and write reports! Get out! Get out, I tell you! Go to the job and be damned! If ever I see you live again I'll sack you."

Strike-a-Light! was the only strong expression used by the tall gaunt man who showed me the 78-mile section of rabbit fence I was to "ride." His section of about eighty miles was further on, and, each fully equipped with a riding camel and a pack camel for transport, it was not with regret that we parted. Strike-a-Light was born tired, and he will never die because he will be too tired to do so. He was so tired that he loathed cooking, abhorred washing and reading. In one respect only was he energetic. He never grew tired of grousing. He groused at the most beautifully browned and cooked damper ever I made. When I asked him what was wrong with it, he said: "I always like my damper perfectly round."

Having parted from Strike-a-Light, I faced the bush alone, thrown entirely on my own initiative, beyond policemen and ambulances, sign posts and water taps. After but a slight apprenticeship to the Australian bush, I was about to be tried before Judge Solitude and a jury of two camels, prosecuted by Mr. I-told-you-so, and defended by Mr. Pride. The trial occupied, to my credit I still think, fifteen months.

Day after day and never a human voice but my own. Night after night lying on a stretcher beneath a mulga tree, watching the stars and the moon and the clouds, if any; imagination stirred by the wailing howls of a dingo pack; nerves shocked by the terrible scream of a curlew. Fighting a way along the fence in a dust storm, listening for camel bells to ascertain which direction they took when freed, fearful always of possible accident which in those conditions, would have but one result. Little matters, one and all, to be laughed at today.

I came to regard the bush as the blacks do. To me it was, and still is, a watching spirit waiting – waiting for a lonely man to make one slip to claim him for its own. Then I regarded the bush as a dreadfully malignant spirit; but with the passage of the years, it gradually changed to one of placid maternity, calmly waiting to take me back, whispering in the trees, singing in the sand: "Dust thou wast, and dust thou shalt become."

The loneliness was felt less when I again began to practice novel writing, and still less when I bought for ten shillings a wall-eyed cattle dog called Hool-em-up. He had formerly belonged to a man who had a passion for dog fights, and at every opportunity urged the beast to violence. One day, however, the owner of a kelpie sheep dog overheard the cattle dog's owner sooling him to fight, resulting in the dog owners themselves fighting, with ill results to the sool-em-on-er.

To obviate further unpleasantness, the sool-em-on-er re-christened the cattle dog Hool-em-up, and consequently it was only necessary for him to shout "Come here," and yell "Hool-em-up", to precipitate a dog fight.

That dog might have been good at heeling cattle, but he was no good at catching rabbits or kangaroos. Yet what he lost in "toe" he made up in determination. Once started he went on until the rabbit reached a burrow or a hollow log, or the kangaroo reached Queensland or South Australia.

Always did he scout ahead, unless chasing something, which was about twenty times in the hour. He would suddenly stop to glare at something with his one eye, his one ear pricked – the other the owner of a licked dog had shot off – his tail stiff and his hackles raised. Then off he would go with murder in the timbre of his yelps and quite inconvenienced by the three-cornered jacks in his feet. But never did he bring back anything from the chase.

Where the fence crossed the dry Paroo, that alleged river was two miles wide. Nothing, of course, grew on it other than spindly, spiny rubbish. The ground was creeked like mosaic work – cracks many feet in depth and sometimes six inches in width. Heaven help the man caught there when the flood waters, instead of rolling along, rise up from the bowels of the earth.

And on this country, Hool-em-up must needs chase an iguana which, to this day, I swear was yards in length. When the dog first sighted this land alligator, he was ahead. With interest, two animals and a man watched the race, an interest which increased when the iguana, instead of climbing a fence post, or ducking down one of the cracks, left the fence and circled back, passing us about 100 yards distant.

The camels stopped, and I waved my hat and cheered. Hool-em-up ran well, but the iguana took matters calmly – until it hit the fence from which it rebounded with astonishing velocity.

No longer calm, with Hool-em-up in sight of his only victory, the iguana ran along the fence towards us. At their approach the camels became frightened. The pack camel charged between the riding camel and the fence, leaving thus her mate to meet the charge. Like a ray of dark green light, the iguana thought only of escape from the slavering jaws but two feet astern. It appeared as though, when yet several feet away, the reptile sprang off the ground to reach the riding camel's near shoulder. There was no passage of time between then and when it was clawing its way up me to reach the top of my head.

Followed an earthquake. It seemed like coming down from a balloon and seeing the four legs of each camel spread outward as though they were dun-coloured beetles. On awakening, I found myself on the wrong side of the fence; and, enclosed in a circumference of 100 feet, was scattered everything which those two camels habitually carried. They were not in sight, but Hool-em-up was – peacefully sleeping in the shade cast by a fence post.

What a mess! Here in a ten by ten mile paddock in February! Fortunately, I knew that the vermin fence made the southern boundary of the paddock, and that to the south-east corner was a dam and two stockmen in their hut.

It was then that counsel at my trial began argument. Mr. I-told-you-so rose to say that I was an absolute failure. Then Mr. Pride arose to say that failure was not yet proved. Judge Solitude, like Brer Rabbit, said nothing.

So, most rashly, with the undamaged water bag filled from one of the water drums, I began to track those camels. By dusk I had followed them barely six miles, and would not have reached that far had not the country bordering the Paroo been soft and sandy.

The night was spent on a claypan that recalled a doctor's advice to sleep on a billiard table to cure insomnia. The fool! Daylight the next morning, hungry but fed with hope of catching up to the camels beyond the next of the eternal sand-ridges, on I went, noting how Hool-em-up appeared to be running faster this day, yet never losing sight of the tracks.

At about two o'clock, when I was at fault in hard mulga country, the manager drove up in his buckboard accompanied by a black boy driving two extra horses. Looking at me as a doctor might look at a dying victim, he said:

"Better get up."

Relating what had happened, I pointed out where last I had seen the camels' tracks.

"Oh! you followed them to there," he said wonderingly. "I

thought you were just walking about admiring the scenery."

The black boy he ordered to hobble the spare horses and then ride to a clump of cabbage trees I had pointed out, from which he was to track and bring back the camels. No longer angry, the manager assisted in making a fire on which the billy was boiled. The black boy presently returned with the camels, and we all went back to the scene of the disaster, where, after a little while, everything again became orderly. When he was about to drive off, I said to the manager:

"I suppose this means the sack?"

"I have never sacked a man in my life," was his reply. "When I want to get rid of a useless man I set him to work scrubbing floors. Just now the floors at the homestead don't need scrubbing."

With a twinkle in his eyes he drove away.

And Judge Solitude smiled at the prisoner.

Camels and a Scorpion

In the far north-west of New South Wales, there is a sheet of water created by heavy rains, named Moonamurtee Lake, and as evaporation in that country accounts for five feet of water every year, this beautiful lake goes dry after a lengthy rainless period.

Right on the west shore two Chinamen used once to occupy the hut, and they made a garden in which they grew vegetables to supply the diggings twenty miles away. Eventually, one Chinaman hanged himself, or was hanged by the other – I forget which – and the garden quickly was claimed by the native tobacco bush which grew there prolifically.

Within a furlong of the hut runs a vermin fence which I rode for nearly a year; and, because of the fish in the water and the countless water birds on its surface, the lake and the hut became a favourite camp, despite the latter's reputed haunting. Usually arriving in the late afternoon, the camels would be unloaded outside the hut door, and then freed to hobble to the water and take in about eight gallons each before making their way to the neighbouring sand-dunes, among which grew the delectable pig-weed and other herbage; for, be it understood, camels will not eat grass.

During the red hot weeks of summer, the first task, after unloading the three camels, would be to gather wood for the billy and the camp oven, erect the stretcher and the mosquito net over it on the side of the hut furthest from the water, and then rush for the lake. After a swim and dressed in clean pyjamas, one would be wonderfully refreshed after a fortnight during which the daily ration of washing water could not exceed two pints.

The reason for sleeping on the far side of the hut was logical enough, for the following morning I would creep into the iron building, and from the living-room shoot several ducks with a double-barrel shotgun, the ducks and the water hens being so accustomed to the place that they would be feeding at early morning along the lake edge within fifteen yards range.

As usual, in mid March, the first evening of my stay at this fine camp the bunk was fixed outside the hut, the camels were contentedly feeding, the fish lines were set, and the damper and salt meat cooked by sundown. With the incessant quacking and honking of the water birds drifting in through the open window, I wrote for several hours before slipping under the net on to the bunk, with matches and made cigarettes.

As I was lying peacefully, with no covering over me, placidly smoking a cigarette, a red hot dagger was thrust, without warning, into my ankle. I smacked the part with my hand, and struck a match, and found still very much alive, a red-brown scorpion almost the size of a man's palm.

Experts tell us that scorpion stings are not fatal, and I do not presume to argue with them further than to state that to a man whose blood is in ill condition through living on soda bread and alkaline-filled water, and whose menu does not contain green vegetables, a scorpion sting is sometimes fatal without any outside or subsidiary conditions to make it so.

Naturally, I did not have with me an antidote, nor did I have any antiseptic. With all speed I got the slush lamp going inside the hut, and with a blunt knife gashed across the stung part deeply. Into the wound made, I poured the blue-black tea from the billy, and then plugged it with a wad of tobacco before bandaging it with a torn-up shirt.

Doubtless the procedure would be frowned upon by a modern surgeon to whom life would be incomplete without a case of knives and a range of antiseptics, but I have known of snake venom being defeated by nicotine, although I must confess that the application of strong tea has not been proved efficacious or otherwise in surgery. It is when a man is placed out of sight of a hospital, beyond telephones and policemen, when his food supplies are low and tobacco down to the last ounce, that he will try anything to prevent incapacity, for incapacity in itself can be more fatal than ten cobra bites.

Unable to sleep, I heated water as day was breaking, removed the tobacco wad and scalded the wound. I know an aboriginal who, when his foot was bitten by a tiger snake, thrust that foot into a camp fire and held it there, but he was no more stoical than I was, and no more frightened. The colour of the ankle would have perturbed Zeno himself.

At breakfast I had ample opportunity to survey the situation. The camels were gone – I could not hear their bells. I was twenty-six miles from the homestead, and knew not the country between the lake and the diggings. At that time I could not expect the chance arrival of motor-car explorers.

All that day I nursed a blue-black leg, and listened for the camel bells, three or four times crawling to the lake on hands and knees with the billy-can. Towards evening the ankle had reached the size of the thigh. No sleep that night, or the following day – pain up to my armpit throbbing as though a rope ran down through my body, which was incessantly tugged by a devil. I would have been less wretched had I had tobacco.

The third night the moon rose about eleven o'clock, and shortly afterwards I imagined I heard the camel bells, having for so long strained my ears to hear them. Ten minutes later I realised it was not imagination. On the far side of the lake the camels were coming back to water, and then I was in no better state for it was out of the question to crawl the full mile round the lake's edge.

Gradually the bells became louder. They rang with the rhythmical timing of travelling animals, and gradually I understood that they were coming back to the place before the hut to drink. There the shore surface was hard, whilst at many other places the surface was soft. Fear of being bogged dictated a familiar watering place.

When they emerged from the surrounding scrub, to hobble across the sandflats, I was at the riding saddle clutching the riding camel's noseline. Three huge putty-coloured shapes finally stood drinking at the edge of the silvery water; and in my white pyjamas I crawled to them, calling endearing names, hoping they would not take fright at the strange white beetle, and rear on their hind legs to bring down their ponderous forefeet upon it. When a man is up against it, he will chance anything.

"Buller! Buller, you old scoundrel!" I cried, tremblingly; and as I reached his forefeet, Buller lowered his grand old head to my level, waggled drops of water from his split upper lip, and allowed me to slip the end of the noseline over a plug drawn through a nostril. I am sure he asked: "What the devil do you think you're doing at this time of night?"

To appreciate Buller please visualise an old gentleman set in his habits, strong in his convictions, and emphatic in his opinions. At twelve-mile intervals along the section of fence, I had erected windbreaks at temporary camps used by many riders before me, and never could Buller be induced to pass one of them. To him they represented a full day's work, and, being a good unionist, he struck work when arrived at one of these camps.

Unhobbling him and the two cows, I hooshed him down, flung a filled canvas waterbag from his neck, and climbed across him behind his hump, to which I clung. With the cows following, we set off for the homestead. One cross gate I opened after putting Buller to ground and crawling to it. Another was but a low one, which he was persuaded to step over.

At the first of the two camps he half-heartedly attempted to stop, but firmly I urged him on, and, after a rumbling growl at this overtime, he went forward. The two cows hung back at the camp and bellowed, but he kept going, bellowing angrily back to them for attempting to mutiny at his decision. They did not stay back at the camp for long.

At eleven o'clock the next morning we passed the second camp, and this time Buller really objected. I believe that my mastery over him was due to the fact that he was not saddled, and that his cows were not loaded with pack-saddle and gear. Of all animals, the camel is the most sagacious, and Buller appeared to know that the then procedure was very irregular, but wholly necessary. We reached the gate in the vermin fence at noon, and through this gate we had to pass to reach the homestead, two miles distant.

I remember hooshing him down to his knees and getting off his back before the gate I had to open. Then exhaustion claimed me.

I awoke as the sun was setting, my feet and one leg badly sun-blistered. Either the sun, or my body itself, had defeated the venom, for the swelling had gone down. My foot had regained its natural colour, and no longer did it pain.

The two cows had wandered off to the nearest shade, but Buller all that afternoon had not stirred from beside me – which was as well, for in each of the surrounding trees were watching impatient crows.

To a wad of tobacco, blue-black tea, and a wise old gentlemen did I owe my escape from the Bunyip, the ever watching spirit of the bush.

The Man Who Lost Count

In a singular respect it is to be regretted that Defoe wrote his masterpiece from second-hand data; for, if he, not Alexander Selkirk, had been wrecked on that lonely island of Juan Fernandez he would have known that notching a stick daily was by no means an infallible method of keeping time!

No man fully appreciates how finely balanced is the human mind, and how utterly it depends for continued sanity on its clear contact with other human minds, until he is cut off from his kind for long periods. The isolation must be complete – an isolation amplified by the knowledge that one is right outside the human world, beyond chance contact with human beings; black, yellow or white.

Personal experience proves that youth is better able to withstand the insidious attacks of solitude than is the elderly man. During 1928-29-30 I felt the fortnightly periods of solitude more keenly than those periods of six and seven weeks before the war.

The inevitable result on the mind of prolonged isolation from human kind is insanity, no matter to what extent the mind is disciplined and employed. Continued sanity does not depend on self-control, for self-control is based on mental activity. It is the slow dulling of mental activity, slow mental starvation which is the cause of the final breakdown,

For more than a year the writer rode the netted vermin fence guarding a million-acre sheep station in western New South Wales. The periods of isolation extended from five to seven weeks, each period divided only by one day spent at the homestead for the purpose of drawing rations and meat and material.

At the close of the first period I was accustomed to conversing with the three camels used for transport, and the mongrel dog, useless save to catch rabbits. With the passage of time, unrealities became realities ever more clearly. The camels and the dog were falsely imbued with the gift of human reasoning and speech, answers to questions being falsely accepted, directions given being falsely accepted as being received.

The days and the nights became a succession of alternate periods of light and darkness. Consciousness of time faded to the point of one's life being controlled solely by the rising and the setting sun. Reading and writing both became boring, whilst mental ecstasy, working like a drug, drove one to imagine oneself as a great and powerful person dictating to the world.

To mark the passage of time by striking off the date on a calendar, by notching a stick, by daily placing a pebble in a tin, or by tying a knot in a piece of string every evening is a weak reed upon which to lean. Inevitably the doubt will be presented that the daily task has been or has not been done, and no amount of retrospection will recall to the mind if it was, or was not, done.

Leaving the homestead two weeks before one Christmas, with a hamper and a bottle of wine to be consumed only on Christmas Day, I adopted the notched stick, the knotted string and the pebbles-in-a-tin methods to make positively sure of enjoying the feast on this feast day. Every morning I reviewed the camps stayed at since leaving, tallying them with the notches on the stick, the pebbles in the tin and the knots along the string.

I so managed it that on Christmas Eve we reached an old hut on the shore of a lake of beautiful water, and early on Christmas morning I shot a couple of widgeon ducks and obtained a nice perch on one of the night lines. I was cooking a right royal meal when the boss arrived – to prove to me that Christmas Day actually was past two days!

For many hours my mind frantically sought the error I had made despite the precautions I had adopted to keep accurate time, a mind hopelessly bogged in a morass of doubt and muddy thinking.

Even when on the State Fences, when one has to keep a diary of work done and distances travelled, the days cannot for long be accurately noted. It becomes too great a task for the human mind to accomplish when it is so driven in upon itself, forced to feed upon itself, to be satiated only by its own destruction.

Fear steadily grows the longer one remains cut off from human kind, the longer one remains close to the naked bosom of Nature. The bush takes on a malignant personality, a spirit exemplified by the aborigines' banshee. At any moment she might strike with one of her hundred weapons.

A scorpion might sting when one is short of water and far from a supply; a snake might bite when potash and pipe nicotine might be unavailing to save; a camel might kick, or bite, or knock down and lie upon one in any unguarded moment. Bad water might cramp a man into helplessness; even influenza might attack and render helpless a man who has not been in human contact for several weeks.

All accidents not of themselves fatal, but fatal when life depends on reaching far distant water.

Fear of all these things becomes ever more intense the longer one is cut off from human contact. For it is unnatural for man to live alone – as the Bible says.

One morning whilst eating breakfast I realised that I had carefully set out eating utensils for two people – enabled to do so with the spare set carried. That had to be the end – at least for a time – of riding a vermin fence! I went straight back to the homestead and demanded my cheque.

The Ration Sheep

According to the Lombroso school of criminology, which maintains that a criminal is born with certain physical traits – such as projecting ears, prominent brows, a protruding chin, etc. – George Bycroft was a villain of the deepest dye whose certain end would be on a trap door. He had all those physical characteristics with which villains are endowed by the great Victorian novelists.

Six feet three inches in height and massively proportioned, beetle browed and iron fisted, the stranger might well be forgiven when in his presence; and yet, as you shall see, George Bycroft had the tender heart of a swooning woman.

For several years, he and a man known as The Midnight Mail – a sobriquet earned by his preference to carry his swag during the night – drove two camel teams from Kyle Station, near Mt. Brown, to Broken Hill with the wool clip. Each man's team comprised twenty-two camels which drew a table-top waggon carrying a mountain of wool.

After the first trip one spring, The Midnight Mail fell sick, and Gorge Bycroft, knowing of my breaking-in by One Spur Dick, suggested to the manager that I take the sick man's place.

"But," I objected, "I may be able to drive mules across the Paroo Bridge when up against it, and I know something of pack camels, but when it comes to pushing twenty-two camels ahead of ten or twenty tons of wool I'd fall down on the job."

"That's the worst of your Englishman," Bycroft roared – his normal voice was a bellow. "You're either Know-alls or Shrinking Violets. Now, look! We puts the humpies in here and we drives 'em for ten days before we strikes the grades of the range. For ten days they don't want driving. All they wants is flogging. If they bolts – well, all the better. The quicker they gets there. Anyways, they'd sooner sleep than bolt. They're always sooners. Sooner do anything than work."

"Well, I'm telling you I know nothing about team camels."

"You'll know all about them when we gets back. I'll do the camel hunting and you can do the cooking. Come on, now. Never let the world beat you. Never let old One-Spur Dick know that one of his lads turned up his toes at a few measley camels."

The reference to One-Spur Dick banished further hesitation. If there was any man's respect I desired to retain, it was his.

The empty waggons were drawn up outside the woolshed and the loading proceeded as Bycroft and I laid out on the ground the forty-four sets of harness placed just where each camel would be "hooshed" down on the long chain lines.

Being the cook of the outfit, it was my task to not only draw rations for six weeks, but to kill three sheep and salt the mutton. And, too, early on the morning of our departure, I placed two live ration sheep in the crate slung from the rear of one waggon.

I was given a man to offside for a mile or so, and when Bycroft gained a half-mile start, I whistled to the team as I had once whistled to the mules, cracked the long-handled fourteen-foot whip with a little luck, and got the team off the mark with the offsider – an experienced bullock driver – straightening them up on the far side.

After the first day the journey became governed by routine. As neither had a watch, Bycroft would arouse me before dawn, timing by the stars. When day broke, we had eaten breakfast, and, mounted on the chaff-fed, stock horse which followed his waggon all day, he would set out for the hobbled camels whilst I packed and stowed away the camp gear. It would be ten o'clock usually when we started on the day's stage. At noon we stopped for lunch, the camels lying down in their harness and placidly chewing their cud for an hour. Then on again until sunset, when the teams would be freed to wander at will.

While I would be cooking the tea, Bycroft would tether out the two ration sheep. After a few days they would drink water out of a bucket, and gladly accept a ration of chaff. Within a week they became quite tame, eating damper and brownie crusts and potatoes, and would nuzzle our pockets for these dainties.

A week was generally spent at the West Camp, Broken Hill, unloading the wool into motor trucks which transhipped it to the railway, and, that completed, bringing out tons of cased rations and flour and wire and corrugated iron, and tar and paints. All this unloading and loading would be supervised by Bycroft, who took especial care with the loading which is an art acquired only after long practice.

When leaving the Hill we had about six pounds only of salted mutton, and the night we camped at Stevens Creek I mentioned the fact to Bycroft.

"Better kill one of them ration sheep tonight," he said carelessly. "I'll hold the lamp for you, being as its dark."

He had already tethered the sheep, and they were picking up the last of their ration of chaff when we approached them with the lamp and the killing knives.

"Which one shall it be?" I asked.

"Oh, any one will do. Take this one."

When I went to throw the sheep, it uttered a joyful baa and sprang at me to muzzle my hand for dainties, and for the life of me I could not get on with the job. No, it was impossible. I realised that I was a sappy-hearted sook, and taking the lamp from the most hardened-looking criminal in Australia, I gave him the knives and asked him to do the awful work.

It was then I came to know that Lombroso and his school of criminologists were a pack of nit-wits, for George Bycroft looked at me ashamedly, grinned sheepishly, shook his head and confessed that if I offered him £50 he couldn't cut the throat of "that bleedin' trick of a sheep."

"But one of us has to do it," I protested. "We will want mutton the day after tomorrow. Do you mean to tell me you can't kill a sheep – and you an Australian teamster?"

"I could kill all the sheep in the flaming country bar them two," he averred. "Anyway, it ain't my job. You're the cook. It's your job. You get on with it, or it'll be morning before we get to bed."

We argued the matter for half an hour, the sheep bunting us, and both of them yelling for dainties, and we then went back to the waggons and our beds each grumbling at the other's squeamishness.

Fortunately, the next night we camped at a dam at which also was camped a droving outfit, and with the boss drover we exchanged one of our sheep for his, whereupon Bycroft, to show how hard-hearted he was, killed the drover's sheep without a tremor.

George was the king of the teamsters. When I got into difficulties, he would halt his team and walk back to lend me a hand, and show me 101 little points of the game. He was one of the few men I have known who never grumbled or lost his temper no matter what the provocation. I have seen him run up and down the long line of camels, his great whip cracking like a machine gun, his roaring voice vieing with the roaring camels tugging frantically at their tremendous load.

In a wide creek his waggon became bogged to the axles. When it was seen that his team could not shift it, we yoked up twenty-two animals ahead of his. Forty-four camels could not shift that huge, now inert mass. We were digging the clay from before the wheels when a twenty-six bullock team arrived at the crossing and, after a conference, the twenty-six bullocks were yoked ahead of the forty-four camels.

Three drivers and the bullocky's offsider abruptly became yelling, flogging, demented devils. The extraordinary team got down to the strain. The bullocks were magnificent. They pushed into their heavy yokes with bellies almost to the ground – and then fell on their noses when the shafts of the great waggon were torn out.

I thought Bycroft would never stop laughing. We were occupied three days making temporary shafts with bush timber, but we got clear of the bog without unloading.

Tramping by the Darling

Into my young blood insidiously was creeping the wanderlust. After all the money spent on me, money wasted, deliberately I turned my back on my profession, flung away the opportunities of youth, became only too anxious to hear ever more loudly and to see ever more clearly the spirit of Australia and its many alluring voices.

To observe a ridge of sandhills was to wonder what lay beyond them. To watch the shimmering mirage transforming a gibber plain into a dream of fairy islands and spires and minarets floating on a palm-fringed lake was to inflame my imagination to the point of ecstasy.

Perhaps it was the sense of freedom, both physically and spiritually, the knowledge that should I want to look beyond the sandhills and peer beyond the mirage, there was nothing but my two legs and a water bag to prevent me. Unlike a child bored with too many toys, unlike a man satiated with love, unlike a man lost because he has no more worlds to conquer, the man smitten with the wanderlust can never, never grow bored or satiated or lost by too much travel, too much freedom. And yet, when all is said and done, the wanderer is not free: he is enslaved by the passion to keep moving, enslaved by a mental force as strongly as his body can be enslaved by drugs. Never is he free to settle in a place and enjoy the greatest gift of all – contentment.

The development of the wanderlust in me unfortunately occurred when there did not exist the fear of unemployment. There was always a job waiting on the next station, on a farm and in a city factory. It is unlikely that such conditions ever again will exist; for it was based on a spurious prosperity brought about by almost unlimited cheap money.

As thousands did before me, and as men are still doing in these days of depression, I asked for my cheque instead of my orders one bright morning in May, and a week later an eager young man pushed a loaded bicycle out of Wilcannia.

It is surprising how much weight a bicycle will carry. It is surprising how easy it is to push a loaded bicycle. It is even more surprising to feel the joy of travelling beside one of the inland rivers – in May. One's lungs breathe an air that intoxicates; one's eyes are freshened and strengthened by the limitless carpet spread beneath the gums and the box trees, woven by the springing wild carrot, parsnip and buckbush; one's ears are appreciative of the Wild's music – fish jumping in the river, the cries of galahs and cockatoo and kookaburra, swan and pelican and crane. The crows seem to be less malevolent, the smiling bush welcomes instead of watching and waiting to pounce.

And there is ever a gamble on what the next cook will be like. Will he be generous or mean? For every cook who has turned me away with nothing but a snarl, there have been ten who gave me a "fair issue" and about three who offered me as much as I cared to take.

An outstanding character was Rainbow Harry, so named because of his love of highly colouring his dishes. He was a big man with grey eyes and a full beard as white as the moleskin trousers he wore. At our first meeting he had me at a decided disadvantage. He was standing on a doorstep, and the effect of this enhancement of his height above me will be understood by any salesman. The cook who can look down on the applicant for tucker is placed as the great man who sits at a table set at the farthest end of a huge room.

By this time I was not so foolish as to offer a cook money. I suggested to Rainbow Harry that, perchance, he could give me some flour. The request made him grow one foot taller; made his eyes stand out from his face, and his beard stand out from his chest.

"What! Flour! I can't get enough flour to feed the hands!" he shouted – to add with astonishing softness: "Give us your bag."

When he brought me about twenty pounds of flour, I found it easier to suggest that a little tea and sugar would not come amiss.

"Tea! Sugar! Think a station's got nothing else to do but feed tramps?" was the roared question, to be followed by the soft request: "Give us your bag."

Some four pounds of sugar and two pounds of tea duly appeared in my calico ration bags.

I thought of meat, for I was tired of fish.

"Stiffen the crows! D'you think I'm running an abattoirs?

Think I can supply every tramp humming on me with meat?" was the shout preceding the whisper: "Give us your bag."

At least thirty pounds of uncooked mutton was handed out, and with a wink and a grin Rainbow Harry wished me adieu. It appeared that his generosity would have bankrupt any station had he not been curbed by the manager; and his loud and indignant denials of what tramps thought him to be was obviously intended to be for the manager's delight.

Fearing for the frame of the bicycle, I yet managed to get the load to the shearing shed one mile up river, where in the shearer's kitchen I found the usual assortment of men resting from their labours of wandering about. There was Butch, undoubtedly understudied by Wallace Beery. During the two days I camped here he never wore anything other than trousers and singlet. He had never worn boots for years. There was Musical Treloar who played his violin by the hour – even played it whilst he tramped. There was The Man from Snowy River, who, in appearance, was a greater villain than Butch: a vast man called Pompey George; and a little, dapper, blue-jowled man named Jake the – but what the something was I did not know till later. It was not included in the introduction.

It was Butch who told me that I need not cook this evening as dinner was ready. It was The Man from Snowy River who inquired if I was "All right" for tobacco. And it was Jake who stepped to within a few feet of me to most offensively eye me up and down. Took his time, too, like a French peasant contemplating the purchase of a cow.

"How much?" inquired Butch unsmilingly.

Jake circled me, his lips pursed, his eyes screwed into pin points.

"Come on," urged the human gorilla. "How much? A bloke 'ud die of fright waiting for you to make up yer mind."

"Seven feet, two and a half," Jake replied at last, adding decisively: "Yes, I must add that half inch."

With that he moved back to the great fire where he had been engaged in grilling a half side of mutton cut into chops and fillets, Butch also retiring. I turned to Pompey George whose measurements were much nearer to Jake's estimate than mine.

"What's he trying to guess – my height?" I demanded irritably.

Pompey George was exceedingly attractive when he grinned. He said:

"No. Not your height – your drop." Observing mental sluggishness, he explained: "The little chap is Jake the Hangman. Was hangman once in England. Pulled out when he had to attend to a woman. And he can't break the habit of estimating a man's proper drop."

Here, as elsewhere when bush tramps foregather, Socialism is practised as it is preached. There was none scheming to make a fortune, or even a comfortable living out of the underdog. Despite outward appearances, these men were carefree and in many respects admirable. They made me welcome to the cooked food as though it was my right, and provided a menu of grilled mutton and baked cod, featherweight damper and strong tea.

When packing up preparatory to pulling out, Pompey George asked if he might accompany me, and, because of his attractive smile and cleanly habits, I agreed. Despite the frosts he bathed in the river morning and night. He carried three shirts, enabling him to put on a clean one every night. I say "night" advisedly, because no self-respecting swagman would carry pyjamas.

Pompey George had one fault – always looking for a fight. Never did a man so love a fight as did he, and never was a man less capable of engineering a situation to produce cause for a fight. I came to see drovers and bullock drivers with ironbark faces and ironstone fists on their very best behaviour in his imposing presence; for a man whose height is six feet three and whose width is about a yard surely does possess an imposing presence, when assisted by yellow hair, violet eyes, and a Rock of Gibraltar chin.

"If there are any likely looking fellers in this shanty we're coming to, never you be backward in coming forward," he said, when we sighted a bush pub between the grey and red trunks of the giant gums forming a 2,000 miles long avenue down which ran the river.

There were several hard, poker-faced men in the bar, but nothing happened, and, on our way again, Pompey reproached me.

"You might have started something," he complained. "I haven't opened my chest for months and months."

Alternatively pushing the weighted bicycle, we camped wherever we pleased. If the weather threatened, in a shearers hut; if it were fine and cold, then beside a roaring fire on the river bank. The fish we caught and grilled on wire netting! The ducks we bought from ancient fishermen or traded tobacco for with the blacks! The men we met – how Dickens would have loved them.

We both had plenty of money. We never stayed at a hotel longer than to take two drinks, and, at one hotel, I gave George his long desired chance. An obnoxious person called me a Pommy with extras, and although I have played in a soccer team calling themselves with pride "The Pommies", this occasion produced anger.

But before I could get going, I was swept aside by Pompey George, sent flying out through the door. The building proceeded to rock on its foundations, and from the doors and windows, and from every crack, poured the yells of men and the dust deposited by countless sandstorms. Men came out of the door one by one as though blown out by an explosion. One issued through a window bringing the frame with him. Some enjoyed it; others appeared disinterested.

Pompey's entertainment cost him three rounds of drinks and £2 for damages.

For a week he behaved with the irresponsibility of a man in love, and then, as wonderful day succeeded wonderful day, he gradually became his old self; quietly humourous, even tempered, sometimes pensive. For an hour or more he would gaze into the heart of a fire, without speaking one word. Now and then Latin phrases would escape him, and once he discoursed on a cricket match played in the park of an English country mansion which seemed to indicate that he was not one of the gardeners.

There were quite a number of men in the bar of a wayside hotel between Cunnamulla and Wanaaring when we entered it late one afternoon. Outside were two bullock teams and a drover's outfit. We had been there about half an hour when one of the bullock drivers who was the worst for wear deliberately upset my glass.

Here, thought I, was a golden opportunity for Pompey George.

I began to discuss the subject of the spilled drink. Began is correct, for I never finished it. An iron-hard fist sent me back against the wall. Oh, Pompey, where art thou? Pompey was outside and I got the father of a hiding, which was thoroughly deserved.

All the way to Wanaaring George grumbled and growled because I was fool enough not to have been sure he was present. As though I would have started the play if I had not been sure. When we finally parted, I took a scrub-cutting job, and heard no more of him until informed quite recently that he had fallen in Palestine. What a man!

The River Pirate

I have informally chatted with a foreign royal duke, an earl, two baronets, a Prime Minister, and an Attorney-General, and no one of these mighty ones had the forcible personality possessed by Father Time.

A quandary at a road junction, a wrong choice, a walk of eight miles – then Father Time, in whom was epitomised the sterling qualities of the Australian Sundowner. For your sundowner is utterly unlike your unclean English tramp and the worse American hobo. He will accept work periodically; he is very generous to his fellows, and very seldom dishonest.

The road I was following led me north-west towards Wilcannia, skirting the east side of the Darling, which it touched only at the apex of the greater eastward thrusting bends. The distance from bend to bend might be eight or ten miles, whilst from road into a westward bend might be anything up to six or seven miles.

Pushing the trusty bike – which required no ground feed and demanded no hunting in the morning – I was faced with the problem of choosing one of two roads when reaching a junction. Both roads indicated that an equal amount of traffic passed over them; and, consequently, it was impossible to discern which was the main track and which the subsidiary leading, most likely, to a lonely station homestead.

The surrounding country comprised box-tree flats, and a climb into one of the tallest trees failed to reveal the sweeping lines of the much higher gums bordering the river. The junction formed a Y – one track going north-west and the other going north-east, and because the westerly one would certainly take me to the river and water, and the easterly one probably across dry and unknown country to a dead end, I chose the former and followed it for four miles to its terminus at a motor and waggon shed on the river bank opposite a selector's homestead.

They have sown wheat in the dry bed of the Darling River and reaped an excellent harvest. They have grown amazing crops of lucerne on the bordering grey flats, but here for the first time I witnessed "The Gutter of Australia" providing dairy pasture. The river was fairly low, and along each side of the slowly-moving stream was a wide border of vivid green water-weed. The selector's cows were feeding on this weed, and now and then they would casually swim backwards and forwards across the river precisely as though they were water buffaloes.

The day was bright and cool; the scene pastoral and peaceful. Near the house, beyond the river, a petrol engine methodically pumped water to a raised stand from which house and orchard and garden were supplied. There was no hint of poverty there. Why the selector kept his car and truck and waggon on my side of the river was because of the better track to Menindee, and he should have erected a signboard at the junction.

Down river a flock of black ducks, almost as large and heavier than Indian Runners, were feeding busily among the weed. In the shallows stood several cranes too sleepy to fish, or waiting for the late afternoon when the small fish would become active.

I had boiled the billy, and was eating a lunch of soda bread and cold grilled perch, when round the northern bend came sweeping a large flock of teal ducks. They passed with whirring wings to settle on the water beyond the black ducks. They were the pilot birds to the strangest craft I have ever seen.

There was that about it which recalled an islander's catamaran, a Chinese junk, on outrigger and a Venetian gondola, but presently it resolved into a most ancient river prau. Athwart it were lashed two long poles, at the extremities were fastened a five-gallon airtight oil drum, making the craft uncapsizable and unsinkable. Fore and aft, and on both port and starboard beams were erected short poles which suspended a bag canopy, and attached to the stern was a large wire netting cage partly submerged. In this cage the crew of the ship kept a supply of live fish. The navigator-captain-deckhand reclined beneath the canopy and languidly steered with a piece of packing case nailed to a sapling which served as an oar when the current threatened to beach this Dreadnought of the Darling.

My first impression of the crew of this floating home was of glistening snowfields. Observing me and the blue spiral of my camp fire, he waved a hand and began to warp his ship to the bank below me.

The selector, who was labouring with saw and hammer in the shelter of an open shed beside his house, called out:

"Good day-ee, Father Time. How's your whiskers today?"

As though he were stone deaf, the mariner stepped ashore and secured his craft to a tree root with an old rusty chain. His every action was deliberate, made without haste or waste of energy, crying out the pride of the ancient in his ship and his home.

"Ain't you talking' today, whiskers?" sang out the carpenter.

Continuing to maintain dignified silence, Father Time produced his billycan, and with it filled with river water and a gunny sack slung from one broad shoulder, he made the laborious climb up the steep bank.

Arrived, he stretched his powerful body to its full height, and, in a mighty voice roared:

"Hey, you! You unwashed son of an unwashed – "

With my pen I can proceed no further, save to state that for two full minutes Father Time offered his opinions of the carpenter, and the carpenter's ancestors back to the Neolithic age. He was a master of elocution, for he never repeated himself and never twice used the oaths in his amazing vocabulary. Rare the speaker commanding such diction. He proved himself to be a seaman, an international interpreter, a blackbirder, and a London cab-driver. Then, when proper climax was reached and the peroration ended, he turned to me with no sign of perturbation or heat in his china blue eyes. The calmness of his soul was unruffled.

"Good day," greeted Father Time in surprisingly gentle tones. "Do you mind if I boil my billy on your fire?"

When squatting over the fire arranging fresh wood against his billy-can, he lifted his head to indicate the selector.

"His name's Redditch. He's living in luxury provided by the money his old mother stole from the likes of you and me. She kept a pub beyond Burke, and smoked cigars. When a chequeman got merry on her watered whisky, she would blow cigar smoke into his glass before filling it, and that would knock him right out, and when he came to he would have nothing in his pockets bar the lining. Two blokes I knew she ruined their minds. When she kicked off she left £11,000 to her son, who would have run to the police had I shot one of them ducks being out of season. If you wish to shut the mouth of a jackanapes, make public the sins of his mother – above a whisper."

Blue eyes beamed upon me. The pink skin of this centenarian – he was a hundred by the shortest estimate – matched and toned with the whiteness of his hair and beard. He looked as old and as strong as the bordering gums; as eternal as the river itself. He could have borne no other cognomen than the one given him by the selector.

"I know all of 'em who lived on this river since 1845," he went on. "I seen Burke and Wills when they was camped at Menindee. I could have gone with 'em, but I knew that before long I would be arguing with Burke. Explorers! They wasn't explorers' shadows. Coming back to old Mother Redditch – the mail coaches used to stop at her pub for dinner at night, and when the travellers were sitting down at table with her husband and him over there, she would say: 'Will ye be havin' goat or will ye take a bite o' galah?' She always asked her poor husband the same question; and, of course, he always nominated the goat. And always she said: 'Indade ye won't. Ye'll be havin' galah.'"

When he had eaten, Father Time announced his intention of continuing his voyage and making port that night at the Twenty-mile Point. I accompanied him down to his ship, and from his larder he pulled a nice chunky cod, careless of the spines of several cat fish.

A grand old man, his actions were ever slow but deliberate.

The hawser he stowed with meticulous care. Gaining the poop, he settled into his lounge, and, with the oar, gently pushed off to gain the middle of the stream. He waved to me once, ignored the carpenter – still too stunned to offer comment – and went sailing down the river like the boatman who ferries souls across the Styx. On the eve of my departure, thinking of the eight unnecessary miles due to the lack of a signboard at the junction, I shouted out to the selector:

"Hey. Will ye be havin' goat, or will ye take a bite of galah?"

The Gentle Grafter

I have no exact knowledge regarding Cockney Slater's criminal history, or of the number of his convictions for petty larceny, but I do know that he was a likeable man, a born optimist, unfailingly cheerful, and generous always in deed and thought. He never spoke ill of any man, and I am not now going to write ill of him.

Our first meeting occurred in 1911 on the road from Roma to Charleville, Southern Queensland, and our last was in 1919 on the outskirts of Cork, Ireland, where I found him established in business as a butcher with a most capable wife to take charge of the cash box. It seems a far cry from an Australian tramp to a captaincy in the Sinn Fein army; and yet, another fellow tramp, one Pompey George, rose to be a major in the Egyptian Camel Corp.

Cockney Slater was undoubtedly a disciple of O'Henry's gentle grafter. He was without viciousness; he was imbued with a code of honour that dictated giving the sucker a run for his money. Picking pockets, or using other direct methods of getting rich quick, was as abhorrent to Cockney Slater as it is to the average decent citizen.

"If I had five bob I could make some Slater's Permanent Polish," he said one afternoon when we were fishing in a bend of the river a mile above Burke. "That's the stuff that gets 'em, but a man wants quick transport before pulling it over."

"A permanent polish! A floor polish?"

"Polish anything from a lady's shoe to a gent's bald head. Hey, what's this on my line?"

It was merely a seventeen-pounder chunky cod which quickly gave up the fight and was drawn to the bank as though it were a corn sack filled with rubbish. Of course, the fish's weight was only estimated, and I am inclined to believe our enthusiasm was responsible for at least two pounds.

"We can get sixpence a pound dead weight for this joker at any of the pubs," declared Slater. "That'll be eight and sixpence. We can shove into him another four pounds which will make it up to ten and six. Off with your clobber, and take him across the river."

"What for?" I demanded, thinking of the temperature of the water in August.

"Trade secret. Get ready while I fixes him."

By this time the fish was dead. Cockney Slater removed the hook and the sinker, and tied the end of the line to the fish's jaw. The jaws he fixed wide open with a stick.

"You take him across to the other side and let him go when I sings out," were his instructions. Hugging the fish to my chest, I kicked my way across the river, Slater paying out the line. The river was high, the current strong, and the colour of the water warship grey. On the farther side I held the fish pointing to my companion in crime.

Being all set, I let go the fish and Slater ran back from the bank as fast as he could, the fish being dragged through the water quicker than ever it swam. This performance was repeated three times, when Slater judged that several pounds weight of water had been forced into it.

Leaving me at the camp, he set off for the township with the fish hanging down along his back, reminding me vividly of a famous advertisement.

He reached Burke about twenty minutes to six o'clock, and sold the fish at the first hotel at which he offered it. They weighed the fish which topped the scale at 23½ pounds, and Slater received eleven and nine pence. According to his code of honour, he spent none of the money on drink, but he did spend nearly eight shillings on bluestone, shellac, and two powders, the names of which he would not state.

The whole of the following morning we spent in boiling and skimming the liquid these ingredients produced, and early in the afternoon we entered Burke with the stuff in two gallon oil tins. When Slater had purchased two paint brushes, our stock in trade was complete. When he varnished his left boot, the effect was startling. There he stood at the kerb, his right boot scored and dusty, his left boot brilliantly polished and brilliantly reflecting the light of the sun.

"Give your shoes a permanent polish, lady," Slater asked a Chinese woman. "Only two shillings the pair, lady. Last for ever."

The lady stopped and gazed at Slater's example on his left foot, fascinated by its wonderful brilliance. She presently walked away wearing shoes that vied in splendour with Cinderella's slippers.

Presently both of us were applying Slater's Permanent Polish to both feminine and masculine footwear, and the shillings came rolling in in a silver flood. Fortune favoured us, for no suspicious policeman came to look on at our labours, perhaps to ask pertinent questions. A man parked a car nearby and entered a bank and, while he was within, Slater varnished a narrow strip of the front mudguard. That strip shone out like the sun from between dark clouds. It was not an old car; neither was it brand new. To the owner Slater suggested that we should varnish the whole of the car for two pounds. The two pounds were paid, and no car in a showroom ever appeared so brilliantly spick and span as did that one.

Knowing Cockney Slater, I realized there was a catch in it somewhere, but just where I could not fathom. The polish certainly was highly successful. It transformed shoes and boots and cars better than and almost as quickly as Aladdin's Geni could have done the work. Commercialised it should have made its inventor a millionaire.

Returning to the river, I asked Slater why he did not buy more bluestone and shellac and his mysterious powders, and he said that rapid transport was far more important. Even then I could not discern the "catch" in Slater's Permanent Polish. The dust on his own polished boot had but to be wiped away to reveal that the polish was as brilliant as ever.

Retrieving our swags, we walked ten miles down river to a lonely bend where we camped for the night, equally dividing between us a few shillings over four pounds.

Now Slater was a hard man to get up in the morning; he was a hard man to get to bed at night when recounting his experiences hoboing in America. The next morning, when I was cooking the breakfast as usual, I picked up Slater's polished boot. The polish was all right. The wonderful gloss still remained. But I could, and did, tear the leather to pieces as easily as tissue paper.

As for the car – well, I hate to think about it even now.

Providing a subject for psychological study, Cockney Slater was remarkable. Ordinarily, he was scrupulously honest. He exhibited no hesitation in dividing the spoils of one day's gentle grafting. He did not drink; neither did he steal. He would not work – until he married an Irish colleen and became a Sinn Fein captain and butcher. Further, he was almost as bashful as I when approaching a station cook for tucker, and yet his brain was ever busy evolving downright swindles which gave the mugs a run.

Before I left his entertaining but dangerous company, he related the following experience without a smile.

There was a couple named Trewan who owned a small selection on the Loddon. Mrs. Trewan was twenty-one stone in weight, whilst her husband was a little more than seven stone. He was a meek and mild little man, and after many years of acute suffering, he went and hanged himself on the sheep gallows near the house. Said Slater:

"When old Mrs. Trewan seen him hanging there, she threw a seven for an hour or so, and then she thinks of all the blowflies settling on poor little Trewan. So out she goes to him, and draws up over him a calico meat bag.

"Then me and Spider Kemp came along, and we called at the house asking for meat. The old woman was going on something cruel, and we couldn't get nothing out of her for her wailing and gnashing, excepting something about the mail coach what was due at seven o'clock.

"We showed her money, and offered to buy some meat, but that didn't have any effect or calm her down any, and off we went feeling sour about it. And then we sights the carcass hanging in the meat bag on the sheep gallows. Says Spider Kemp to me:

"'You go back and pitch to the old tart, and I'll soon cut a couple of pounds of chops.'

"Back I goes and engages the old lady in a one-sided conversation till I hears Spider Kemp letting out a roar. I seen him tearing off down the track below a cloud of dust. That was eleven years ago, and I've never seen him since."

Kissing the Capitalists

Alf the Nark was a bush cook with an unbreakable habit of throwing off his apron and jumping on it when his cheque was three months old and £30 high.

We met, not for the first time, in the smallest bar in Australia, where but five men could drink at once, where the landlord's front adipose was kept pressed to the counter in order that his rear adipose should not sweep the bottles off the shelves.

At the moment of meeting, Alf the Nark was speechless. When he greeted me he was on his feet, his body was steady. His eyes were wide open and his mind seemingly alert; yet he was speechless. His jaws moved; so did his tongue; but he was unable to utter so much as a whisper. Always after his third drink he became speechless. This was a great pity. Sober, his anecdotes were memorable; what they would have been like when watered with whisky caused one to sigh as though bereaved.

The smallest bar in Australia was at Pooncarie, on the Darling. For three weeks we lived in that bar by day, and by night slept with the centipedes on the woodheap. Only towards the dawn of each day did Alf the Nark regain lingual control for an hour or so – until the bar was again opened.

The parting had to come eventually – from Australia's smallest bar. Broke, we rolled along the track northward to Menindie, our gunny-sacks filled by the publican's wife and the publican's pockets filled with our money. Now and then Alf the Nark would halt, lay a restraining hand on my arm and emotionally endeavor to talk. It was evident that some matter of great import weighed heavily on his mind. His black eyes ringed with crimson reflected the anguish created by his disability. Then, resignedly, he would march on, leaving me to stagger after him, my mind filled with forebodings.

After many strenuous efforts to regain speech victory was finally achieved when he placed his hands on my shoulders and said earnestly: "Hug yer chains, lad! Fear 'em not, but hug yer chains."

Thinking he referred to the chains cast around us slaves by the capitalists, I grunted acquiescence, and lurched on by his side with the feeling that something was behind me, dogging my footsteps – something I dared not turn round to face.

"Fear 'em not but hug yer chains, lad. Hug 'em and kiss 'em. They won't hurt. Don't knock 'em orf. Hug 'em and kiss 'em, and you'll be free of 'em the quicker."

Glancing at his profile I noted with particular clarity his Roman nose and the point of his long chin protruding between the black hairs of his drooping moustache. I could make nothing of his philosophy, for I had never feared the capitalists, and thought lightly of their chains cast about me, but I did bar hugging and kissing any capitalist of any race and creed. Presently he said, with a "Hail, Hitler!" kind of salute:

"You see, I don't fight 'em. I lets 'em alone. 'E thinks 'e's teasing me, frightening me, and 'e's disappointed 'cos I don't knock 'im orf. Hug yer chains. Hug 'em and kiss 'em."

Engaged with my own more pressing problem, the almost irresistible temptation to look behind, and restrained only by the fear of what I might see following me, I no longer pondered on the incongruity of kissing the capitalists. Together we trudged from river-bend to river-bend.

Never did shipwrecked mariners want a drink more direfully. To drink water was then impossible. To stop to boil the billy was equally impossible. If I did stop the thing behind me would catch up and jump on my back. There was a mob of horses standing in the shade of several wind-tortured box-trees; there were sheep panting in the shade of a sandalwood-tree growing on a sand-bar stabbing the flank of the river; and even the blowflies were swarming in the shade made by the occasional old man saltbush. To me the shade was forbidden by the thing forcing me ever onward, and Alf was too occupied with kissing the capitalists and hugging them to notice the heat.

"Look at this one crawling up me arm," he said presently. "See, I'm not frightened of 'im. He might 'ave two 'eads and six lobster claws with two eyes to each claw, and he might be painted yaller and blue, but 'e don't frighten me. I'm not knocking 'im orf for 'im to holler for 'is mates. No, not me. I got more sense. Hug 'em and kiss 'em, says I."

Only then did it dawn on me that he had not been referring to the capitalists. When with song I tried to charm away the thing at my heels Alf the Nark determinedly assisted, but at length the torture became unendurable, and with a yell 1 sprang round – to see nothing but the grey track winding away into the dark green of the river box-trees.

"Now, now, 'Ampshire," implored my fellow-sinner. "Now, now, hug yer chains. Kiss 'em. Don't let 'em think you're afraid."

The sun was westering when again we came to the river to select a temporary camp site at which to boil the billy and eat a little. We both knew that to stop for any length of time would be impossible that night. We stood above the river, the like of which no other country can show. Steep and deep the banks appear, as though fashioned by man with giant scoops, so evenly sloped and so straight are they between the bends. The stream was low and the banks were as slippery as grease. We each held an empty billy and a canvas water-bag. Our tongues were swollen with thirst, and the kookaburras mocked our distress. To attempt to reach the water in our weakened condition would have resulted in sliding into the river, and our chances of getting out again would have been equal to those of a mouse in a half-filled bucket of water.

"You're the youngest," Alf the Nark truthfully said, "I'd get to the water all right, but me 'ands shakes so that I'd spill all of it outer the billy."

I pictured myself crawling up the inclined grease-board of a bank, presenting the thing ever behind me with a wonderful opportunity; and, like a man reprieved, I sighed relief when Alf pointed out a fallen tree sprawled down the bank further up the river.

Like the banks the water was dull grey. Twilight was swiftly tinting it to molten silver. The rings made by the jumping fish moved outward sluggishly, too sluggishly for our throbbing eyes to follow them. Beside the tree roots we argued which should go down to the water, finally agreeing on both going down – Alf to protect my back. All the kookaburras in the Western Division were gibing at us.

The going was easy until we reached the level of the last rise. Without the tree branches no man could have proceeded without shooting down into the river. Hearing Alf's grunts behind me, knowing my rear was well guarded, inch by inch I neared the blessed water, until at long last I sought for firm foothold whilst I filled the water-bag from the billy. Then I saw lying along the branch to which I clung a five-foot diamond-marked snake.

"Look out! Don't touch it," I yelled.

"Now, now," said the crooning voice behind me. A hand on the end of a hairy forearm slid over my shoulder. The hand gripped the snake behind its head, and withdrew it from the branch across my shoulder. Fearful of relaxing hold on the branch, for several seconds I could do nothing. "Now, now. It's all jake. You mustn't be afraid of 'em. Hug 'em and kiss 'em."

It had looked so real, that snake, and even as I filled the water-bag I wondered how Alf the Nark could distinguish between the "capitalists" and the real thing. Comforted by his presence at my back, I completed the task, and together we laboriously climbed back to the high ground. Presently the flames of the fire were wrapped comfortingly around the billy. I sat on my swag with my back against a sapling, secure from rear attacks. Alf the Nark squatted on his heels beyond the fire, trying unsuccessfully to cut chips from an evil-looking tobacco plug.

Then through the hot air I saw the snake's head wriggling out from his shirt, and, when I heaved myself into a crouching position to spring away from it, he noticed my anxiety. Laying down the plug and the knife, he deliberately drew the reptile partly from his shirt and kissed its head.

"I keep on telling you, 'Ampshire," he said gently, "that the great thing is not to take too much notice of 'em. Hug yer chains and kiss 'em I says. You see, this here snake ain't vicious-like. What we sees now we don't see ordinary times. Consekently these sort don't bite. They ain't dangerous. Once I 'ad a little nigger baby what insisted on ridin' on me shoulder and tuggin' at me 'air. Did I bash 'im? No, I didn't. I just let 'im stay there as though I was enjoying it. If I 'ad bashed 'im 'e'd 'ave come back with all 'is relations. Don't I know 'em!"

"Did you ever have anything spring on to your back, and wind its arms round your neck and throttle you?" I inquired plaintively.

"No," he replied with conviction. "But I've 'ad 'em crawl up inside me trouser-leg, squirm up past me belt, and come out of me shirt collar to wriggle round me neck and go inter me 'ead through an ear'ole. Even then I took no notice; not even when he sang yims and 'The Face on the Bar-room Floor' for hours and hours. It don't do to notice 'em.

"I did once on the track outer Wanaaring, but never again. I lorst me block and fought one what was like a football with all eyes and no part on 'im where a mouth could be. Like a fool I knocked 'im orf me, and I jumped 'igh and came down on 'im with both boots. You ought to 'ave 'eard 'im holler. I dropped me swag and bolted, and every now and then I looked back to see 'undreds of millions like 'im rolling along the track after me. No, 'Ampshire, I never fights 'em now. I 'ugs 'em an' kisses 'em."

We ate and drank in the ruddy firelight; the bullfrogs, a mopoke and a party of ducks our orchestra. Afterwards we smoked. In earnest Alf the Nark battled with the demon of despondency which rode me, but which was of less importance than the demon waiting for me on the other side of the tree against which I pressed my back.

When the moon came up we slipped into our harness and followed the track. I implored my partner to walk behind me. I knew that the thing had instantly taken its position there immediately I left the guarding tree. Obligingly, Alf the Nark did so.

Once we stopped to boil the billy and to rest for an hour, when my partner gained another opportunity to discuss the peculiar mannerisms of the "capitalists." We boiled the billy again at dawn. All that morning we continued to tramp until we reached a shearing-shed about noon.

Utterly exhausted, we lay down on the wool-room floor, the swags for pillows,

We slept.

I awoke at sundown. The Thing no longer was behind me, no longer threatened to catch up with me and pounce. Alf the Nark was sleeping placidly. The point of his long chin, protruding upward from his mandarin-like moustache, was like a bare hill rising from dark scrub. A diamond-headed snake was half-way out of the open neck of his shirt. With a stick I managed to get it right out.

It was dead. It had been killed by the kookaburras at the very least four days previously.

Wells and Water Troughs

Just fancy going to work by the same train or tram six mornings in every seven, starting work at the screech of a hooter, and working under the watchful eyes of a foreman until the hooter screeches again to knock off! If that has to be done to enjoy the pictures and the beaches in company with a kissable mouth, then such joys will never be for me.

In a former article I mentioned appreciatively the Australian custom of being sacked or leaving a job at a minute's notice. How irksome it must be for both employer and employee to have to wait even a full day before parting company!

No, No! A hooter would send me mad. So would a foreman. Which is not to say that hooters and foremen are not necessary evils, for without both, many men and women could not work at all. As an inspector on a Government vermin fence once said: "Men can be divided into classes: men who can't work unless the boss is looking at them, and men who can't work if the boss is looking at them."

When he said that I sat down and did nothing until he had cleared off.

You see, there are so many kinds of work in the bush at which a man must be trusted to do a fair thing. If he is a born slacker, he will not last long, and will be "put on tramp" as he should. And here it is that we come to the second Australian custom I hope never to see die out – the mutual spirit of give and take.

I do not know the station where the Arbitration Court's ruling regarding hours is adhered to. There never was any necessity to give a ruling laying down the number of hours to be worked in one week. In the first place, no station could be run with men starting and stopping work at fixed hours. In the second place, the old custom of give and take was quite satisfactory both to squatter and men.

It is the rule that men living near the homestead gather outside the office at 7.30 a.m. to receive orders for the day. The work set out seldom cannot be performed later than four o'clock. I have been set work that has been done well and comfortably in two hours, and had I asked for further orders for that day, I would have been considered a nuisance. Consequently, no man rightly can feel annoyance if he is asked to do urgent work at seven o'clock in the evening.

There was certainly the practice of give and take at Two Wells in the south-west corner of Queensland, a place then of magnetic attraction to countless animals and birds. Placed in the middle of an unnatural dust heap having a diameter of half a mile, the two wells were sunk within one 100 yards of each other. In one, the water was as salt as that of the sea; in the other, it was almost fresh. A windmill raised the fresh water, and a petrol engine pumped up the salt water. Both wells supplied one set of reservoir tanks that fed a line of troughing in each of the converging three paddocks and, because of the number of stock and wild things watering there, both wells were worked hard.

Nearby was a bush shed, and a windbreak protecting three tents. A humorous, ancient, wild-eyed and wild-haired Irishman acted engineer and cook and sheep skinner. It was the business of two scrub cutters to lay a ribbon of scrub branches across the path of the sheep flocks on their way to and from water; for only at the far ends of the paddocks was there left a little ground feed, the objective of this being to minimise drought-weakened animals travelling eight or nine miles to water, and eight or nine miles back again the next day to feed.

Time, six o'clock in the evening of a hot, still January day. Temperature well above the century. In the vicinity of the troughs, thousands of strutting galahs and cockatoos; above the troughs a constant whirring of wings and a babel of noise. No emus were present, for they had taken their fill at noon. Here and there in the near distance solitary kangaroos were sitting up, suspiciously regarding the camp and the troughs at which they must drink or perish. Further away little spurts of dust rose to hang motionless above the dust heap flung upwards by bounding fleas, which presently resolved into swiftly arriving 'roos. Of rabbits there was none. A heat wave with a shade temperature of 119 had killed them all.

"I wish to Gawd it would blow," growled Paddy, observing how the kangaroos' dust drifted not at all. "Why they don't put an engine on to that fresh water well beats me. Got to use both wells to maintain a supply, and the mixture about ninety salt and ten fresh. Them poor critters walkin' miles and miles to get a drink of sea water in this heat! The dam mill hasn't gone all day. I had to shin up the mill and turn the fan wheel to get enough water for us."

There was no hint of Ireland in Paddy's voice, but the brogue was strong in Irish Muldoon. In his youth this man of middle height and large girth had studied for the priesthood, and if ever you have been cornered in a bar and compelled to listen for anything up to two hours to light hours and densities, magnitudes and angles and systems, then you have met Irish Muldoon. He had long forgotten all that was known by Sir James Jeans.

"Tanks full?" he asked in that soft, pleasant voice of his, nothing further from his mind than the celestial bodies when he was sober.

"They could be fuller. The mobs are coming in now."

From north of west and from due south, steadily rising brown clouds of dust rose into the red-flecked bronze of the sky, each cloud whirred upwards by the close-packed lines of travelling sheep. The vast dust columns marched towards us with the steadiness of tramping giants – that to the south mushrooming into a cloud having the precise aspect of a water cloud, snow white, its western face tinged with pink by the westering sun.

Now we could see the dull grey lines leaving the scrub at the foot of those gigantic dust columns. The western one blotted out the sun which, striking upon that to the south, painted the column with ever-moving splashes of crimson. Louder and louder came the sound of eager baaings, faster and faster moved the leaders towards to the water which had lured them for so many weary miles. And presently was added the low rumble of thousands of hoofs which churned up the dust that hid the almost countless followers.

"I suppose we had better get going," suggested Irish Muldoon.

We set off each to a line of troughing.

Now Paddy had slaved all day attending the engine and the pumps, skinning dead sheep, and cooking for the camp. Save for the midday hours, Irish Muldoon and I had swung an axe against tree branches in the sun which so heated the ground that it would ignite a dropped safety match. Yet there was no suggestion made that this was after working hours; that we were not paid for the task ahead of us; for this was not a matter for the owner of the run – who lived in idleness in England – and ourselves, but between ourselves and poor, helpless, water-famished animals. Your bushman may be rough and hard, he may never grease his hair or manicure his nails; he may always spend his cheque in a pub, or indulge in every city vice when on holidays, but he is a sentimental cuss with animals.

Here at Twin Wells, night after night, we each arrived at the water troughs with the sheep. Outward from the troughs spread the flood of wool. More densely rose the now stationary dust columns merged by close proximity into one. A mad, straining, trampling, moaning surge of flesh and bone and wool, with here and there mounds of wool heaving above the general level, each mound marking the place where a sheep had fallen and was being trampled to death. Dust-choked and heated, we scrambled from mound to mound to rescue the fallen. Then to the troughs to seize a foolish sheep which had been pushed into it, and was blocking the flow of water.

So it went on. The leaders, having distended their bellies with brine, forced their way through the streams of arriving sheep to take position several of hundreds yards distant where they waited, stolidly chewing their cud. With the passage of time the weaker sheep arrived, sheep which lurched and staggered, glassy-eyed, gaunt despite their wool, their mouths dry and as hot as fire. They went down in dozens in the scramble, poor beasts that when lifted moved strengthless legs frantically to get them to the water. And having drank and drank they laid down with their bellies distended close beside the troughs, refusing to get up or to stand up when lifted.

Gradually the dust thinned. Behind the halted leaders massed sheep in their hundreds, heavy with water, tired to the point of exhaustion by that long walk. About the troughs the press of sheep eased to reveal vacant spaces. All about were sheep lying down, muzzles resting on the ground, eyes closed or almost so. Others lay dead, their last ounce of waning strength used up, expended in effort never to be rewarded.

And now through the hanging dust came the spectre of

drought. Strange shapes that moved a little forward, fell, moved again, fell and moved onward yet again, tongues lolling from scorched mouths, some with an eye or both eyes plucked out by the crows. A little rest, and then one more effort; another little rest and then one, oh! just one more effort to drink and drink and drink.

There was Irish Muldoon straddling sheep and walking them to his trough. There was Paddy screaming oaths and curses, and carrying water in a tin to pour down the throats of sheep doomed to death. He said he did it to save as many as possible, to lighten the work of skinning the dead ones the next day. The liar!

Evening after evening the western sky was like the wall of a slaughter house. Day after day showed the fiery heat of the torturing sun. After the sun had set, the afterglow reddened this field of horror, the standing water-filled flocks, the individual sheep lying down between them and the troughs, and between the troughs out along the paths the flocks had taken from the scrub lines. Far and near, black dots moved sluggishly about dun-coloured mounds, crows feasting on the bodies of animals which had failed to come in. Kangaroos were creeping closer on all fours. Others were hopping short distances. Yet others were sitting up waiting for men to leave the water which they must get or perish.

Faces red with dust, perspiration gluing our clothes to our bodies, we would finally go back to camp and pour water over each other. The dusk was deepening, and flocks were lying down close packed for protection against foxes. From each flock individual sheep left to drink again, and to return slowly.

Over a pannikin of tea Paddy would curse the squatters for breeding sheep to suffer thus, and, in the natural order of things, Irish Muldoon would uphold the squatters. Their voices would rise high in vocal combat.

And when finally we went to bunk, stretchers brought out from the tents, lying on them without covering until after midnight, the ceaseless cries of the wild came from the water troughs; the warning thrump-thrump of kangaroo tails, the snarl of a dingo, the spitting quex-quexing of quarrelling foxes. The world hidden at long last by the merciful darkness.

Crabby Tom

By far the most important person on any station is the cook. He has it in his power to create for others heaven or hell, for the sky will be bright, and energy at full strength, after a breakfast of well-cooked grilled cutlets and well-made yeast bread; while life will be dull and not worth living if the cutlets have been grilled to cinders and the bread is more suited to putty in window panes.

As a class all cooks are difficult. Their tempers are uneven, and one never knows the moment when a cook will tear off his apron, dance on it, raise his hands high, and depart, swearing that never again will he feed such low, grousing, lazy crawlers.

There was Ted Ellis. No man ever lived who knew more sea shanties than he. These he sang the livelong day – until someone came along who offered him a "taste". It was always the taste that did it. Within an hour Ellis was heading for the nearest pub.

There was Crabby Tom. Invariably, when he arrived to take charge of a kitchen, he was on the verge of delirium tremens. I say "on the verge" because he would be too drunk to enjoy them, and only when sobering-up did he see things which did not exist.

I first met Crabby Tom when he arrived at a place called Wombra Lake, meaning in the local aboriginal dialect, Big Lake. Just where was the lake I never discovered, despite the fact that then I was riding three paddocks totalling in area something like 199 square miles.

My fellow stockman was away on a trip, and for some time I had to do my own cooking, when the boss rang to say that he was sending out a cook on the truck next day. And during the next day I had visions of beautifully cooked meat, and freshly baked, feathery yeast bread. It follows that my interest was aroused when, on sighting Wombra Lake after a long day, I observed a man running round and round the two huts.

Having unsaddled and freed the horse, I was able to give further attention to the sprinter. He was about sixty years old, wore nothing but underpants, and showed remarkable stamina. Now and then he would glance over his naked shoulder, utter a loud yell, and speed up. With the regularity of clockwork he would disappear round the corner of one hut and reappear round the corner of the other, quite oblivious to my presence.

It happened that in the scabbard attached to the saddle I was holding was a 0.32 rifle, and when he again hove in sight, I allowed him to pass me before firing off the gun and pretending to chase an imaginary horror. With that, Crabby Tom pulled up and came about with rasping breath.

"Did you get him?" he wheezed, hair on end, eyes dilated, teeth bared in a terrible grin.

"Wounded him," I admitted sorrowfully. "But he's cleared out. He won't come back any more. Better come in and we'll get some tea."

"Right. But you keep the gun handy. I ain't no shot. I never killed anythink yet," he said earnestly.

"Leave it to me. Did you bring a drink out with you?" I inquired, desiring to know the amount of the stock, if any.

"No. Old Starlight," meaning the boss, "took a full bottle off me. Blinking shame, and me dyin' for a drink."

The poor wretch sat on a form against the table in the kitchen while I got the fire going, and, later, unrolled his swag and made up his bunk. I was in two minds about ringing Old Starlight and giving my views about dumping a madman on me, when Crabby leapt two feet off the ground, vented an ear-piercing shriek, climbed the table, and swung himself up to one of the roof cross-beams.

"Look out! It's just behind you!" he yelled. "It'll get you! It'll get you!"

Endeavouring to pacify him and allay his terrors, I made tea, and, when he refused to eat or drink, ate a hearty meal, believing that a stormy night lay ahead. And a stormy night it was, too. No doctor handy to give him a shot or two of morphia; no policeman in the vicinity to yell for if Crabby Tom got his hands round my throat thinking he was strangling a green man with blue hair and red eyes. A situation, indeed, to make one exercise what little brain one might have.

"Look out, mate! It's behind you again!" Or – "Shut the door! Can't you see it's trying to get in?" Or it might be in stuttering wails: "Hug! Hug!" and he would frantically brush things off his person, or from the beam supporting him.

With a man in such a mental state, pleading and argument are useless. The only efficient method of dealing with such a person, should morphia not be available, is to club him into unconsciousness with a mulga root; but to this method is attached some slight risk of being charged with the crime of murder, because judgment and finesse are qualities rare in the average peaceable man.

About nine o'clock I gave Crabby Tom half a bottle of pain killer, but to my disgust it had no effect on him. At ten o'clock I was getting "fed up." At eleven, when Crabby was barricading himself into the fowls house in company with twenty squarking hens, I contemplated rolling a swag and going away into the scrub to sleep. After all, I was not being paid the handsome sum of thirty shillings a week and tucker to nurse a lunatic.

However, there are occasions when one has to do small odd jobs without hope of gain, and about midnight I determined to experiment on Crabby with Dr. Browne's chlorodyne. From five to thirty drops Dr. Browne advised for cases of nervous debility and a hundred other complaints.

Now Dogger Smith once told me without batting an eye-lid that he had drunk two full bottles when he anticipated an attack of D.T.s, and allowing a reduction of 75 per cent to counter exaggeration, I gave Crabby Tom half a bottle. Or it might have been a little more, because in twenty minutes he had regained normality and drank a pannikin of tea, and ten minutes after that he was sleeping in his bunk.

Blessed rest! Exhausted, I lay down to sleep, the two scared cats coming to sleep on my feet as always they did. Peace! Wonderful peace at last! The night so quiet! Aye, a little too quiet. I could hear no sound from Crabby Tom, no snore, not even his breathing.

He was lying on his back. His face was dull grey. His eyes were shut. There was no movement of his powerful chest. I thought of the looking glass to make sure he was dead. For hours I slapped his face and shook him. For hours I walked him round and round the room. It was full daylight when I collapsed and he was snoring in healthy sleep.

But his D.T.s were cured, and the trouble and fright he had rendered me were worth it all, for he proved to be the finest cook in my experience.

All cooks have bad feet as well as bad tempers, brought about by standing on hard floors in slippers. A cement floor will cripple a man in no time. Yet to offset this drawback, there is always a job waiting for a good cook, even in these days of depression. Cooks, who have to labour seven days in the week, are always scarce: a good cook is as rare as water in the Paroo River.

The day must come when a bushman will have to turn cook, and I found that a knowledge of cooking is no weight to carry, and a trade of value when held in reserve.

My first batch of bread was not a success. There must have been something wrong with the yeast, and after forty-eight hours, I baked the dough hoping it would rise in the oven.

Yes, it must have been the yeast. When, in disgust, I threw a loaf out of the window, it cracked a cement-hard clay-pan star fashion. The second batch was a trifle better, although it had not risen a fraction of an inch in sixty-four hours. In the quiet of the night, acting similarly to a body-snatcher, I buried about thirty pounds of dough in the ash heap.

And when the hands came into lunch the next day, the blacksmith said with a grin:

"Have you seen them mushrooms out by the ash heap?"

It was the mushroom season, and I have a strong passion for mushrooms, but decidedly it was not the season for that buried dough to rise and shame me.

Broke in the City

Today – even today – there is in all Australia but little necessity for an unmarried man to be dependent on others for a bite to eat and a billy of tea. When a young and robust man stops me on the street to tell the old, old story of being short of threepence for the price of a meal, he thoroughly deserves to continue thirsty. In the first place, his story proves him to be quite lacking in originality, and, in the second, his request reveals astounding vanity, prompting him to think that all men save him are fools.

I never did have the slightest acquaintance with the fear of unemployment in the bush, but unemployment in a city was, and ever will be, a nightmare. Once out of a city job, I would get out of that city with the speed of an escapee from justice. No other land in the world is so kind to the down and out as is the real Australia. It offers him unlimited firewood, water costs him nothing, and possession of a fishing line and a gin trap assure him of food. But a man with domestic responsibilities is as securely chained to the industrial chariot as are his brothers in the old country.

I went broke in Melbourne – awoke one morning to find myself possessing capital amounting to seventeen pence, no knowledge of any trade, no knowledge of how to set about competing in the wild rush for casual labouring work, and no friends. I could have wired to One-Spur Dick for financial assistance, but it would have been a repetition.

You see, the week before I had gone broke, too. I then wired to One-Spur Dick urgently requesting the loan of five pounds. He wired the money that same day, but, unfortunately, I did not get it until after the Mildura train had pulled out the next morning. What happened at his end was this.

At three o'clock, when he was unyoking the bullocks, and his offsider was throwing off the load of wood on to the station woodheap, the bookkeeper gave him my telegram. One-Spur Dick read the cry for help from the city wilderness before the bookkeeper left him, and he said:

"Wire him a fiver at once. I'll sign the chit directly I've turned out these colourful hornies."

When they were having dinner that evening the blacksmith indignantly demanded an answer to –

"Wot's the good of sending a measley five pounds to a man in Melbourne? Strike me pink! That wouldn't last Jimmy Woodser a day, let alone Hampshire!"

This so worried One-Spur Dick that he insisted on signing another chit for five pounds, and he urged the bookkeeper to dispatch the money first thing the following morning.

Accordingly, at nine o'clock the next day the second remittance was telephoned and telegraphed some 800 miles. At eleven o'clock, when the bookkeeper was settling down to his work, there entered his office Tommy Ching Lung, the station gardener, who laid on the desk five sovereigns. He said:

"You sendum these five pound, Hampshire, quick. Ten pound no good. Hampshire, in Melbourne."

So that, in the space of four hours, I walked from my hotel to the G.P.O. three times to collect a total of fifteen pounds; and instead of catching the Mildura train the next morning, I lingered among the fleshpots.

With the arrival of the second term of bankruptcy, and realisation of the fool I was, I would, indeed, have been laid low had I again wired for assistance. I was in a pit of my own digging, and pride dictated the urgency of climbing out of it the best way I could. How far from Melbourne the Railway Commissioners would have conveyed me for seventeen pence, I knew not, but I did know it would not be far beyond where Sunshine now is. Beyond Sunshine lay hundreds of miles of open cocky country, where the wintry winds of June are most unkind, and where it always rains, or seems to be always raining. And carrying a swag down Collins Street offered no appeal despite its possible originality in the twentieth century.

Uncle most considerately advanced sixteen shillings on a cigarette case; and with this money I bought a job from a labour bureau and a rail ticket to Neerim. At no time in my life – not even at the war in the winter of 1916-17 – have I felt as cold as I did waiting for the Neerim train on the Warragul station.

I understand that all the land round Neerim is very lovely –

during the summer. I would not have thought it, but I am open to conviction. I was there just a month, but I saw little of the country, and nothing of the town. At dawn one would step off the verandah into ten inches of mud, and toboggan down the side of a mountain for the thirty cows. The boss and his wife would assist with the milking. That done, one would step out of the ten inches of mud on to the verandah, and eat breakfast. How I missed my early morning tea, the night-before tea in the billy heated to be drunk whilst a cigarette was smoked, and one listened for the horse bells.

If it did not rain, it sleeted; and if it did not sleet, it snowed. To me the real Australia appeared to be on the other side of the world. No wonder that the Kelly gang got going – they had to do something to keep warm. Bankrupt in Melbourne, I had been like a child blindfolded and turned round and told to walk ten paces. On the bandage being removed, I expected to find myself in Sunny Australia – not at the South Pole. Alas, my blood was as thin as vinegar, and I had no backbone. I called upon the gods to witness the oaths I took never to go broke again in a city.

The boss said: "I've got to go to Melbourne for a week. Finish that ploughing, and, if you've got time, get to that sucker bashing in the lower paddock."

That was at the beginning of my fourth week, when the rain let up for ten-minute periods. I completed turning the mud with a single-furrow plough, and went to the sucker bashing like the local baker went to his ovens – to get warm. But there were the cows to be eternally milked, and the separating to be done, and my clothes to be rung of water; and when the opportunity came, I gave a week's notice to the housewife.

"What's the matter with the place?" she wanted to now. "You foreigners are never satisfied. I can't understand why you don't go back to England, if you don't like Australia."

"The place may be all right, but I left England to come to Sunny Australia – not to the Antarctic" – was my complaint. "I want to get near to a hundred square miles bush fire. I want to see if the sun still rises and sets. The smell of bullocks in a team on a saltbush plain is bearable, but rain-soaked cows in a small shed are beyond my powers of appreciation."

The boss came back the day before I left. I saw him

overlooking the ploughing, and, strangely enough, he found no fault with it. Then we went along to the sucker bashing.

"Hum! Haven't done too bad," he said, with evident satisfaction. "How many axe handles did you break?"

"Break! I broke none!"

"Broke none!" he echoed. "Do you mean to tell me you never broke an axe handle?"

"Yes. Why should I break axe handles?"

He regarded me as though I grew wings. Then:

"Well, you're the first man I've had who didn't break axe handles at sucker bashing. Did you use an axe, or did you use your teeth? The last man I had broke two a day. The man before him broke on average four a day, and the man before him broke seven in one morning. Now, what are you leaving for?"

"Feel my clothes," I pleaded. "They haven't been dry for a month. Build me a hut with an open fireplace, and with a hole at the back of it to inset a whole tree trunk, and give me ten pounds a week, and I wouldn't stay."

I was not far off being broke when I returned to Melbourne. I had enough money to get me to Mildura and the woodheap, but I could not go north and face One-Spur Dick, and the blacksmith, and Tommy Ching Lung. They would make nothing of the debt, but I could not stand their grins and well-intentioned gibes. Pride demanded restitution before explanation.

I went disk ploughing with eight horses in the Wimmera. It was in July, and, if I was seldom warm, I was at least seldom wet. Harvest came. I earned two pounds and ten shillings a week and tucker tending sixteen horses – two teams, the first of which I hooked into a harvester at ten o'clock, the second at two o'clock, and the first again at six o'clock. In my spare time I sewed 4,000 bags of wheat, for which I received twelve shillings and sixpence a hundred.

Eight weeks that harvest lasted. I mailed the fifteen pounds to the boys up north. To them every Sunday I wrote the same message: "Seeing you soon."

But never a word about the cows and the axe handles. To them, months afterwards, I swore that the cocky was my uncle, who had made me his heir. To myself, morning and night, I swore that never again would I go broke in a city.

A Cure for Snakebite

It is a singular fact that a particular scent will invariably recall to mind a scene or a person. The scent of carnations will recall to my mind a pair of laughing blue eyes; a snake will always bring out of the past a man known to his friends as the Storm Bird.

He was a man who, most tragically, lived 200 years too late. Had he lived 200 years ago, he would not have had to wait for an obscure biographer to bring him forth from obscurity. Had he lived to rival Captain Kidd, as assuredly he would have done, his "life" would have fallen to the task of every famous historian.

Alas, he lived in those prosaic days before the Great War, when, as you know, piracy, and even bushranging, were not considered the pursuits of gentlemen, when the community basked in a doe-like complacence established by an efficient police force. Instead of being the carefree stockman he was, in the reign of Queen Elizabeth the Storm Bird would have been royally licensed to beard the King of Spain.

"I was camped with a bloke in a hut like this one in o-four," he said, "when I was preparing to climb into my bunk for the night. We had several kittens in that 'ut, and when Alf Stodger got atween the blankets, he said: 'Blast you! Get out of it.'

"I said: 'Wot's up with you?'

"'E said: 'Blinded cat bit me toe.'

"I don't take no notice of 'im being interested in a Garvice, where the cook was about to arst the gardener for 'is dorter's 'and, but after a whiles I'm layin' back smokin' me bed-time pipe, and it strikes me that for the first night since I 'noo 'im, Alf Stodger wasn't snorin'.

"Ain't you asleep yet, Alf?," I says.

"When 'e don't answer and I can't 'ear 'im breathin', I takes the slush lamp to 'im, and finds 'im as cold as a dog's nose. Now that makes me think a bit, and I remembered wot 'e said about the cat. So I pulls orf the blankets one be one, and among 'em I finds a saltbush snake about seven inches long. Which is why I always makes me bed afore I gits into it."

Which was why I then made mine for the first time that week!

We were in residence among a conglomeration of iron sheets, designated a stockman's hut in all official returns, and situated thirty-seven miles from White Cliffs. The Storm Bird was working on contract, building a set of sheep yards, and he slaved with amazing vigour from dawn until dark, piling up a comfortable cheque.

He was imbued with the ambition of visiting New Zealand, but at the time I was unaware that this ambition was of life duration, and that he never got nearer to New Zealand than the first wayside hotel. His intentions were always good. But the flesh was always weak.

"I'm gonna work right through this Christmas," he declared. "I'm wantin' another 'alf 'undred to give me a good three month's spell. I'll 'ave enough when I've finished this job."

A day or so later he said: "It's gonna be a dry Christmas, but it wouldn't be so bad if we 'ad a few bottles out 'ere to wet it, sort of."

Thus it came about that I asked the boss for permission to drive the buckboard into White Cliffs to purchase a tinned Christmas pudding, and thus it was that on Christmas Eve there reposed under my bunk a nailed case containing the Christmas pudding, a box of cigars, two bottles of whisky and a dozen of beer.

We had solemnly sworn not to open the case until eleven o'clock on Christmas morning. At noon Christmas Eve we knocked off work, and, so that Christmas Day should be a real holiday, I set to work cooking tucker enough to last several days, whilst the Storm Bird became busy on the woodheap cutting a pile of firewood. We determined to rise early the next morning and clean out the place before the holiday officially started.

I had two teal ducks roasting in one camp oven and a damper cooking in another, when my camp mate suddenly ceased singing "The Face on the Bar-room Floor" to utter a yell of anguish.

On rushing out, I found him wildly striking at something with the blade of the axe, and the something proved to be a forty-inch speckled snake.

"'E got me, 'Ampshire! 'E got me on the 'and!" screamed the Storm Bird, standing up from chopping the snake into small pieces.

"Show it me," I ordered, overwhelmed by my complete lack of toxic knowledge in this crisis.

The snake had bitten his left hand at the edge of the palm. The punctures were plainly to be seen.

"Suck it! Come inside! We'll have to cut it open!" I cried, and ran on to the hut. When he staggered inside I was sharpening the butcher's killing knife on a steel.

"Cut me 'and orf, quick," besought the Storm Bird.

"You may as well be dead as live with only one hand," was my opinion. "Hold your hand firmly on the table. Shut your eyes."

I sawed into the wound with the blunt knife, but the victim uttered never so much as a whimper. We had no permanganate of potash, so I repeatedly filled my mouth with water and squirted it through our pipe stems into the terrible gash I had cut, having read somewhere that nicotine is a makeshift antiseptic. When a ligature had been fixed, I asked him how he felt, I myself feeling very sick.

"Crook," he wailed. "I can feel the stuff actin'. They say whisky is a good antidote. Wot about breakin' a bottle?"

I opened up the cellar and gave him half a pint of raw spirit, took a dose myself, and then rushed away into the night paddock to yard the buckboard horses. Then back into the hut to see if the Storm Bird was dead.

"It's gettin' me orl right," he said drowsily.

"Walk up and down," I urged. "Have another drink. I'll put in the horses in two ticks."

It might have been five ticks, not longer, when I had the horses harnessed and the buckboard at the door. Inside I rushed to grab the open case and two canvas water bags; the case to put on the driving seat, the water bags to strap to the side rails. In three more ticks I had got the Storm Bird on to the high seat, and, with the case and two pannikins between us, we started on our thirty-seven miles' rush to the nearest doctor like a fire brigade answering a call.

"Don't go to sleep, now," I pleaded. "If you do, you will never again wake."

"It's gettin' me. It's paralysin' me arm," he stated with resignation.

"Take another drink. The poison in the bottles will counteract the venom. Keep awake now, or I'll have to start punching you. Take a deep noser this time. You stick to the whisky. Give me a bottle of beer."

Thus he was made busy and his mind kept off the horrible death waiting to pounce on him if I failed to get him to the doctor. His piratical aspect had given place to the solemn appearance of an undertaker who had not shaved for a week and had not washed his neck for a month.

Twelve miles out of White Cliffs we reached a mail coach change, and luckily the groom had in his yards a dozen fresh horses. An explanation of the urgency of our case produced a rapid exchange of horses, and in less than a minute we were on our way, two half-broken horses tearing along at a gallop.

Now and then the patient would take a half-pint of whisky to keep the venom at bay and dash off the head of a beer bottle against a whirring tyre that I might be refreshed. We had forgotten the ligature, but it had come off and the danger of gangrene was removed.

We entered White Cliffs with the dash of a Marathon-winning four-in-hand, pulling up outside the hospital in a cloud of dust. The Storm Bird was nearly dead. He could not articulate when the doctor asked the reason for our abrupt arrival.

The doctor smiled whilst he washed the wound and stitched it, and then he lectured me on the difference between the bites of poisonous and non-poisonous snakes.

I was a newchum, but the Storm Bird was certainly not a newchum. A long time afterwards he said he had not reckoned on my surgery, but even that was better than a dry Christmas Eve.

Waiting for Rain

I have long reached the conclusion that, of the money Maker and the money Getter, the latter is the much better off. Having been both, there is authority for this opinion. The employer has the worry of making money and of going bankrupt if he ceases to do so even for a short space of time, whilst the employee has but to wait with patience for the pay days.

Making money is a gift; waiting for a pay envelope is a habit. Habits being more general to the human race than gifts, there will always be many more money getters than money makers.

Joe Foster – one time known by the cognomen of Skylark – was a born money maker. He had that cheerful, buoyant disposition which not only attracted to him money, but friends. But it was not until he was forty-five that there began to arrive a fine house, a motor car, and boxes of cigars. Before "he took a tumble," he made big cheques sinking dams, and because he had built up an efficient plant of horses and gear, the Western Lands Board allotted him the leasehold of 30,000 acres of fine country.

After all, perhaps, it was the woman he married who actually cultivated in him the habit of clinging to the money he made. Anyway, I am quite sure that to her courage and her faith in Australia was due their present Adelaide home and their lives of comparative security after a period of horror through which the weaker sex, sic, again proved its strength.

When the Skylark was granted the leasehold, he had about £400 in cash, and his plant was worth easily another £500. He spent over-much on a house for his bride, and he spent too quickly on improving the property and in stocking it. This coming at the beginning of a two-year drought, brought him to the verge of Carey Street.

The peculiar thing about an Australian drought is that not only is it difficult to foretell, but it is difficult to realise when it actually has begun. A drought may be likened to a mountain, to reach the top of which one has to climb a succession of lesser ridges, each appearing to the climber to be the real summit. After a six-months' period of dry weather, a splendid rainfall will dispel the caution the dry period has engendered in the heart of the squatter. He believes that one good rainfall will be followed by another; when, instead of that, it ushers in a much longer rainless period. He gambles on the probability of rain more than he should do.

Before one May, when two inches of rain fell in three days, it had not rained for seven months. Everyone was joyful, for it seemed certain that the comparatively short drought was over. At this time I had more than £300 saved, not due to any inherent virtue but to a preference for taking a holiday on tramp rather than among the fleshpots of a city. The Skylark put to me the proposition of taking me into partnership and paying me a wage of £3 a week and tucker, and thus it was that I became a bloated capitalist.

With my capital we carried on hopefully. When, after another dry period of five months, sheep went down to two shillings a head, we bought 1,800 ewes, for the dam was still almost full and the drought-defying saltbush in splendid condition.

I am a great believer in divining for water. My partner was an expert, and he selected with a piece of bent wire the site for a well, accurately estimating the water stream to be between fifty and sixty feet below the surface. We found water at that depth, but it was brackish, a little too brackish for the stock to drink without dilution with fresh water.

During the mid-summer months we laboured at the well-sinking. 4,000 sheep on the property was overstocking at the beginning of a long drought; and, because we did not realise that when it rained two inches in May, it was the prelude to a long drought instead of the end of a short one. By the end of the summer the dam was dry and the sheep were forced to live on the brackish water of the well.

We could secure agistment nowhere. No one wanted to buy sheep; all wanted to sell. The price of fat sheep soared, but no one had fat sheep to sell.

How easy it is to be wise after the event! It would have paid us to muster the sheep and slaughter half of them for their skins, giving the remainder a better chance. But what squatter could do that when every squatter eternally hopes that it will rain the next week? When in every little cloud he sees the forerunner of a mass which will drop water and transform the dust heap into a paradise.

So the lambing time came. Because there was no green feed, because the ewes' milk was limited, every ewe with twins abandoned one. There formed little parties of motherless lambs, watched by the eagles and the crows and the foxes, weak little mites which ran bleating towards us like lost and frightened babes in the wood.

For hundreds of miles around, the vermin gathered over this drought-stricken district to grow fat and slothful. They multiplied amazingly. They ate the lambs alive, and then began their horrible work on the weakest of the sheep. I came to understand how it was that some men, when they catch a crow alive, delight in torturing it.

In a light cart, the Skylark and I drove about skinning the dead sheep and killing those sheep whose dreadful end was otherwise certain. A cloud in the north-east would cause us to smile until it slowly vanished in the scarlet sky above the setting sun.

"Perhaps it will rain tomorrow!" the Skylark's wife always said when we ate dinner, undimmed hope in her eyes, the horrors of the day in ours carefully kept from her. It was not the slow and inevitable approach of bankruptcy, the wastage of our savings and our labour, dreadful as that was to us in our helplessness, but the vivid never-to-be-forgotten scenes we witnessed every day in the animal kingdom – the cruelty and the heat and the thirst.

"Perhaps it will rain tomorrow!"

"There's a heavy cloud in the north. It might work up into a thunderstorm."

"It's going to rain! I saw the ants carrying their eggs up into a tree!"

But it did not rain.

Frustrated hopes and the horror of the greatest drama Australia produces, cowed us two men. Both of us would have given up the battle long before we did had it not been for the grim determination of a frail woman.

"Perhaps it will rain tomorrow. Let's keep on," she would urge with assumed cheerfulness, undimmed hope in her eyes, faith in the real Australia ever in her heart. The stacks of sheep skins in the cane-grass shed grew in number.

Every lamb perished. Hundreds of sheep dotted the land minus their skins. Sheep died which were not found till long afterwards, and from the rotting carcasses we pulled out the wool and bagged it.

"I'm damned sorry I got you to come in with me," the Skylark often said, and as often I would reply: "What's £300 anyway? Nothing venture, nothing win. There's more to be got where that came from."

There was old MacIntosh. His wife came one day to say he had not returned home the evening before. We found him in his sheepyards, where he had been all night long, slaughtering his mustered sheep and piling them into a mountain of unskinned mutton. He kept on singing "The Wild Colonial Boy," and was still singing it when they took him away to Broken Hill. Old Mrs. MacIntosh found sanctuary with the Skylark's wife.

There was Matthews, owner of a big run. Once he ran racehorses, once he was rich. The mortgagees closed on him and gave him £250 and his car with which to start life afresh. But he was too old to begin again in this life, and with strychnine hastened the start in the next.

"Perhaps it will rain tomorrow!"

Dozens of women were saying that daily, dry-eyed and hopeful when in the presence of their men, haunted with fear of the future when alone in their red hot homes.

My courage failed me when but 300 of the 4,000 sheep remained to be skinned. Skylark had a buyer for the place at £200 when normally it was worth £5,000, and he wanted to sell and pay me half, but I had no dependents, my old bicycle, and a pair of legs. I deserted the ship like a rat, and so would the Skylark have done but for his wife who was the real captain.

"Perhaps it will rain tomorrow!"

And when the tomorrow did come and the brave new world arose from the vast dust heap, she and the Skylark rose with it. Today they and old Mrs. MacIntosh live somewhere in Adelaide.

You see, the real pioneers of the old days, and the real pioneers of these days – are the women.

The Musical Hut

If you ride westward from Winton, Queensland, for ninety-four miles, you will reach the branch track which will finally take you to Charleville. Beside the junction grew a great bloodwood tree, and nailed to the trunk was the bottom drawer of a once valuable rosewood bedroom chest, then utilised as a letter-box.

It was a year when I was young; when life lay ahead with a promise as glamorous as the mystic land lying beyond the sunset, and I rode a horse and packed another, and camped o' nights beneath trees in the vicinity of a dam or bore, and knew not care. And so, following the south-west track from the junction, I entered the country of Melody Sam.

The reason behind Sam's going bush was never rightly known. One day he arrived, and for seven years he stayed, six of which he lived alone in an iron hut, riding two paddocks and mixing with his fellows only when mustering throughout the shearing. He had never been known to read or to play cards, and was not a conversationalist, his leisure hours being occupied with playing on his violin. And that, they told, Melody Sam played with exquisite skill.

By repute he was known for many miles around, and the little iron home came to be called the Musical Hut. It was only by chance that the manager called one day to find its lonely tenant dying.

Melody Sam lies at the foot of a giant gum near the homestead, and his violin hangs on the office wall. It had been there but a week when I first saw it, and the Musical Hut had been vacant ten days when I settled into it and began to ride the paddocks he had known for six sad and lonely years.

It is as well to have a mental picture of the Musical Hut. It was a long, low building of corrugated iron, bordered on the front side by three pepper trees. At the back was the well and windmill and water troughing, and beyond that were the sheep yards. The interior of the hut was divided into the living-room and the "bunk house"; for, in those days, stockmen and shearers slept in bunks in tiers, much like those in the forecastle of a ship. The hut's situation at the end of a track dictated its isolation, and, unless anyone came especially from the homestead, none called to give news of the world.

It was quite a nice hut as huts went in those days. The afternoon of my arrival I spent in sweeping and cleaning, and browsing among the old books and papers left by the tenant who occupied the place before Melody Sam. At tea time a ginger cat arrived and entered with such quiet confidence as to proclaim that Melody Sam liked cats. Later, it returned from the bush, and, one by one, brought in six kittens.

Weary – temporarily, of course – of travelling anywhere, I settled down to the job, working to a routine, most days spent in the saddle, every evening occupied with reading or writing. The weeks went by, and summer came in with a sudden heat wave which forced me to erect a rough bunk on the narrow verandah.

Havelock Ellis has written much on the psychological effects of solitude on the human mind, and what he has written is convincing enough to compel belief that he experienced it. Others, also, have written on the subject, but they lack the authority of personal experience, and are unable to appreciate the significant fact that as human minds differ, so the effects of solitude vary with all men who suffer it. Solitude may be personified by a stalking tiger-cat which will inevitably claim its victim, and final madness is hastened or delayed by the manner in which the victim exercises his mind.

It was nine o'clock one moonlight night when I first heard Melody Sam playing on his violin when he had been dead nearly three months. Not a zephyr stirred the air or the drooping leaves of the pepper trees. Outside, lying on my bunk, wearing only pyjamas, the topmost blanket folded sideways to be pulled over me only towards daybreak, I smoked and listened to Melody Sam whilst little cold shivers played over my skin.

The music was soft. It was so soft that only when lying quite still could it be heard. At first I thought it came from the bunkhouse, then from beneath the pepper trees, then up in their branches, then in the living-room. It was impossible to decide at what point it had its origin; it seemed constantly to move about, the low plaintive wail of a violin.

It made me wonder what kind of a man Melody Sam had been. They said he was tall, pale of face, sloping of shoulders. He never smiled. His eyes were dark, almost black, and of great intensity. His hands were finely shaped, and when in the sun he invariably wore gloves.

What had sent him into the bush? Not the quest of adventure which had sent me, I felt sure. Tragedy? It appeared most likely. A broken love affair, perhaps; or possibly the death of one he loved exceedingly well. The manager said that when he died he was smiling, and that he whispered a woman's name.

Now, if a man is very unhappy for a long period, during which he has lived in one place, I could find no logical reason why his spirit would want to return to that place to haunt it. There are places which I want never to see again, and yet to others those same places might be the background of happy reverie. But here at this lonely hut where Melody Sam had known agony of mind, he was returned to haunt it with his violin.

I have heard, and even taken part in, argument concerning the problems of metaphysics, survival of life after death, and time. I have listened, too, to allegedly clever people discoursing on these same problems from public platforms, and never do they get any "forrader". They invent extraordinary words to affirm their cleverness, and theorise and argue, but they never prove anything whatever. For ages men have propounded theories and sought to solve these problems, and they would have been better employed making bricks in so far as any results have been secured.

Some ten days after the first haunting of the Musical Hut I again listened to Melody Sam's soft playing, so low, and so sweet as to be elfin. It was another such night as that first, but moonless.

Eventually, because of the state of the country, further flocks were put into the paddocks I rode, and a man named Dirty Dick was sent to live and work with me. His habits certainly were not dirty, but his language, which lacked artistry, certainly was.

He built himself a bunk beneath one of the pepper trees. Never once did I mention to him the spiritual activities of Melody Sam, because, firstly, I did not want to be laughed at, and secondly, because I did not want it thought that the Tiger Cat of solitude was catching up to me.

Dirty Dick had been with me more than a week when, having dropped off to sleep early one quiet night, I was awakened to see him standing over me.

"Hey!" he whispered. "'E 'as come back. 'E is playing on 'is violin. Can't you 'ear 'im? I'm gettin' outer this. I'm not stoppin' 'ere. I never liked 'is eyes when 'e was alive; they must be somethink awful now 'e's bin dead five monce."

And leave he did. He rolled his swag and departed for the homestead at eleven o'clock that night.

The manager rang up the next morning to hear about the haunting. He understood from Dirty Dick that Melody Sam walked around the place, arrayed in his shroud and playing with exceptional verve. Not one of the men would take Dirty Dick's place, and the manager came out, determined to stay until he laid the ghost.

He had a scientific mind, as was proved once or twice when I considered the weather too hot to ride the paddocks, and he quickly laid the ghost by the heels after we had wandered around with the lamps looking for Melody Sam. The tune Melody Sam played was Tosti's "Good Bye," and Tosti's "Good Bye" was the manager's wife's favourite gramophone record. When the record was played at the homestead, it could be heard at the Musical Hut, but not of sufficient volume to be easily distinguished. Either along the telephone wires, or because of unique conditions, in certain climatic conditions, the gramophone music was conveyed eleven miles.

Whitewashing a Police Station

The summer had been long and hot, and the autumn rains delayed in coming. For a year almost I had lived at the edge of a great gibber plain in the far north-east of South Australia, the small hut of iron sheets and its wide verandah roof of cane grass being situated above a lone water-hole in the bed of a creek.

At noon every day there came to the creek a flock of fourteen emus, and at sundown there arrived Iky Mo, Eliza, Dad, the Old Man, Ethel and Flo, and Blue and Brown – otherwise a family of eight kangaroos. It is needless to mention the many birds.

The two dogs and the five cats came to tolerate both the emus and the 'roos which arrived with the regularity of sunrise. Over five months their numbers neither increased nor decreased, the country being in fair condition and offering them no hardships.

Then one day in May they failed to appear. The camp at eventide seemed strangely deserted. They came not again, and even when I saw the buck rabbits sitting on the highest points of their burrows, I did not guess the reason for their desertion; no, not even when I noticed how the rabbits were spiritedly twitching their nostrils.

About a fortnight after my friends vanished, there came along a half-caste dog-trapper who told me that down around Broken Hill it had rained about two and a half inches. The south wind had brought northward the smell of rain-soaked earth and the promise of springing green herbage, which proved an irresistible magnet to all things which flew and ran.

Perhaps it was the south wind whispering of cool days and cold nights to come which aroused the migratory instinct within me, for that evening I rang up the manager and asked if the half-caste could take my place immediately.

Thus it came about that with a bank book proving a credit balance of £88 and a station cheque made in my favour for £30, I met Blue Peter, a stocky little man with red hair and blue eyes, and a winning smile. Together, we tramped towards Hergott Springs, each bicycle loaded with a swag and tucker.

For the reason that I liked the sergeant and kissed the sergeant's daughter, I am not going to mention the name of the township this particular police sergeant controlled. He was an unorthodox policeman who, however, knew his job and his people, and efficiently ran a huge district, the capital of which was a two-pub, post office-cum-store, twenty-house town. Beside the police station was erected a one cell lockup.

Arrived in town, Blue Peter went along to the baker, and I had the station cheque transferred to my bank account which was thereby swelled to £118. That was late in the afternoon, and whilst waiting for my companion, I sat on the wooden kerbing on the sidewalk outside the store. Then the sergeant strolled to my side.

He was a jovial looking, white-haired man, with kindly brown eyes and a grim, determined jaw.

"Where you come from?" he asked gruffly.

"Way down from Swanee River," I replied with unwaiverable flippancy.

"Oh – have you! And where are you going?"

"To my Old Grey Home in the West, sergeant."

"Well, well, well! Many a true word spoken in jest. Now you just take a little walk with me."

And before I knew what was what, I was safely lodged in the one-cell prison, the walls of which were washed grey.

On the hard trestle bed I unrolled my swag and made myself comfortable, for the sergeant told me I would be there all night. Then a trap door in the door proper was slid upwards and a pair of dark-brown solemn eyes regarded me in cool and calm judgement.

"What are you in there for?" asked the sergeant's daughter.

"I'm here because I told the sergeant I was making for My Little Grey Home in the West, and he kindly helped me to my destination."

"Oh! Are you hungry?"

"I am."

"What is your name?"

"My friends call me Hampshire."

With that the trap door dropped into place.

Half an hour later the Sergeant's daughter brought me tea and bread and butter and jam on a tray. She unbolted the door and walked in with the provender after she had seriously besought and gained my promise not to escape. It turned out that the sergeant's lady and I originated on either side of Portsmouth harbour, and the sergeant's daughter and I discovered mutual interest in the George Hotel, in which is still the bed Lord Nelson occupied during his last night ashore; and talked of his flagship, the Victory, now in dry dock for ever, and the plaque in the high wall above the spot where the gay Duke of Buckingham was assassinated.

She had left with the tray when I heard outside Blue Peter pleading to be locked up with me. He was pleading not with the sergeant, but with the sergeant's daughter, who, without much demur, opened the door to admit him and lock it again upon us both. Having heard of my fate, Blue Peter stored his machine, bought three bottles of beer and a pound of tobacco, and decided to camp with me.

The next morning the sergeant said to him: "What are you doing in here? How did you get in?"

"Well, I was looking for My Little Grey Home in the West, and I reckon I found it last night when your pretty daughter opened the door."

"Well, well, well! Had breakfast yet?"

"Yes, sergeant. Your daughter did not forget to bring it."

The sergeant returned about an hour after that, and hailed us before the "beak." Without visible means of support, was the charge.

"Plead," snapped the "beak."

"Guilty, you honour," replied Blue Peter, without hesitation.

"Seven days," announced the Court.

I never regained breath until I was back in the cell, and then began to remonstrate with my fellow prisoner. He said: "What are you worrying about? We've got board and lodgings for a full week. We'll get three good meals a day and a real rest."

The sergeant came in to say: "Now, boys, you play the game and we'll get on all right. I want the station whitewashed. Do a fair thing and you'll find I won't be hard. What about it?"

"A little gentle exercise will do me, sergeant," assented Blue Peter, and, because it was useless to kick against the pricks, I concurred with him.

The Law immediately relaxed its vigilance. Blue Peter and I

got to work making up the whitewash, and at noon the sergeant's lady announced lunch. She and the sergeant and the sergeant's daughter and the two prisoners sat at a table in the sergeant's kitchen. The sergeant's lady was about fifty years old, and she and I talked Portsmouth till nearly two o'clock, when the interested policeman suggested work. The sergeant's daughter wanted to mutiny, but received no support.

At five o'clock the sergeant instructed me to purchase from one of the hotels two bottles of beer with the four shillings he gave. The work and the bottles of beer gave to us prisoners an excellent appetite, and, after dinner, whilst the sergeant went hunting for the illusive desperate characters, we sat in his parlour with the sergeant's daughter running the gramophone. When he returned without any desperate characters, he locked up for the night the two he did have.

Three excellent meals and a bottle of beer every day for a week. As Blue Peter said: What more could any man desire? The sergeant was delighted with the newly-whitewashed police station, and contemplated charging us with disorderly behaviour in order to retain our services another week to have the front fence repaired.

Our last night I bought four bottles of beer and the largest box of lollies in the store for the sergeant's daughter, whom I had come to know was madly in love with me. When the sergeant, on the following morning, advised us to get employment, I showed him my bank book in proof that I really did have substantial means of support.

"Goodbye, Hampshire. I wish daddy would lock you up again. Come back soon, so that he can," cried the sergeant's daughter.

Her eyes were very bright, and she wanted to be kissed.

She was only twelve.

Chasing the Rainbow

The present world trade depression, from which – we devoutly hope – the nations are about to emerge into prosperity, is by no means the first of such phenomena experienced by men. Perhaps not so universal in scope, every civilized community has known the cycle of seven years of plenty and seven years of famine.

Trade depression is much like war and drought in that, when suffering it, men and women are much more given to retrospection, more inclined to look back with pleasure on the "good old days." In fact, we are ever looking backwards: the aged love to talk of their youth, the soldiers will always talk only of the humorous side of military life, and the bushman, retired, will invariably dwell only on the best side of bush life. To appreciate life, like wine, life has to be measured by time.

Looking backward, many of us enjoy tolerant amusement from our wild rushes to secure the pot of gold beneath the rainbow. We were always so sure of reaching it, always so blind to the fact that the rainbow arching above the pot of gold was an illusion.

I once saw the coloured bars of a rainbow over the sugar plantations of Queensland from a station in north South Australia. Bill the Bo'sun pointed it out to me with stories of the money to be made cutting sugar cane. It appeared that men earned cheques on which were written fabulous amounts, sums of money far greater than those earned by shearers. No entrant in a race to a new diamond field started off so quickly as I did for the pot of gold beneath the sugar rainbow.

I believe it was less the urge of gold than the excuse to look beyond the mirage, or, in this instance, beyond the rainbow; for, when Bill the Bo'sun and I weighed anchor, it was the rainbow and not the gold that most attracted.

700 miles we pushed loaded bicycles to Cunnamulla where ends the western railway, and there the first man we met was Bill the Bo'son's long-lost friend. I can see that man now, standing motionless on the sidewalk, his eyes wide with astonishment. He had twenty-to-four-o'clock feet, a white face and beer-stained moustache, and violent red hair. Bill the Bo'sun called him

Daybreak, and that night we camped at the Bushman's Home.

The following day, realising that these old friends determined to commemorate the meeting in a manner much different to that of laying a foundation stone, I sold my machine and left for Brisbane and Mackay. It eventually became apparent that there were at least 40,000 other rainbow chasers in Australia, every one of whom were squatting outside the several mills. Cane cutting had started, the mills were working at top pressure, and at each hundreds of men were waiting for a millhand to suffer an accident which would give one of them the unfortunate man's job. The pot of gold was beneath the rainbow without doubt, but one could not reach it for the scrum. Rainbow chasers always think that they alone can see it.

Broke, again disillusioned, I took work on a pineapple plantation near Brisbane, and from it graduated to a vineyard on which some of the best Queensland wines were vinted. Dry and sweet hocks, madeira and port, chablis and sherry, were words with which I became familiar, and it was not long before I could tell one from the others with my eyes shut, knowledge easy to acquire at a shilling a bottle.

Nowhere else in Australia I found a happier community than that one of the pineapple growers formed chiefly of Germans. Every week one of them would give what they termed a "night," to which everyone was invited without an invitation direct. The houses being built on piles – the space beneath was devoted to carts and fruit packing – one had a varied choice of amusement. In the living-room one could discuss cooking and clothes, babies and scandal, whilst drinking wine or coffee out of glass and china; play poker, and drink beer out of a tin pannikin under the house; flirt beneath a paw paw tree; or dance on the verandah to the music of an accordion. One could displease only by leaving before dawn.

There is no gainsaying that the German and the Scot make the best settlers. They have the land sense more deeply implanted in their hearts than have either the Englishman or the Australian, and they become much more quickly assimilated by a young nation than do the Latins who cling to certain districts and to certain streets in town or city.

The Germans among whom I worked permeated a community; they did not dominate it. The old people passionately loved their native country but hated militarism. The second generation poked fun at the Kaiser and bet on the tests when not discussing the last "night" or the "night" to come.

There were the FitzSchorns. The two girls worked in city offices, and during the evening, if they were not playing tennis, they were reclining on the verandah reading novels. Beside the house, the wife and a small son would be labouring either end of a crosscut saw, and down by the creek the lord would be smoking a huge pipe and debating agricultural questions with his neighbour. It was always thus when passing their place.

There was old Mrs. Paul. I used to go another way in order to escape her pressing invitation to step in and taste some delicacy, which meant the opening of a bottle or the tipping of a demijohn.

There was old Gus who had the most penetrating voice in Australia. The day after a "night" he would be sure to start arguing with his family who, at a signal given by the wife, would rush him and bear him off to the stoutly-built woodshed where he would be incarcerated for hours. Without cessation, he would state his amiable intention of what he would do when he got out with the volume of a sound which hammered the hilltops and echoed across the dells for miles around.

I rented an acre of ground, and tilled it, and planted it with tomato plants. I cut about 4,000 ti-tree saplings up which to train the plants. They grew and grew like Jack's beanstalk, and the settlers came to look at them and tell me how forward they were, and how much money they were sure I would make. I would have made it alright had not 3-ounce hailstones smashed the flowering plants into the mud. The "night" the settlers gave to show me their sympathy will never be forgotten.

Our railway station was only eight miles out of the city, to which some Saturday evenings I would escort a young lady. We would return by the last train, unofficially designated "the drunks' train." The department was considering replacing the ever replaceable windows with iron bars.

Returning from the city alone one moonlight night, after leaving the station on the full night walk, I saw ahead a girl dressed in white. When she took a left turning I decided she must be one of my employer's daughters, and I hurried to catch up with her. Evidently she did not recognise me, for she hurried on, too. And when I broke into a run, she ran. Slowing to a walk, she ceased to run. One of the girls was of those who fish for a squatter and fail to hook a stockman, and I became sure this was she. Determined to secure the honour of escorting her, I began to race, but she, too, raced, and ran equally as fast. She must have been winded at the same time as I was, for when I walked again she walked. Over the first hill we proceeded, separated by about a hundred yards, then down the further side, across the bridge, round the slope of another hill, and on to the permanent lagoon beyond which was her father's vineyard. The road took a sharp turn closely to border the lagoon, and she, instead of keeping on the road, walked straight ahead across the silvered water which, in places, was reputed to be twenty feet deep.

For several moments I stood at the lagoon's edge and gaped, and watched her reach the far side where she vanished among tall trees. To prove a certain hypothesis, I inquired if either of my employer's daughters were out that night, or was likely to have walked in her sleep. It transpired that wine at a shilling a bottle was too easily obtainable. Bottled sunlight, the weekly "night," and hospitality in general, were beginning to have its effects.

When the war came, a son of German parents and I joined up together, and during the birth of the A.I.F., many of those old Germans contracted for transport work for the new army.

Boys into Camp

At any meeting of Diggers, whether it occurs on the street, or at a social function, by far the great majority delight in discussing the lighter side of army life. Seldom do they mention the grim realities of modern war.

Natural – perfectly natural! Who talks of death when life is so attractive? Death as a subject for conversation is possibly interesting to the Ancient, but we of the A.I.F. are not yet ancient. No Sir! Not by a long shot. When we get together the 19 years that have passed are wiped out, and we are again members of the Australian Imperial Forces, living, during those epic years, the lives of gods.

A week or so back, a man whom I knew in Egypt, England and France, hailed me with a shout in Collins Street. He invited me to his house for tea. Proudly he showed off his wife and family of four almost grown-up children. He was going grey, like I am, but the old twinkle was still in his eyes. After tea, whilst his wife cleared away, he led me into the garden and to a seat beneath an ornamental tree.

"Now," said he with a chuckle, "we can talk about Cairo."

What comes to the digger, in this year of grace, out from those epic years of war? Does he vividly remember the oath he took to murder the sergeant-major? Since then, most likely, he has had a pot or two with the sergeant-major. Does he remember the route marches, the everlasting stews, the flies of Gallipoli, the mud of Flanders? Probably he does, but he prefers to remember the Mademoiselle from Armentieres, the "bloke" who wore the top hat belonging to the mayor of Corbie, the "ving blong," and the "mob," meaning that wonderful band of comrades whom he never has had better.

There was that example of comradeship I shall never forget.

Having emerged with the crowd from a Hastings theatre, and when walking along the street with a lady friend, a gruff voice behind us said loudly:

"You want to salute there, Australia!"

The voice saying the same thing again, I turned to observe two red-caps walking behind us, and asking my friend to walk on slowly, I went back to them and requested to know if they were shouting at me.

Before either could reply, a digger rushed up to demand anxiously:

"What's the matter, sergie?"

Explaining that these military policemen were shouting at me to salute officers, he stepped back a pace.

"Salute officers!" He echoed, dawning astonishment spreading over his frost-bitten face. "Salute officers! Don't you know that we don't salute foreign officers in our army? How long you been sodgers?"

I left him arguing Australian military law to rejoin my anxious friend, and a minute later he edged up alongside to whisper hoarsely:

"That's the way to fix them –. Lend us a coupler bob, sergie."

In these memoirs, therefore, it will be that extraordinary person, the Digger – his likes, his antipathies, his humour and his renowned casualness – whom I hope to present to this generation. As a figure he stands four-square with all that is manly, courageous and chivalrous. At work he hated all regulations which impeded his getting on with the job; in his leisure – and there was not enough of it – his natural sporting instincts were given rein. When he "pinched" the "old man's" whisky it was for the gamble or sport in the act rather than for the whisky itself.

When a young man joins a peace-time army he is like a new boy at an old-established school. In the peace-time regular army the recruit finds himself in a minority among men older and more experienced than himself. They exert steadying influences on him from the start of his military career. He has become a cog in a mighty machine which was running smoothly before he was born, and should he not properly fit, the machine throws him out.

With us it was wholly different. We were all parts of a machine which had yet to be assembled. We were mostly all young. We were all new boys in this newly opened school: a tiny bit fearful, a mighty lot proud, interested in the masters, as keen as a Malay kriss.

Although we were all new to this school, there was a leavening of "boys" who had attended another school – the British Regular Army. Many of these were undeniably smart. When I arrived in the camp the officers were there, the sergeant-major was there, the tents were there. There were no horses, no G.S. waggons, no equipment, and remarkably little tucker. The only man in uniform, other than the officers, was the bugler, and we never saw him until a few moments after he sounded reveille the next morning. We thought him a fine fellow, and not till long afterwards did we come to look on him and his bugle with disfavour.

Then the mechanics began to assemble the machine. They placed all the cogs in ranks and marched them about in sections of four until the sharp edges were worn off and we began to look more alike. We were marched along the roads, thrilled and heartened by the old Boer War songs we soon learned to sing: "The Red, White and Blue," and "We're Soldiers of the Queen, My Lads."

Then the horses arrived.

They had been roped a little on the far-western stations, and, I think, some of them had been ridden – once. We took them from the railway yards to the camp with only two bolts. And in camp they issued us not with Australia's sensible national saddle, but with the Army Creighton.

Undoubtedly the Creighton saddle is a comfortable one, and to it one can lash a lot of gear, but in the sunset country where they allegedly break in horses they use close-fitting saddles with knee-pads. We were expected to ride these fiery steeds on an iron-hard, padless, fore and aft concern that was as slippery as any greasy pole.

How the horses did enjoy themselves!

So did the fellow who drove away on a water-cart. The cart, of course, was empty. The horse had never seen such a contraption before, and tried hard to get away from it. The driver bounced out of his seat to straddle the boiler-shaped tank, and every time the cart bounced so did he. My! He rode the boiler like Tom Mix.

Men poured into the camps from the recruiting depots. They carried portmanteaus and suit-cases, and, of course, wore civvies. You could tell from where they had come: the western bush, the nearer farms, the city. In no respect did they bear uniformity each to the other save in physique and health. In those days the "quacks" turned down a man if he showed the most trivial defect. They had 100,000 men from which to choose 20,000.

Despite the fact that the Master Engineer, Lord Kitchener, had drawn up blue prints of the machine he, and others with him, saw one day might be urgently needed, the feat of gathering together 20,000 men into battalions, and regiments, and units, together with the requisite number of horses and rifles and full equipment, and dispatching them overseas within a few weeks of the outbreak of war, was one of which Australia may be justifiably proud.

What hard cases there were! I wondered what has become of Mouldy Alec and Tired Tim and Square Face. Square Face became my cobber, when the long and the short of it was never better exemplified. Not that I was over long, or the Square Face was under height. He would be, I think, five feet ten inches in his socks, but he was about five feet wide and four feet thick – a cubic mass of muscle. He had but to use one hand to put any man on his back on the ground.

There was Fly-spot. Luck certainly assisted him to pass the "quacks," for he was so high. I used to see him sitting in a tent at Maadi holding hands with a witch. I thought she was telling his fortune. But Fly-spot was learning Arabic, and in no time spent his evenings off duty dressed up like a Gypo, and he ended by becoming an efficient Secret Service agent.

Not whilst we remained in Australia did we get to know each other. There were too many outside influences arrayed in skirts. Every Sunday the camp was crowded with visitors. The ladies brought out hampers, and their lovers or husbands lit small fires and boiled the family billy and forgot the stews of which already we were sickening.

Mouldy Alec wanted to know why my sweetheart or wife did not come to visit me, and, on being told that I was a stranger in a strange country, detailed off one of his sisters to "nurse" me. She was a fine girl with beautiful auburn hair, and never a policeman loved a cook as I loved her. Her hampers were wonderful.

"Andy" Fisher, accompanied by Mr. W. H. Hughes, looked us over one day. I happened to be at work on the officers' woodheap when they came along and stayed for a "pitch." Andy's soul leapt out through his eyes and bored right into a brain to see what was going on there. No wonder they made him Prime Minister. For more than an hour he had been talking to the boys individually, even without an officer escort. Not till years afterwards did I come to understand the one flash of pain I saw in those piercing dark eyes.

"To the last man and to the last shilling" was no empty, vain, silly boast. He visualized our future better than we did. He regarded us as his own boys, and, as we now know, he delayed our departure from Australia till every possible measure for our safe transport had been taken.

"Well, good-bye, and the best of luck. I wish I were young like you." With which, his head erect and his back like a ramrod, he walked on.

There was a certain amount of secrecy getting away from Brisbane. The Emden was somewhere below the horizon. We left camp in the middle of the night, walking the horses to the wharf. It was a long way, and there were no bands to play us off. An easterly half-gale made the transport roll badly, and sent to the deck a goodly number of us. Those of us who were less sick, or not sick at all, had extra work to do. The poor horses had a touch of the strangles, which did not improve matters.

And then, to our chagrin and astonishment, they pulled us off at Melbourne and parked us at the Showgrounds for some three weeks. We thought to hear that the war was over any day, and that we should be disbanded just when we were beginning to know each other. We did not dream of a huge fleet of transports which were to carry 30,000 Australians and New Zealanders, and thousands of horses, to the very foot of the Pharaohs' pyramids.

All Aboard

There are 700 horses on the Anglo-Egyptian – Transport A.25. During the dark hours they have been dozing whilst leaning against one side of their stalls because they cannot lie down. A hoof thud – silence – a chain rattle – silence – long silence – a squeal and loud hoof stamping – silence again. At five o'clock in the morning one would have thought there were but seven horses on the crowded lower decks, not 700.

The alley-ways are narrow, and one must walk warily between the long avenue of horses' heads. Some there are who like to remind the guard that "Feed-up" is now not far off. Time drags. The only continuous sound is the methodical, never-ceasing labour of the ship's engines.

From the foredeck are to be seen the motionless stars, stars which are in the heavens, stars which float upon the sea. The eastern sky is sable-grey and cloudless; to the west the heavenly stars blaze from an invisible horizon more brightly than the stars on the sea.

Then out of the night come shadowy ships; ships forward and ships aft and ships on either beam. The Anglo-Egyptian is surrounded by ships. They steam across the magic sea as though founded on solid earth with the water running by them, for their positions never vary. For days and days each ship has maintained its position in this mighty convoy.

Now Night is being sent helter skelter by advancing Day, and from out of the darkness come all kinds of ships from the luxurious liner to the stumpy tramp; ships with one funnel and ships with two funnels; ships with black hulls, ships with green hulls; ships from the Orient, P. & O., the Clan, the Holt and other lines. There are brightly painted ships by which runs a sun-flecked sea. Three lines of ships – nine, nine, and ten. 800 yards between each ship. And, following these three lines, come two lines of grey-painted ships from New Zealand, in each line five ships.

Ah! There is the old Ibuki still stoking up. More smoke is pouring from her funnels than from all the funnels of the convoy of 38 transports. Square Face said they poured oil on the 100 tons of coal they shovel into her furnaces every day purposely to make smoke to attract the German raiders.

Beyond the distant starboard line of ships is that Japanese warship. Far ahead is the thin smoke of the Melbourne. Away to the west, so far that she looks like a grey match, rides the Sydney. And somewhere down below the rim of the sea is the Emden.

Well, here is the day. A sergeant is rousing the men below. The horses have become restless, anxious for breakfast. A bugle call floats over the water from a trooper. On all the ships are 30,000 soldiers, nearly 8000 horses, and possibly 5000 seamen. The cubs were answering the call of the old lion, and Matthew Mark succinctly if impolitely said:

"If old Queen Lizzie was to wake up and see this little lot she'd forget to pick her teeth and damn the King of Spain."

The weather became hot as we approached the tropics. Our decks were not of spotless wood, and neither did our ship sport sun awnings and provide stewarts to run about with iced drinks as they did on the Orvieto which carried the "Heads." Our decks were of common iron, but we were blessed with the absence of women in the persons of Army nurses, and our attire was left to our choice.

We wore towels as loin-cloths, and, of course, rubber soled canvas shoes. It became fashionable to wear our hair clipped close. We cleaned up below in loin-cloths, we ate in loin-cloths, and we spent our leisure in loin-cloths, and in pyjamas we slept anywhere but in the regulation hammocks provided us.

Mouldy Alec and I chose the roof of the horse-boxes built along both sides of the forward well deck. The roofs were gently sloping seaward. To prevent slipping down into a watery grave we fastened a rope around our waists and tied the other end to an upright fronting the stalls. I can never understand how it was that I got out of my rope, to find myself on awakening with both legs dangling over the sea. Another foot – !

Lying on that roof o'nights, yarning to Mouldy Alec, we used to watch the masthead and stern lights of the ships ahead and abeam and aft of us, and debate what would happen if the Emden they could not find sneaked in among the transports and let things rip. What a chance she had of sneaking up from astern.

The Osterley overhauled us, kept in close on our starboard that the passengers might have a front-seat view. She drew away ahead, and her skipper was reprimanded for coming anywhere near. Had the Emden captured her, a note, a letter, a snapshot found among her passengers would have made Von Muller wise. He would have sneaked in from astern too. He was the kind of man who would have welcomed such an end to his ship, knowing that he could not continue raiding indefinitely. And what an end, surrounded by sinking transports!

Never at any time did I come to love animals as well as I did those seven horses in my charge. After a week or so of shipboard they became almost human. When exercised in the long alley-ways, they walked with the straddling gait of old seamen. At the end of mess I used to take them each a piece of bread loaded with sugar, and I had to pass the twin rows of horses' heads in which were jealous, nipping teeth. The uproar from my seven at the far end of the alley-way was terrific.

The captain on the bridge said:

"I have noticed that when the men have been at mess some time, the horses directly below me suddenly stamp their hoofs and squeal."

"Oh!" said the O.C. "I'll wait and hear it."

When pandemonium broke out below, they sent for the sergeant-major.

"What's all that trouble down there?" he demanded.

"Trouble, sir! No trouble, sir. That's only Upfield feeding his horses."

"Feeding them!" broke in the Vet. "On what?"

By the time the Vet. got down all the bread and sugar had disappeared, and the mokes were yawning with satisfaction. I received a lecture on the fattening qualities of wheaten bread and sugar, and asked if I had a brain, and what did I mean by upsetting the carefully worked out diet. The Vet. danced with anger, and a big black mare playfully bit my ear – an equine Oliver Twist.

After that I delayed the much reduced bread and sugar issue until the officers were at mess. Even so, I had to watch the sergeant-major.

Then we got the flag-wagging craze.

Mouldy Alec took it up with tremendous enthusiasm, and quickly became proficient. For an hour or two every late afternoon he would stand on the wheel-house roof with his flags, made from the backs of shirts. He delighted in sending messages to all who might read them on the other ships, and I do believe that he had the makings of a fine novelist in him. One message he repeated over several days.

"The O.C. has killed the ------- captain. Ship in charge of the first officer. Armed party told to shoot the ------- O.C. on sight. The ------- Vet. has lost his reason. Shall I sink the ------- ship?"

It went on for several days, and then the captain received orders to:

"Stop that flag-waving fool on your wheel-house roof. Repetition of one adjective boring."

The morning came when the escorting warships were galvinised into furious activity. The Melbourne fired up and moved westwards. The Ibuki stoked up and sent a twisting roll of smoke so heavy that it rested on the water behind her. Then the Melbourne came back and the Ibuki steamed to meet her. They two hovered about on our port beam, and the Sydney rushed away on an undoubted mission.

"Something doing," surmised the intelligent Corporal Luffter.

There was. Word came down that the Sydney was off to give battle to a strange warship. We strained our hearing to hear the sounds of the guns, but could catch only the hissing of the passing sea suds. Then an officer ordered all hands to the mess deck, and there announced the beaching of the Emden.

How we cheered! Then he announced that the officers were shouting for all hands to commemorate the victory. We cheered harder than ever, and rushed the small bar with our tin drinking pannikins.

Now we were safe from possible raiders, and dared strike matches on the open decks. Our Corporal Luffter busily wrote a long letter to his "girl." Someone picked it up and nailed it to the order board.

"The guns roar and the shells scream," wrote the lover. "The heroism of the troops is splendid, magnificent. Calm in the face of ghastly death, they fight like tigers. At last victory is in sight. The enemy staggers back, is sinking, torn and shattered and done for. We cheer and shake each other by the hand. The battle is over and once again I can think of you, my dear one."

I would not have been Corporal Luffter for £1,000 an hour throughout the next fortnight.

Later we learned the details of that fight of Cocos Island; of the manner in which the crew of the Emden fought their ship when outgunned by a superior vessel. When outside Colombo the Sydney passed us on her way into the harbour, and we could never understand why we received orders not to cheer the very gallant German survivors she had on board.

When in the harbour we were warped to a New Zealand transport, and from our holds to hers were transferred tons of horse fodder. Then, on the way out, our steering gear jammed and we rammed the mole. That put us back to anchor off the coal-wharfs until the damage had been assessed. Orders were given that no man was to go ashore, and some of us smiled and estimated the distance from the coal-wharfs to ship.

It was an engineer named Beaky who led the "push." He ought to have been a colonel, for he was a born leader of "pushes." With our money in our mouths, shoes laced round our necks, and arrayed only in towels tied round our middles, some sixteen of us slid down a rope and silently swam for the coal-wharfs. The water was warm, the swim easy, and I thought of sharks not at all.

Without mishap, we found steps leading up to the wharf's decking, and there we put on our shoes and began the long walk round the harbour to the town.

That proved arduous for men cooped up on a ship for five weeks, but once arrived we were made to forget our weariness by the welcome of the population. Thousands of natives escorted us through Colombo, gesticulating and screaming with mirth.

Baldy Benson said that the only pub worth going to was the "Goldface" Hotel (!), and he was about right. With an escort of about 4,000 running beside our rickshaws, we arrived at that splendid hotel on the seafront – sixteen white sahibs each dressed in shoes and one towel. Within we found the front of the bar polished to brilliance by the dress shirts of generations of tea planters and travellers, and now across that bar leaned semi-naked men with hands outstretched for the product of Messrs. Bass.

There came to stand in a side door two gentlemen in evening clothes and monocles. One inquired of us our race, and on hearing it the other withdrew to return in a few minutes with a dozen of their friends from the Ceylon Tea Planters' Club across the way.

Joyfully they became our hosts, and the Bass shares rose two points. Baldy Benson and a tea planter dressed like a duke step-danced on the bar. Did it well, too. Our hosts were much grieved when we insisted on spending our money to save the bother of taking it back to the ship in our mouths.

At the moment of our departure our hosts decided to accompany us to the coal-wharfs, and about twenty rickshaws were hired to transport the party. It was hands across the sea and all that kind of thing whilst being run through the town.

Arrived at the wharfs, the problem arose how to get off to the ship those of us unable to swim. It proved to be a vexing problem, for it was doubtful that the non-swimmers would be able to swim before sunrise.

Beaky, the Engineer, the colonel-who-should-have-been, found a way out. The swimmers among us heaved into the water a heavy squared log of seasoned wood, then jumped in after it and pushed it out a little way. The tea planters considerately picked up the non-swimmers and dropped them off the wharf, and those of them who still remained incapable of swimming were hauled on to the log. Silently, save for Blue Evan's sleepy threat to kill the sergeant-major, we pushed the loaded log out to the ship. Mouldy Alec, of course, had to mention the probability of sharks. He was that kind of man – an imaginative pessimist.

There were no non-swimmers when we reached the ship, and one by one climbed the rope to the central hold door, which was open. There the O.C. and the sergeant-major were waiting to welcome us home, and for the rest of the voyage the sixteen who went ashore did all the guard duty.

That was nothing, anyway. They talk about the night in the Ceylon Tea Planters' Club to this day. There were but ten days remaining of that epic voyage across the Indian Ocean, and then Egypt with all its glamour, its colour and its mystery, and on our ship there were a hundred gay cavaliers eagerly looking forward to delving into some of those alluring mysteries.

Ducks for Christmas Dinner

In 1914 I thought that nowhere in the world could there be a climate the equal to that of Central Australia during the winter months. After two winters spent in Egypt, I must confess that Egypt leads by a neck.

The Light Horse were sent to Maadi, south of Cairo, the infantry being encamped at the foot of the Pyramids. Both places were ideally situated for all ranks, because all ranks were as particles of steel attracted by the magnet of Cairo. The tramway people did a tremendous business! Each train was packed to capacity; the roof of each tram was packed to capacity, too.

Under their grey moustaches the "heads" swore, and in effect said: "Now, my lads, you're for it." How many times we presented arms, how many times we saluted by numbers I have forgotten, but it was somewhere in the ninth million! And, having transported the cogs, the cranks and the pistons, across the Indian Ocean, the mechanics built up the machine, so to speak, and began to give it a series of "runs." Squeaks were eliminated, and in a remarkably short period the new Australian military machine was "run in."

Throughout the A.I.F., though, there was one universal quality which distinguished the Digger – the quality of personal initiative. In the Digger the Commanding Officers had an intelligent, educated, thinking man, a man prone to criticism and respect only those leaders of proved efficiency. It seemed almost that we were expected to be nice curly-headed boys, whereas we were young men who were tasting life in its fullness, keen sportsmen and impatient of anything which did not help the war forward towards a victorious conclusion.

At no time was it proved to us that saluting would win a war. We liked saluting our immediate officers because, being constantly in touch, we could appreciate their abilities; but at no time could we divest our minds of the idea that to salute all officers, even foreign officers, was a mark of servility, an act akin to pulling the forelock to the squire. It was an anachronism, suitable to a musical comedy, but out of place during the war when bayonet exercises and rifle practice and trench digging are of vital importance.

In Egypt, where rain is a rare phenomenon, water and damp are never taken into consideration by builders. Hordes of native carpenters entered and for a space took charge of the camps. They rushed up mess-sheds and canteens, and later erected long lines of sun-shelters for the horses. Within the mess-sheds there were formed individual messes of ten to sixteen men, and, with the approach of Christmas, plans were discussed concerning the Christmas dinner. Each mess appointed a Secretary to receive levies with which to purchase game and beer.

Without thought, I proposed Square-Face as our secretary – and after a pregnant silence someone seconded the proposal! Had I foreseen that Square-Face would make me his secretary I most certainly would have remained silent. We collected £2/1/7½, of which £1 was to be spent on fowls.

The night before Christmas Eve the secretary and his secretary went into Cairo and returned broke. And in Cairo Square-Face left the £2/1/7½.

"Have you ever been in gaol?" I asked him caustically.

"Me?" he exclaimed, astonished. "Think I'm a fool?"

"Have there been occasions when you ought to have been sent to gaol?" I pressed.

"Plenty," he replied, grinning. Then seriously: "Now look! We've got to get busy. We've got to buy £1/1/7 worth of beer, and a quid's worth of game. I can fix the game all right, but we will have to borrow the beer money."

Between us we "put the acid" on nine or ten officers – without success; but fortunately we found the sergeant-major in a generous mood.

On the morning of Christmas Eve, Square-Face reported on sick parade, and a more robust gorilla-man never wore uniform. Throughout that day I verbally flagellated him about raising the money for the poultry, and he persistently put me off with:

"Don't worry. The game is all right."

When the day drew to a close, however; when dozens of men had finished plucking fowls and ducks and handed them over to the cooks, the game for our mess appeared to be far from "all right."

At midnight he aroused me, and, having dressed, he led me out into the bitter cold night towards the houses of Maadi occupied by wealthy Europeans. "Now, not a word, Joe. No argument. Do as you're told – and the game will be all right."

"What have you got that stick for?" I asked defiantly.

"Shut up!"

"Why the chaff bags?"

"Shut up, d'you hear? Leave it to me."

Made desperate by the thought of no game on our table for dinner the next day, I spoke no more and accompanied him to the high wall skirting a three-storied, flat-roofed residence.

"Go quiet. We don't want to rux-up the nigger at the gate!" he whispered. "Gimme a leg up."

He referred to the Egyptian custom of posting a native night watchman at the gate of every house of importance. These men occupied shelters similar to sentry boxes.

When I had heaved him up to the summit of the wall he leaned downward and pulled me up with one hand. Silently we dropped down on the further side to find ourselves in a vegetable garden. It then became apparent that Square-Face had, like a professional burglar, taken pains to become familiar with "the lay." He led his accomplice to the door of a commodious fowl house. My heart began to beat quickly, and my flesh grew cold, when from within came the low quacks of sleepy ducks. Never before had I robbed a fowl-house, but I had kept ducks, and I knew the uproar they would make directly they were touched.

But the Master Cracksman had forgotten nothing.

The contents of the bottle he had that morning stolen from the M.O.'s tent he poured onto the rag he had tied to the end of the stick. It was impossible to mistake the smell of chloroform. The drug-saturated rag was gently inserted into the fowl-house through the partly open door. One duck quacked. We could hear the "flop" when several fowls toppled off their perch.

A few minutes later Square-Face handed out to me to bag eight ducks and eight hens without a single protest from the birds inside the fowl-house. Having tied the mouths of the bags, we slipped back to the high wall, where he lifted me to the top and then handed me up the heavy bags. The first I lowered as far as I could before dropping it to the ground; the second I was lowering when the first of the eight ducks regained consciousness.

The native watchman began to scream and swing the old-fashioned rattle attached to the end of his pole. Within five seconds every watchman in the district was copying him. And every duck in the two bags awoke to join in the protest.

"You idiot!" snorted Square-Face as we raced back to the camp. "Why didn't you ring their necks before you put 'em in the bags? Where're your brains?"

From the commotion at our rear I estimated that at least 25,000 natives were in hot pursuit. Nowhere save in Egypt could human beings create such uproar. Once I fell – still hugging the game – and Square-Face gripped me with his free hand, jerked me to my feet, and pulled me along. After a minute or two the ducks grew drowsy, or became out of breath, and to this day I cannot understand how we made our escape.

Arrived at the camp we made direct for the rubbish pit, into which the regiment had plucked the feathers of all the game, and into that same pit we plucked our game, cleaned and trussed the birds, and then, without waking the cooks, laid our tagged fowls and ducks beside those awaiting cooking the next day.

Now the people of Maadi were most kind to us. They set up a tent and distributed books and papers, and took a general interest in our well-being, and the crime I had committed weighed heavily on my conscience. On our way out of camp the evening of the next pay day, I said to Square-Face:

"I bet you five bob you dare not accompany me to the robbed house to make restitution."

"I'll take you," he said without hesitation. "It's a bet."

Thus it was we were shown into a magnificent apartment at about seven o'clock. There entered a short, tubby, red-faced Frenchman, who politely asked us to be seated. He was in dining kit. As I proceeded to relate the incidents of the robbery, he paced about the room blowing out his cheeks, snorting, and ejaculating oaths until he had worked himself into a vile temper. In notes I offered him 250 piastres.

"Come!" he cried dramatically. "Your money I refuse. Bah! To your judges I will take you. Forward!"

Out of the room he drove us like a couple of sheep. Across the hall he drove us. On the far side he threw open a door and drove us into a room where, seated at a dining table, were about a dozen men and women. Some of the men wore decorations. All were arrayed like their host. Jewels glittered in the hair and on the throats of the ladies. Gripping us, holding us on either side of him, he addressed the diners in impassioned tones in French. Round the table rippled laughter, which swelled into shrieks and roars. I could not move; I stood frozen. Among the diners was our own O.C.!

Our prosecutor ordered places to be set for us, and when we had warmed under the influence of the "ving blong," they made me relate the adventure all over again. A grand dame beside me insisted on thrusting the big end of a hearing trumpet against my mouth. Square-face was like the game – "all right." He had a young mam'selle cuddling his left arm and whispering, "Ah, mon soldat!" And our host trembled like a jelly and gasped repeatedly: "Quack . . . quack . . . quack."

Now surely this not very creditable incident goes to prove that the Digger was not lacking in initiative. After all is said and done, it is initiative which wins a war! Docility, servility were all right in the old days, when armies marched together in close-packed masses of men, when the close contact of individuals demanded nothing more than muscular strength in the common soldier. Modern warfare demands brains of a high order, and the soldier who is able to think, to practice initiative, will always be superior to the saluting, goose-stepping automation. Anyway, we Diggers think so.

Time rolled onwards. The machine they built in Egypt ran ever more smoothly. Men cursed as they were hardened and tempered. The officers gained confidence; the voices of the N.C.O.'s became brittle. The bugles incessantly sent forth their brassy orders. Egypt became an armed camp – and the Egyptians never made so much money in their lives!

Then, from the infantry brigades came the unmistakable signs of a move. At last! Where to? Where to? The battalions moved out; some led by their bands in broad daylight, some marching away in the dead of night to the tap-tap-tapity-tap of a kettle-drum.

Gallipoli! They had gone to Gallipoli. At the First Australian General Hospital all were working to receive the first trainload of wounded.

For us the war had started.

Laughter and Death at Gallipoli

The detachment of which I was a member arrived off Anzac Cove at dawn of 20 May, in a former British Railway Company's steamer, the Clacton. Daylight revealed us poised on a glassy sea half a mile off towering, sheer-faced hills overlooking the beautiful Suvla Bay to the north, and the low country which rolled out into the headland of Gaba Tepe to the south. Nowhere along that coast were there coastal hills as high and as sheer as those directly opposite us.

What a place for an army to take! The sharply rising land back from the beach could be negotiated, but that wall of shale and conglomerate backing it, rearing above it, would defeat the climbers of Everest. They called it Plugge's Plateau. From beyond the level summit drifted seawards the faint cackle of rifles and the tat-tat of machine guns. Unmistakably the firing line was beyond Plugge's Plateau.

The narrow beach supported mountains of cased rations, square-shaped mountains of brown and yellow. Every time I look across the Yarra at Flinders Street I am reminded of the beach at Anzac.

Alongside the Clacton came a small pinnace warped to an ungainly barge. In charge of the pinnace was a diminutive child in naval uniform whose orders were obeyed by sailors as old as the child's father. They and we transferred a pile of stores, and, sitting on the stores, we cast off for the journey to the shore.

From a great distance we heard the dull boom of a gun. I had lit a cigarette and gazed with grave interest at the mighty walls and turrets and narrow gullies taken by the battalions who had marched out of Egypt. I noted the shadowed, barren escarpments and the green-bushed gullies. A clap of thunder cracked overhead, and the water to starboard was white-splashed as though an angry god had cast into the sea a handful of pebbles. Immediately above us hung a little woolly cloud.

The child in command stood on the engine-room deck-light. He said in small piping tones:

"Cox'n, keep under cover!"

The distant boom of the gun again reached us. The cox'n

crouched against the wheel around which was built a steel shed. The child remained standing on the deck-light. His round face was expressionless save for a hint of aloofness – and he had probably been under shell-fire several times every day since April 25.

When the second shell arrived I found a case of bully beef to be much too small. It burst in the same place as had the first, spewing its load of bullets and its iron splinters beyond us.

"Starboard a point!" ordered the child, and I thought he was going to yawn.

"Aye, aye, sir!"

We bumped against a jetty in the making. We worked at unloading the stores. Three or four times did we crouch against a ration stack when Beachy Bill dropped H.E. And the sun continued to shine, and the waves continued to lap against the round stones. It was a beautiful early summer's day, and a man we had never seen, and who had never seen us, was deliberately trying to kill us. If I could put into print what we named that gunner!!

At Anzac I found a Digger different from him who had romped in Cairo, and had tramped, tramped, tramped over the loose desert sand. The digger here was less ebullient. He still smiled, but in his smile was more expression, dreadful experience. He had been a youth – now he was full grown. On the voyage from Australia I had seen him naked save for towel loincloth and canvas shoes. In Egypt I had seen him in smart uniform and loaded with equipment.

Here he stood midway between the extremes. Here he wore heavy boots and trousers with the legs cut off to make shorts. If he wore a tunic he wore no shirt. Often he was naked from the waist up and from the knees down, and his body was darkened by the sun like old ivory.

I camped with a man named Taylor, in whom I discovered strength of a kind much different to that possessed by the Herculean Square-Face. He was of slight build and his eyes were of the clearest blue. All I ever saw him wear were shorts and boots. His facial expression was exactly like that of the child commanding the pinnace and barge. He had conquered fear. He told me that he would not leave Anzac. He never did. To Taylor I owe a debt.

Those early days were comparatively peaceful – behind the line – to what they afterwards became. Beachy Bill, situated somewhere among the southern flats and orange groves, indulged in regular "hates". Early morning and late afternoon it would rake the Cove, and at odd times attend to the barges and small boats. Between "hates" we need think only of Anafarta Annie, alleged to fire from the mouth of a tunnel driven into a cliff north of Chocolate Hill.

That phase gave place to another. Beachy received more ammunition and replaced the regular "hates" by dropping a shell or two at any time during the daylight hours, so that one came to expect to hear a railway train at any moment.

In addition to Anafarta Annie, the enemy trained a .75 to speed a shell low over the spur running from Table Top to the north end of Anzac Cove. That gun gave no time to take cover. The sound of its discharge arrived with the shell.

The third phase quickly followed the entry of Bulgaria into the war. Further to increased ammunition supplies, the enemy used heavy howitzers, and the shells from these guns dropped into those places hitherto considered to be immune. It was possible to see their shells from their point of apex dropping downwards. And every shell so seen appeared certain to drop on one's head. Sometimes the Goeben came down into the Sea of Marmora and took a hand in the game. So distant was she that her guns could not be heard.

Her great shells would arrive silently, slowly, tiredly, so slowly that one could see them revolving languidly as they sped with incredible slowness to pass low over the beach into the sea. When they did fall on solid ground their bursting was like no other.

Off duty, Taylor and I would walk up the spur running down from Plugge's Plateau, and from a jutting ledge survey the great sweep of Suvla Bay, the distant Chocolate Hill, and the hill range beyond. We saw the Queen Elizabeth remove the top of Chocolate Hill, and we watched the Russian Woodbine, a warship having five funnels, rake the enemy's right flank with her small guns, which rat-tatted like an outsize machine gun. A bullet "placked" into the soft earth at our feet, and when a second bullet arrived there was no mistaking that we were the objective of some sporting sniper.

We walked up Shrapnel Hill through Monash Valley, entered the trench system, burrowed into a narrow tunnel, reached a small excavated chamber, the far wall of which was screened with bushes. In the chamber was the man we had come to see. On a tripod rested a rifle fitted with telescopic sights. It was pointing at the bush screen. Through the leaves we could see across a steep gully to the far slope.

The sniper who occupied this chamber was dead. He had been "got" by his opposite number. He was Taylor's brother, and Taylor's face was a mask.

A month after that we walked warily round the north point and into Mule Gully. Coming back, Taylor, who was behind me, sighed immediately after he had, so I thought, trodden on and snapped a stick. He had said that he would never leave Anzac.

After that my nerves began to go. I missed Taylor's strength.

I looked down into a shallow and narrow gully watching the Indian transport drivers cooking their evening curry. The early evening was very quiet. Against the sunset sky the hills of Imbros Island were painted blue-grey. Without a second's warning the .75 shell whistled by me to explode exactly in the cooking fire. War! It was not a battle! It was not a fight! It was a plague going on day by day and month by month. Nowhere was there safety. There was immunity for no one. Whose turn next?

"Look!"

A great fountain of water seemingly stood pressed against the side of the Triumph. All about me fell an extraordinary silence. Then men were shouting, and through the megaphone the Naval Beach Commander was roaring orders, his voice even then not without its cold haughtiness. The pinnace crews poured from their dugouts and raced to the boats. I gained the jetty without noting how I got there. Then I was on a pinnace which was gathering speed to rush away to the doomed ship. A vast sailor said:

"Blimy! Wot chew doin' 'ere? You swim?"

I nodded. An iron-hard elbow crashed into my ribs. The sea engulfed me. Back again on the beach I saw the Triumph heeling over. With terrible certainty she went over, her decks washed by foam as they went under. Then only her red bottom was to be seen for a little while. The pinnace boats were steaming over the place where but a few minutes before her guns were belching great flames and masses of smoke. Four destroyers came north from Cape Helles, their bows white with curling water. A plane – it might have been two – sped across the calm sea from Imbros. Down in the dark depths the submarine rested on the sea bottom.

Day and night, regardless of the bursts of shelling, the repeated attempts to destroy the jetty, the Beach Commander walked that jetty with his stick and his megaphone. The jetty was his quarter-deck, and all hands were made to realise it. How he escaped the shrapnel and the H.E. was a miracle. I used to stand and watch him, and implore the gods to give me courage like that.

A dark night – a black night – a calm night following a swift-passing thunderstorm. Jacko is restless. Out from the darkness, from the very seaward end of the jetty, comes the Commander's voice:

"Who are you?"

From further out a bass voice replies:

"Pinnace boat, sorr."

Possibly the sailor on the pinnace is expected to give a number, for the Commander says in cold, sarcastic tones:

"Of course you are a pinnace boat. Do you think I take you for a ruddy submarine?"

In the quiet of the last evenings that followed a voice from the summit of one hill would shout imitatively:

"Who are you?"

"Pinnace boat, sorr," would come from another hill-top.

From a dozen vantage points would float down the chorus:

"Of course you're a pinnace boat! Do you think I take you for a ruddy submarine?"

And the Beach Commander would smile in his wintry manner, and ceaselessly pace his quarter-deck until the hour struck.

There was a tall, lean man dressed in khaki slacks and shirt. He was a major and wore neither Sam Browns nor shoulder crowns. He was specialist doctor from Sydney. He carried a sack and collected beef bones from the cooks with which to make broth for the patients in the tent hospital beyond Shrapnel Gully.

A small crowd of men were bathing from a barge moored beyond another barge piled high with empty water-drums. Beachy Bill placed a shrapnel shell but a few feet above the empty bathers' barge. Fifty men scrambled ashore across the water-drums like angry ants. One man stood on the highest point of the water drums, looking back, looking down into the empty barge.

He was naked. In his hands he held his clothes. He appeared to stand like that for a long while. Then his clothes dropped from his hands, and he sprang down into the barge in which he was about to dress. When he again came into view, he was partly lifting, partly dragging another man, bringing him across the water-drums. The drums sounded hollowly.

"Stretcher bear-ERS! Stretcher bear-ERS!"

From beyond the summits of the sheer-faced hills, from the top of the gullies, the rifle and the machine gun cracked most all the night through. The gullies were alive with men and mule-drawn, two-wheel carts. The soft hissing commands of the Indian mule drivers were accompanied by the rickety-clatter of the cart wheels. "Pull up here!" "Let these stretcher cases pass!" "Right away!" "Blast!" There's a hundred semi-naked men getting a heavy gun up a wall! "Go on – go on!" "Who the hell's blocking the road now?"

Sibilant oaths in an unknown language. The incessant cackle of rifles. The Midnight Bees! Always they are droning by, down to the beaches and the silent sea – those invisible bullets.

Dawn will break in an hour. A single star is drifting shoreward, casting a faint sheen on the black water. Beneath it floats a shape which resolves into a destroyer. Against the sky, so close does she come, we can see the mass of men causing her to list to port. Pinnaces and barges bring them to the jetty. The jetty deck rumbles beneath their boots.

Daylight! A man with a white flag crossed with crimson heads a procession from the sand-bagged Casualty Clearing Hospital out to the barge moored to the jetty. Following him stagger a party of men, many of them splashed with the white of bandages. Behind them other men carry stretcher after stretcher. The enemy gunners do not fire. The barge moves out to the green and white-painted ship. The bearers return.

The flies! The flies are almost everywhere. The lice! The lice are everywhere. It is possible to escape the flies: the night will defeat them. From the lice there is no escape, night or day. Even the colonels and the generals have their fair share.

Nine little soldier boys sitting on the beach peering intently into the seams of trousers and flannels; nine little soldier boys subconsciously prepared to act when the next "train" is heard. One of them throws back his head and roars with laughter. The others grin and demand to be told the joke. The laughing man shakes with the power of his emotion, and he holds out a corn-covered hand.

"Cripes!" he gurgles. "Look at that little bloke! He's got two green spots on 'im. He's a descendant of the louse what crawled over Helen of Troy. Ain't he just lovely?"

Laughter – and death.

A fat sailor is sitting beside the open manhole-like entrance to the engine-room of a pinnace. He is mending his trousers and sits in his flannel. A shell whines, screams triumphantly, rushes down towards him. The fat sailor leans forward, dives down the "manhole," gets stuck. Half a thousand men hold their breath, release it in guffaws of laughter. The shell plunges into the water beside the pinnace. Two white legs wave frantically above a wide stern.

From along the beach:

"Stretcher bear-ERS! Stretcher bear-ERS!"

Laughter and death; anguish and laughter.

So it goes on.

Hammer and Tongs in the Somme

It is doubtful if any man was able clearly to visualise the tremendous destructive forces created and pitted against each other along a front of many hundreds of miles. Along that front, day in and day out, year after year, was an incessant thunder of guns, incessant human activity. Hundreds of thousands of men literally faced each other; behind them were hundreds of thousands of men holding lines of communication; and behind them yet hundreds of thousands of men and thousands of women making munitions and driving ambulances.

To learn how the war was going it was necessary to read the newspapers.

A point of interest and one in which we may take pride is that the comparatively small Australian army became outstanding for its valor and its dependability. Throughout the entire course of the war no army received such a signal compliment as did the Australian army as when it was rushed to the Somme to stem the victorious German flood consequent to the crushing defeat of Gough's Army Corps. Almost then did the Germans win the war.

The Brass Hat had little time for the Digger. The Digger was too casual, too intolerant of military pomp and regulations and snobbery to please the Brass Hat. He had long made up his mind that he was brought across the world to engage in and win a war, and he could not see how frills and ceremony were going to accomplish it. But of him the Brass Hat wrote:

> "These Australian battalions and companies are exceptionally effective if given much fighting to work off their energies. Their keenness and efficiency are too great for normal defence."

Which was why when there was any "back-slack" to be taken up the Digger was set to do it. For this reason – not because the Diggers were disliked, for they were not – the A.I.F. suffered the highest percentage of casualties of any army of the Allies. Despite the occasional sneer levelled against the Digger for an alleged lack of discipline, Haig said after reviewing the 2nd and 5th Divisions:

"They could not march better if they had received years of peace training."

In 1917-18 for every raw Digger going up to the line there were two returning after being patched up in the hospitals. Candidly, no one went back eagerly for a "second issue," but no man I ever saw went back with a glum face.

In any party of Diggers numbering from three upwards there was the "dag." In him was the pure essence of the Digger spirit. He saw humour in everything, he would scrounge anything, he was always broke and yet always successful in "raising the wind." Like our aborigines, he had no sense of property values and would share his last cigarette by breaking it in two – and then stalk the O.C.'s supply.

In the dog-box railway truck which conveyed me to the Somme were forty of us, and of that number thirty-eight were "dags." It was early summer and we travelled in jerks and starts with the wide side doors open, lounging on our kits, smoking and yarning, and singing and playing poker.

That night, shortly after ten o'clock, we were stopped just before entering the station at Abbeville to await a threatening air raid. On one side of the several trucks was an anti-aircraft battery, and along the other a row of huts occupied by a Chinese labour battalion. During the course of the raid a Jerry laid two eggs on the battery, and after the gravel and things had stopped falling on the roofs of the trucks, several of the Chinese darted into our box and burrowed like ostriches among our legs and kit.

Heartrending yells arose from one end of the truck – slapping sounds. Two further bombs dropped sufficiently close to enable one to see by the explosion flashes two Diggers each belabouring a Celestial stern with a belt. To our visitors, the horrors of war without came to be preferred to the horrors within, and they departed even more quickly than they had arrived.

Finally the long line of dog-boxes was halted on a siding in a forest of stately trees, and from here we started our long march to Divisional Headquarters. The roads were white with dust, and when we emerged into open country, comprising chiefly pasture land, with a small village nestling here and there around one or more poplar trees, the heat became intense. With us was a huge 4th Divi. man who sang and whistled. He had three wound stripes. He said to me:

"You're looking crook. Fever?"

"I think so. Malaria. I've had it before."

"Give us your rifle. Hey, Blue! Here's a bloke crook. Take his coat roll."

They relieved me of half my equipment as though it were a normal thing to do.

The officer in charge, a captain, reminded me of a careworn professor of mathematics. He had a large nose, he wore glasses, and his chin receded. To him Blue said:

"Have you got a drink about you, sir?"

"I – er – I have not," replied the captain, regarding Blue as though he had never seen a Digger before.

"Perhaps some quinine, sir?" pressed Blue persuasively. "Bloke feelin' a bit crook."

The Captain did have aspirin, and he gave me two tablets, and from his own water-bottle into a collapsible metal tumbler he poured a draft with which to swallow the tablets. The draft contained brandy. Blue regarded me suspiciously, and more than once tried to smell my breath. The captain regarded him now and then with calm meditative eyes.

We camped that night beside a mighty aerodrome, and while we ate breakfast the next morning machine after machine swooped down to fire bursts of bullets at a target when directly above us. Marching out, the road skirted the 'drome. The sunlight sparkled on squadron upon squadron of French 'planes drawn up into lines like toy machines on a golf tee.

In the burnished sky, so high that it was difficult to see them, aeroplanes floated like wisps of gossamer. Of what nationality they were it was impossible to distinguish. We could not hear their engines, although the road was empty of traffic. Only towards noon did we reach a cross road along which flooded a river of motor traffic, going one way – to the south-east and to the line. Huge trucks carrying small mountains of horse fodder, huge tarpaulined trucks, cars carrying staff officers, a fleet of buses crammed with French soldiers, despatch riders and empty ambulances. In the square of a small town where a military policeman directed traffic, we sat in the shade of a house and ate our lunch.

I remember that we passed through a town named Allenville when somewhere on the horizon sprawled the dustheap which had been Corbie. We were delivered to Divisional Headquarters, despatched to several companies. In a doorway of a house in a street a man shouted. It was Square-Face. It was like arriving home.

"You're looking crook," he said, grinning as though offering me a compliment. "The old malaria? Come in and have a deep noser."

Like the prodigal's father he led me into a well furnished room. There were books and a reading-lamp on a table, easy chairs and a writing desk. Snug quarters, to be sure. Evidently they did the digger well on the Western Front. From a cupboard, Square-Face dragged a case of whisky. Another man came in. We drank heartily – twice. The generous Square-Face presented the other man with a full bottle. He gave me a full bottle, too. We drank again. Then he said he would show me "the office" and my quarters.

"Can't you put me up here with you?" I asked.

"No do," he replied regretfully. "This joint belongs to a Tommy colonel. He'll be back any minute."

Perhaps because of the heat of the day, I had been expecting a thunder-storm. I had taken no notice of the incessant rumble of thunder, but when it increased in volume towards sundown, it occurred to me only then that it was gunfire. Down south they were at it hammer and tongs.

Thunder from dawn till dark! All night long the line marked by Verey lights. The air constantly vibrating with the hum of raiding plane engines. The "thrump – thrump" of bombs. Over there a dump on fire. The roads trembled beneath pounding hoofs and groaning wheels, and the solid tyres of huge trucks.

Marching men, ambulances, G.S. waggons, ammunition waggons, and lorries, marching men, always marching men! Further up – long lines of men loaded up with timber, wire, water, bags, cases of small-arm ammunition, and hand grenades. On either side, in front and behind, gun after gun, battery after battery, wallowing in their pits. Away east, to the north, and to the south, countless men "standing to," men crawling about between lines of barbed wire, now and then flood-lit by bursting lights. The whip crack of rifles, the rat-tatting of machine guns.

For tens of thousands it had become normal life. That there had been any other kind of life seemed difficult to realise.

After the passage of years, life in Australia came to be regarded in retrospect as a pleasant and leisurely dream; or as though we had migrated from one planet to another.

Here we found men from other distant planets, and we became planetarily, worldly, nationally conservative. The Australians seldom mixed with the Tommies. They never mixed with the New Zealanders or the Canadians. But in any argument behind the lines the Scotties and the Australians mixed like blood brothers. Everything was O.K. if Australian and Scottish divisions went into the line together.

Precisely what is myalgia I do not know. It attacked me in the spine, and I was taken to a field hospital close to the crossing of two roads. There, several times each day, we could hear the low whine of heavy shells which "thrumped" into Amiens, and I thought of the Goeben's shells arriving at Anzac. The quack gave me castor oil, and "went crook" because it was a physical impossibility to keep it down. Why they should torture a man's body with something against which it violently revolts is difficult to understand. I sometimes think that medical science is exceeding slow in progress.

Then there was that casualty clearing station. Why establish a C.C.S. between an important railhead and a huge aerodrome, both legitimate targets for the enemy? The Germans came at night to bomb the 'drome and the railhead, and anti-aircraft shell splinters and dud shells fell among the long lines of joined E.P. tents.

We men were all right. It was a place we stayed at not long, but the doctors – our cleverest surgeons – and the nurses were there for weeks. I could issue Number Nines any old time, but surgeons and nurses are not made in five minutes. In fact, they are not made at all; they are born.

Knowing the Digger, I can quite understand how an English

school teacher came earnestly to seek information, regarding our native peaches. Was it right that our native peaches had the stone on the outside?

The prickly pear farms we owned! And the gold mines!

It was just as well that the Government in its wisdom, permitted us to draw but a portion of our pay. Farms! Gold mines! Why, we seldom owned a razoo!

The Man Who Thought He Was Dead

We were camped, the dog and I, on a wide bar of sand which rolled westward across the flats to stab the flank of the Darling River. We were on tramp, the damper was baked, and I smoked cigarettes whilst entering into a diary the small events of the day.

The stillness of the wild enveloped us. Not a sound in all that vastness reached my dull, material ears.

Yet there was a sound which the dog heard. He sniffed once and pricked his ears.

Slowly along the back of his neck the hair stood up, and deep within him rumbled a growl. Even then the blanketing silence lay heavy upon my ears and I heard nothing.

Moments fled, and I held my breath to accentuate the silence. The sound which eventually I heard seemed a very long way off as might sound a small, softly played organ in a great cathedral. Surely I was not hearing heavenly music; surely I had not reached the milestone of the sundowner's life? Yet music it was, most certainly it was. The notes rose and fell in rhythm and in perfect time. The tune seemed familiar, or was it the slow intoning of a grand hymn?

To the best of my knowledge there was not a habitation or a human being within at least eleven miles. And never yet have I known a swagman travel on a dark night singing hymns.

Gradually the music became more distinct. There was now no doubt that someone out there in the blackness of the night was not singing or playing an instrument, but humming in a very high pitch. But the tune? Ah! I caught it at last. How often had it been played during the war, that hymn of praise, that hymn of sacrifice, that most wonderful hymn of triumph, the acme of man's musical genius – the Dead March in "Saul!"

Yes, that was the tune without doubt, nor could there be any doubt that the hummer was mentally unbalanced. Had not the dog been there I should have been inclined to doubt my own sanity, but in such a situation a dog can be relied on always to prove one's sanity or otherwise. It was evident, therefore, that a lunatic was approaching.

There are many such afflicted wanderers, especially along Australia's outback rivers and creeks. Poor souls, whose minds have been clouded by loss, by overwhelming adversity, by drink, they are mostly quite inoffensive. Even so, it is better to be prepared at such times, since it is futile to yell for a policeman.

Beyond the radius of firelight there was nothing visible other than the box tree just to our rear. The hummer was now very, very close, yet it was quite a while before there appeared a tall, dark figure emerging from the pervading blackness of the night. My suspicions of the man's sanity were confirmed when he was made out to be approaching with slow, measured steps.

Continuing the humming, the figure drew near. First I saw that he was a very tall fellow, then that he also was very gaunt, and, finally, that his hair and eyes were dark, as well as his trimmed beard and moustache. Yet in striking contrast, his face was dead white – the colour of a corpse.

Without interrupting the tune he hummed, he came to the fire and stared down at us from its further side. The lines of his face were then plain; lines that drew down the mouth and puckered the forehead into a vision of despair; whilst his eyes, wide open, were expressive of deep sorrow. A face, indeed – it must be written – the face of a soul in hell. Standing there, gazing down at us, he hummed the tune to the end.

Infusing as much cheerfulness as possible into the greeting, I wished him "good night." He answered in a somewhat unconventional manner, the while his face retained the fixed expression of grief. He said, much as a child repeating a lesson:

"I'm dead! I'm dead! I'm dead!"

Having it in mind to tell him that he certainly looked dead, I invited him to a drink of tea and pointed to the sugar bag. But the offer made no more impression on him than it would have made on a gum tree. Thrice more came the reiteration:

"I'm dead! I'm dead! I'm dead!"

Half turning, he raised his right foot, and when he brought it down hummed the first note of the Dead March. Slowly, with funeral steps, he passed from sight, leaving me with an amazed sense of unreality. Softer and softer did distance tone the tune of death and life, until at last my straining ears could catch no more.

He had gone.

Was the visit an hallucination induced by solitude or damper-destroyed digestion? I was assured of my own mentality only when I examined the tracks on the further side of the fire.

Two hours later the dog sprang up and barked. This time a figure loomed from the darkness without a sound. It was much shorter than the first, and it drew near with quick springing steps. He carried two small swags as well as the usual billycan and the canvas waterbag. He said cheerfully:

"Good night. Have you seen me mate? Tall bloke. Name of Dead March Harry. We was camped about five miles up the river, and I left him to cook the tea while I went to have a look, see, at the fish lines. Gone when I got back. Gone without his swag, without me. I knoo then that he's got one of his hummin' turns. Oh! a lot of trouble in 'is time. Went nutty on a tart and she turned him down. Well, so long. I'll soon catch up to him 'cos he don't go moren't half a mile an hour. Good night!"

I met Dead March Harry two years after that night. It was when he enjoyed a period of sanity. I really believe he knew more about the stars that Sir James Jeans.

Pimple's Elixir

When Pimple brewed his famous elixir he was cooking at Deepwater Well, situated midway between the homestead and the outstation of Nonning-Nonning. A young-old man with an inventive brain, he lived in a world of his own; and, because his culinary labours were limited to feeding Silent Joe and me, he could devote much of his time to his experiments.

Silent Joe, too, lived in a world of his own. There was small chance of being entertained or bored by his recitals of voyages to the nearest pub, twenty-odd miles distant, for he could not talk, had never talked, and found me obstinately backward in learning his finger language. Hence, we three – two stockmen and the cook – lived in peaceful relationship for several years,

For eighteen years Pimple had been cooking at Deepwater Well. The camp comprised two pine-built huts, set close together and joined at both ends by walls of canegrass to keep out the duststorms. Pimple's occupancy of the kitchen-dining hut made it definitely his. Attached to it was a lean-to shed housing his private electric-lighting plant – petrol-engine, dynamo and storage batteries.

Pimple was fresh-complexioned, sandy-haired and blue-eyed, slight of frame and flat-footed from wearing slippers. A lifelong succession of boils had earned for him his nickname. He never went away to see his relations; never went as far as Flanagan's Hotel on the river; it was whispered that he feared meeting with a wife who was after him for alimony.

All his wages went into patent medicines, electrical appliances, books and gadgets. The mails came irregularly, yet every one contained parcels for Pimple, and the junk stored away in his hut must have cost hundreds. One mail would bring him a book on wireless and a manual on card tricks; another would bring electric bells and wireless parts and gramophone records.

What with Pimple's several gramophones, the wireless and the station telephone, life was not as dull as might be imagined. Pimple would invite any passers-by in for a drink of tea and for news of Dead March Harry, Larry the Liar and Henry the Eighth. They, of course, roamed up and down the river with the timetable regularity of mail-boats.

Strangely coincident, the boss once brought out two petrol-cases filled with grapes and a mailed book for Pimple called "Fox's Twenty Thousand Recipes." It being February, we had ceased to regard grapes as a luxury, and, this being so, it seemed natural for the homestead gardener to send out two more cases of grapes the next day by the station truck.

"Wot in 'ell are we gonna do with 'em?" Pimple demanded when I got back that afternoon.

"Make a pie or something," I suggested.

"Pie, me neck! Even the fowls are sick of grapes. If that yaller-faced baboon 'ud sent out a bag of oranges I could have made some ginger marmalade with some synthetic ginger I've got. Drink of tea on the stove."

The fact that Pimple delayed the announcement of a drink of tea being on the stove proved his mental perturbation. Always was this sentence the first to fall from his pink lips on one's return from the paddocks.

I stepped into the kitchen, whereupon a bell rang, and a wall-indicator showed a figure 1. The door would have automatically shut behind me had it not been wedged open to let in the air. There, at one end of the hut, was Pimple's private stove, with the steel plate-racks over it. Beyond the table, on a long bench, were the wireless set, one or two gramophones, a washing-machine into which you stuffed your moleskins and then turned down a switch for sixty-five seconds, and various boxes containing an extraordinary array of patent medicines, with which he was everlastingly trying to stop the boils on his neck and the bunion on Silent Joe's foot.

Two electric bulbs hung from the rafters. If you went out through the back door the bell indicator showed 2, and should you then enter the dynamo-house it would show 3. Pimple was rigging up wires to connect with the ball-valve of the horse-trough to make the indicator show 4. For many months he had been nutting out a gadget to shut off and put on the mill over the well by pressing a button at the head of his bed. Some day Pimple is going to be world-famous, for he has courage of a high order. When a course of patent medicines fails to give results, he will not hesitate to try a mixture of several and make his own estimate of dosage.

"What have you got this time?" I asked him when I was sipping black tea.

"This? It's a book giving 20,000 recipes," Pimple replied, "I ain't looked at it yet properly, but it tells you how to make anythink from a hair-dye to a permanent soap bubble."

The bell rang when Silent Joe stepped on the doorbag,

"Billy on the stove," Pimple said, becoming normal,

Silent Joe grunted, and made for the billy. His drooping moustache reached his wishbone, and his washed-out grey eyes revealed a state of perpetual sandy blight which Pimple with all his arts could not cure. Having cooled the tea in the pint pannikin with a dash of water from the hanging canvas bag, he grunted again and clicked his fingers.

"Yes, Bill brought two more cases of grapes," Pimple explained, understanding the deaf and dumb signs. "Wot are we gonna do with 'em?"

Silent Joe shook his head, giving his attention to the book of 20,000 recipes. I was about to retire to my bunk, when the speechless one again worked his fingers with lightning rapidity. Looking at Pimple, I watched a beatific smile born on his youthful face.

"Give us the book!" he cried. I waited. Pimple read avidly. "Crummy! That's a good idea, Joe," he said, looking up at Joseph. "The problem of them grapes is solved. The book says – wait a moment – it says smash up the grapes, let 'em stand for a night, wring the juice through a dishcloth, add four pounds of sugar to every gallon of liquid, skim over twenty-four hours, and then bottle. That'll do! I'll make champagne outer them grapes."

His eyes were alight with a great enthusiasm. Silent Joe's tongue licked his grey moustache as a cat licks its whiskers after a drink of sweetened powdered milk. The silent one's watery eyes went dreamy.

In course of time, Pimple filled twenty-seven beer- and whisky-bottles with grape-juice, and he and Silent Joe spent an hour lashing down the corks with tie-wire and string. We all swore an oath that not one bottle would be broached until the lapse of six weeks.

The maturing wine was carefully deposited under Pimple's

bunk, that being deemed the safest place – from Silent Joe. When Pimple became interested in the manufacture of synthetic petrol from mill oil, he quickly forgot all about the new wine in the old bottles.

Not so Silent Joe. He brooded on it. He lost all interest in the sporting papers. Then he lost his appetite. Next he complained of griping pains, and signalled Pimple his opinion that they were due to the intake of dust raised by the successive sandstorms. Pimple gave him some Black's Gripe Relief, but it didn't live up to its name. Then the sufferer suggested that what his stomach really wanted was a little something to warm it. It was a tragedy that the pub was so far distant. He wondered if a little of the grape wine might relieve him of his agony.

For the sake of peace we agreed to break a bottle of Pimple's wine. The cork had to be dragged out with a cork-screw. The liquid was as flat as the well water. A sip was enough for Pimple and me, but Silent Joe appreciated it.

"A bit stale," he said with his fingers.

"Too right! It wants gingerin' up a bit," Pimple agreed. "Where is that recipe-book?"

He found it behind a spirit-driven air-fan, and fell to studying the page devoted to "Champagne."

"Says 'ere that a little brandy may be added to the liquid to hasten fermentation. H'm! There is no brandy. I've got it! Where's the methylated spirit?"

Frantically he and Silent Joe ransacked the place, at long last to find the spirit among the junk in the lean-to back of the fowlhouse. They called me to the kitchen, and we decanted the brew into a large bread-mixing tin. Silent Joe had forgotten all about his gripes. When Pimple added to the brew a full pannikin of metho, we tasted it. Silent Joe with his fingers said that it was a positive improvement. Pimple was doubtful. One sip made me shudder.

To subdue the methylated spirit, Pimple added half a bottle of vanilla essence. It didn't taste quite so raw then. Silent Joe was willing to drink the lot, and we had to be firm with him. Pimple poured in a bottle of pain-killer, and then a pannikin of yeast. On impulse, he added three remaining pills from a little box.

"If she don't get a kick now, I'll burn that recipe-book," he said.

The three sips and the smell gave Silent Joe the ache. He rang up the boss to ask for a week's leave to go to the Hill to have a tooth out. The boss advised him to have them all out while he was about it, and off went our comrade on a chance-passing truck.

While he was at Flanagan's Hotel, Pimple and I agreed to tell him on his return that all the bottles had burst. During the recovery, Silent Joe went hunting around to find the broken bottles to gain a little relief by smelling them.

As time passed we forgot all about Pimple's wine. He connected a wire with the horse-trough ball-valve, and his indicator showed 4 every time one of the dogs went for a drink. His mind was occupied with matters of a more lofty nature than maturing champagne.

The autumn came – blessed relief after the wind and dust of March and April – and one morning the boss rang up to say that Old Ben, with the bullock waggon, should arrive that evening on his way outback with a load of rations.

We first heard Old Ben coaxing his bullocks up the far side of the sand dunes beyond the rubbish-covered flat, and we went to the front door to watch the team crawl over the summit of the surrounding sand barrier a quarter of a mile distant.

"There they are!" Pimple announced when the heads of the leading bullocks showed above a declivity between two sandhills. The others fol1owed, pair by pair, and there finally came into view the top of the small load of rations. We could now see Old Ben, bobbing about on his gammy leg, and hear his unique expletives between the shotlike cracks of his mighty whip, over which old age was losing command.

When the team stopped right at the pinch, Old Ben was beside the polers. He ran along to the leaders, and, because he was ancient, one-eyed and limpy, he tripped over his long whip and scooped the sand into his long, ill-kept whiskers.

"He always falls down when he gets excited," Pimple said. "I tipped that them bullocks would get stuck in that bit of sand."

The windless evening permitted us to hear every word of Old Ben's impassioned speech as he lay on his side on the ground.

"Come down outer that, Frosty," he roared to the figure on top of the load. "A-laughin' up there like a young gel wantin' to be kissed."

"Ah! Frosty Frank's offsidin' to Old Ben," Pimple observed. "Fat lot of good sending 'im to offside to a bullock-driver! Poor old Ben. Seventy, if he's a day, and still drivin' bullocks. Marvellous! I suppose we'd better go along and lend a 'and."

By the time we reached the team, Old Ben's efforts with the whip had turned the bullocks into stubborn sulkers. When the flats of shovels failed to achieve movement the driver cried with tears in his usually bright eye:

"Let 'em stay there till they does pull it out. Let 'em stay there all night, all to-morrer, all next week, if they wants t'. Ten useless animals, and a light waggon, and four ounces of loadin'."

By the time we got Old Ben to the tea-billy he was done up. He sat at the kitchen table, obviously depressed by his inability to get thirty hundred-weight of loading over a bit of a sandhill, when in his youth, as he said, he had driven pink tabletops over deep-dyed sand mountains. I felt sorry for this defeat of age. Softly, I suggested to Pimple that a spot of his patent brew might do the old fellow a little good.

"Care about a drop of wine, Ben?" Pimple asked.

"Too right! Got any?" The years fell away from the bullock-driver like ancient garments. After the shock of hearing that the brew actually existed had worn off, Silent Joe fell to cat-licking his moustache.

Pimple got out a bottle, wiped off the sand, and untwisted the tie-wire while he called for the corkscrew. The cork flew out at the head of a long, seemingly never-ending stream of foam. The foam-streak swerved from the wireless set on the bench to Old Ben's white whiskers, and there it paused. I waited pensively for the roar of anger.

When the foam ceased there was not a drop of liquor left in the bottle. Old Ben had jumped to his feet. He opened his mouth to volley his rage. Then he shut it, and he passed his fingers down his saturated whiskers. Then he sucked them. Finally he beamed his appreciation.

"Got another bottle?" he asked, desperately hopeful.

Pimple managed to fill a pint pannikin from two bottles. He handed it to Old Ben. Silent Joe evinced intense excitement. Pimple filled a pannikin for him. He gave Frosty Frank half a pannikin. My issue did not taste ill, but it was I unlike any wine I ever drank.

After ten minutes, Pimple had the wireless and the four gramophones all going, at once. Frosty Frank walked in and out of all the doors just to hear the bells ring and to watch the indicator numbers appear and disappear. Old Ben went into raptures about his prowess with the whip back in the 'sixties. He moved the table to represent a team of fifty-eight bullocks which he swore drew two table-top waggons in tandem across the Blue Mountains. He ran up and down the table yelling: "Come 'ere, Pieface – come 'ere, Pinto," and never fell down or over.

Someone began to sing "Roses Round the Door." At the time I took little notice of the singer. Silent Joe was dancing around on his poor feet, and through a haze I came to see that it was he who was singing about making mother love him more. The telephone bell rang, and kept ringing, but no one took any notice of it.

It was getting dark when we thought about the bogged bullocks.

"I'll get 'em outer that if I 'ave to flay the 'ides orf 'em." roared Old Ben. "They thinks I'm old and done for. Why, I was never younger in me life."

"Gimme a shovel," urged the no longer Silent Joe.

Away we went in the gathering darkness of falling night: Old Ben treading on air; Silent Joe talking as fast as any man could, fearful that should he stop he never would talk again; Frosty Frank playing Red Indians; Pimple strangely grave. He said that he remembered slipping the three pills into the brew, but he could not remember if they were White's Backache Pills or Wilson's Liver Pills, as both were the same colour and size.

Arriving on the sand-ridge in the pitch dark, we worked like demons to make the bullocks pull out the bogged waggon. Old Ben, with wonderful agility, ran up and down the team cracking his enormous whip like a machine gun whilst we belted at the bullocks with shovels and pieces of timber. Our prolonged efforts, however, were of no use. The bullocks were lying down. They refused to get up, to move, even to nod their heads.

Then Frosty Frank said that Old Ben had flicked out his eye with the whip. Pimple lay down and went to sleep. Silent Joe went on talking. One by one we dropped from sheer exhaustion.

Next morning, on sitting up, I was amazed to see the waggon down on the flat and the bullocks lying down under their yokes and cheerfully chewing their cud. Mystified, I stood up to look around for the telltale tracks. I saw that the bullocks had pulled the waggon off the sandhill whilst we had been sampling Pimple's wine, and that we had mistaken a row of sand-hummocks beside the track for a team of bullocks.

Pimple couldn't understand it. Frosty Frank didn't try to. Old Ben awoke and asked for more wine. When Silent Joe got up, he went on talking. He has been talking ever since, even in his sleep.

A Dog-proof Fence Job

Should you desire to see flies – you would be an extraordinary person if you did – visit the north-west frontier of New South Wales. If you would experience real dust storms, and would appreciate sunny Australia, by all means take train to Broken Hill, and from there travel some 200 miles by mail car to Yandama or Quinambie Station any time during January and February. Most certainly you will be tormented by the flies, choked by the dust, and slimmed by the heat; but you will never recall the name of Sturt, Australia's greatest explorer, without "living" with him and his companions every minute after he left Cawndilla Lake, which is beside the Darling above Menindie, in January, 1845.

Modern explorers who rush around in motor cars and huge trucks make me smile. When they name pot-holes and ant-heaps as lakes and hills, the mud of the former sucked by a lone prospector, and the elevation of the latter used by a stockman to spy out possible feed for his weary cattle before ever the "explorer" was born, I get that tired feeling. How I would like to have one in my power and say to him:

"Here are two camels and equipment and tucker for a month. You can get water at such and such a bore. The water will be a little salt, but that is neither here nor there. Work along this 22-mile section of dog-proof fence, and don't let me see you for a month. It is unlikely you will see anyone, black or white, but that's nothing as lots of men go two to three months without seeing or speaking with anyone. Now get going, my son, and crack hardy."

One can so easily imagine the chuckles and back-thumpings among the old timers of "The Corner."

You face north – it does not matter if you face south, but we will say north – and beyond a narrow flat covered with low bush and widely spaced wind-wracked mulgas you will see a huge wave of sand; here topped with a curling sand-cap, there gouged by a giant scoop. No car ever built could surmount it; it is doubtful if an army tank could make headway up those slopes of fine, light-red sand.

Beyond it lies another narrow flat, and beyond that another

sand wave, and so on and on for miles and miles, six or seven sand waves to be surmounted with every mile travelled northward. Picture a storm-lashed ocean suddenly petrified, each wave fifty to seventy feet high, each wave miles in length, a land killed by the head of Medusa held aloft by Perseus who refrained to look upon it. Save for a panting eagle perched on the limb of a dead sandal-wood tree, and a wide-beaked crow or two, no bird life.

The South Australian Border Fence is an everlasting switchback, a netted barrier six feet in height, topped by barbed wire, which takes a man's ingenuity to scale and which baulks any animal. Running north-south, it is opposed to the full force of the westerly hurricanes of winds and sands.

"You can have no idea of that region," Sturt wrote to MacLeary in 1845, and, with MacLeary, I had no idea of it until the inspector wrote offering me a job riding twenty-two miles of that fence. Twenty-two miles! Why, I could do that on my head, I thought. I found that the 22-mile sections were exactly twelve miles too long.

There was Martin, such a staid old gentleman who could not go without a sip of water after two days. Just a sip to wet his cud, or determinedly he would hobble off to the nearest bore. Emily was a gay widow or a placid cow – according to the mood of the moment. When it was really hot, when the ground burned the rubbery soles of their feet, they would go on strike by making for the nearest alleged shade and camp. And I having removed the loads and got a billy going over a fire, they would get up and come to stand over it, their heads steadily thrust into the uprising hot air and smoke in which, in all that land, there were no flies. Between their heads would be mine, and the slab of salt meat and the slab of rock-hard damper, too, because when not thus protected, it was impossible to convey food to the mouth without flies adhering to it. No butter, of course, and the frying fat kept in corked bottles.

The flies had a liking for canvas and would blacken the tent used to cover the load on Emily so that it looked like black American cloth. To escape them meant breakfast before dawn and supper after dark. There were evenings when the camels never moved their heads from the hot air of a camp fire or a rubbish fire until darkness vanquished the flies. I used to smear a mixture of axle grease and kerosene round their poor eyes. About my head I wore a woman's veil, but firing two such veils with cigarette smoking, I gave the flies best and suffered not silently.

The fence job was the most heart-breaking of any I have attempted. Every little bit of obstruction had to be kept clear of the bottom of the fence to allow the drifting sand to trickle through the netting mesh. Once rubbish was allowed to collect against that barrier, in no time where there had been a fence there would be a sandhill, over which gamboling dogs and foxes and rabbits could enter New South Wales. With a rake I would remove all such rubbish for a mile or more. The next day a windstorm would sweep from the west millions of football-like brittle buck bushes. The whole surface would appear to move, sliding eastward to be halted against the fence, to pile up against it higher and higher, until tons and tons of dead buckbush would steeplechase the fence into New South Wales. Work undone within an hour; work having to be done again and again.

I have found the fence on the summit of a sandhill twenty and thirty feet high, instead of the regulation six feet, swaying in the wind, or it might be lying flat, and all day I have laboured to remove successive "topping" of posts and netting. A storm had blown away the summit of that hill, and the next one, or the one after that, would build it up again, necessitating rebuilding the fence.

And the wonderful water! How the laundry people would have appreciated it! Arrived at a bore head, the steaming hot water ceaselessly pouring from the angled piping, all that was necessary to wash clothes was to hold them on a stick beneath the gush. No rubbing, no soap required. After the fifth wash you could blow holes through a shirt. Both sides of the bore drain were studded with soda and alkalines, and to obtain drinkable water one had to go half a mile down the drain. Even at that point the water was too brackish to make tea, but with plenty of sugar it was possible to drink coffee made with it.

No wonder that Sturt and his heroic band were dismayed by this land of sand and wind eighty-eight years ago. If the sun rose like

Alaska gold – much more yellow than the Australian mineral – it prophesied a day of roaring wind and stinging, choking sand, in which nothing could be done save to crouch in the lee of a pack-saddle – to face the storm to have one's eyes filled with sand; to turn from it to have one's face a crawling mass of flies sheltering in the windbreak caused by one's head.

The strangest storm I ever experienced swept across this country one afternoon in November. The day was still. Cigarette smoke rose in a straight spiral. The camels crouched in meagre shade. Every time I moved out of that meagre shade I became dizzy. In the nearest station homestead they said it was 119 in the shade – proper shade, of course.

Above the sand-gashed horizon rose a long, low cloud, having a much greater density than the usual sandstorm. At distance it appeared to hover just above the ground, rolling eastward with the irresistible solidity of a sandhill 200 feet high, stretching from the north to the south. When it drew near at the speed of a trotting horse its aspect was much like a terrific, Medusa-frozen sandhill come alive.

It frightened me. In it there seemed to be no possible chance for a human being to breathe. There was no time to pack and ride away before it. From black it had changed to dark red, terrifying in its relentless approach, sinister in its silent march. I believe that had there been a rabbit burrow near I would have thrust my head down one of the holes, and at the last instant it was the tent fly beneath which I wormed a way for shelter.

With a gentle hiss it covered up, blotted out the sun, created a darkness known by the Egyptians and the Israelites. The darkness lasted for about two minutes, when the light came back and the sun shone again. Still no wind. Every surface presented by tree branch, the camels, equipment, fence posts, even the fence wires, was loaded with sand precisely as such surfaces in a cold country may be loaded with snow.

It is the land inhabited by the remnants of a tribe of the great warring Dieri nation, which ousted another in the long ago, and settled all the way up the Barcoo delta from Lake Frome to Lake Eyre; the latter named after the explorer, the former after a Captain Frome, once Surveyor-General of South Australia.

Opportunity came to visit Lake Frome with a Dieri native and a half-caste. When we wanted water they would uncover several roots of a needlewood tree, break them and place beneath the breaks any tin receptacle with us. Then they would fire the foliage, and the fire would drive into the tins from half a pint to, in some cases, over a pint of drinkable liquid.

When near Lake Frome we fell in with a party of natives who could not, or would not, speak English, but who responded to certain Masonic signs. That mystified Sturt, and it mystifies me to this day. The only explanation appears to be that of coincidence; for the origin of Masonry is comparatively recent compared with that of the sign language of the aborigines.

Anyway, it gained for us open sesame, gained for us "official" permission to proceed, without which neither the full-blood nor the half-caste would have gone on.

From the summits of the eastern sandhill on a clear day it is possible to see the summits of the western sandhills across the mud flats, which are designated a map on all maps. In dry weather wild dogs may cross by rigidly following their own made pads. At all time those pads are death traps to both cattle and horses, whilst, after a heavy rain, there may be stretches of water an inch or so in depth, which last a week or two in winter.

If there be such a place on this fair earth of ours favoured by Satan as his back yard, it is about Lake Frome and the S.A. border fence in summer.

Fun for the Afternoon

Since early morning the heat had been so severe that the flies had taken refuge in the meagre shade cast by the mulgas, and the 101 one species of ants had remained deep within their nests.

In the more pronounced shadow given by a small grove of cabbage trees the fence-rider's three camels watched me at work with such lofty indifference as to make me feel foolish, labouring as I was in the sun when the temperature within the black shadow of the bloodwood tree at the nearest homestead was 119 degrees. Though, to be sure, that registration of heat, together with a remarkable lack of humidity, away up on the South Australian Border fence, is much less trying than is a hundred degrees in Melbourne.

It was about three o'clock when the bull put in his appearance, as I was waiting for the billy to boil. The camp was situated beneath a stout leopardwood tree – so called because its trunk is spotted green and white. There, where the camels had been unloaded the evening before, were the riding and the pack saddles. Close to the tree was the stretcher bed, on one end of which was the tucker box and on the other my current cat, red mouth gaping, flanks working like bellows. Round about lay the saddles, the water-drums and gear; and from various branches hung the meat-bag, the flour bag, and the bag containing smaller bags of dried fruit.

The scenery of rolling sandhills and stunted trees, although not exactly idyllic, was certainly peaceful. I was sitting on the stretcher making a cigarette, and Tum-tum was drinking water from the billy-lid, when, with startling abruptness, from directly behind me, the Intelligent Bull snorted sharply. There, at a distance of a mere twenty yards, he stood, a tawny picture of 900 pounds of magnificent fury, his head held low, his fore-feet snapping upward from the knees and tossing sand high above his back. Most decidedly the visitor had called on business!

A camel may unlimber into a gallop from a standing position in about three yards. The bull accelerated to top speed in about three feet – and it was then I made the initial mistake which was to prove so costly! Instead of snatching a blanket off the stretcher to meet the charge like a gallant matador, I shinned up the leopardwood tree hard behind the cat, and when the bull flashed by I was inelegantly lying along a bough twelve feet above the arena.

When I had obtained a more comfortable seat where the bough joined the trunk, and when the cat was on my shoulder and spitting at the bull, the opportunity of viewing the situation was presented. The bull stood, face about, giving himself another sand bath – and then in a flash he charged!

Physically the bull was in excellent condition, but the hollows punched into his flanks indicated his want of water. Doubtless he had lingered too long beside a dried-up water-hole when the other cattle had moved to the bore; and now he was mad with thirst, his mind governed by panic as a man's mind may be so governed.

He bounced along over the heated ground; the camels, despite their hobbled fore-feet, lunged away in three directions, and roaring with terror, sped quickly. Bellowing with rage, the bull sped quicker still. And, placing Tum-tum on the branch, I slid down the tree and ran to the riding saddle.

While I was fumbling with the straps to release my rifle, the Intelligent Bull spun round, and came charging back. Without the rifle I rejoined the cat!

The bull now began to earn his sobriquet. Beneath the tree, he regarded us, with displeasure in his blood-rimmed eyes. When he tested the tree hopefully with his head I expected him to back and then to dash out his head in the attempt to butt down the trunk. But not so. Instead he walked round and tested the tree's stability from several sides. Then, to demonstrate his annoyance, he tossed over the stretcher and walked across it to examine the contents of the wrecked tucker box. He nuzzled the water drums and kicked them with his hoofs until the seams burst and all the precious water wasted into the sand. Then he deliberately trampled on the pack-bags and finished by turning over the saddles and tossing them several times.

Having thus demolished the camp, the Intelligent Bull took up a stand about a dozen yards from the tree to glare at us, throw sand over his back and snort, knowing full well apparently that in time I should surely drop to the ground, alive or dead. Time was of no consequence to him.

By the time the sun was nearing its setting I was desperately parched. The situation was becoming serious, for, even at night in that country, and at that time of the year, one must drink. The water drums were empty, but the water bag, half filled, hung on the fence and the water in the fire billy was not yet upset; but I was more than a few yards from these small supplies, and twenty miles from the nearest source at the station homestead!

Hope suddenly burned brightly, however, when the Intelligent Bull walked away, as though tired at last of this cat and mouse game. Yet, when I attempted to reach the ground and the rifle, back he came at a gallop. As soon as he saw me in safety he walked away again – and this time I gave him a hundred yards. He bellowed loudly and appeared to be looking in any direction save at me.

On he went. To the ground I dropped. Back he charged, head down, tail elevated. Back up the blessed tree I clawed my way to reach the cat's side. Oh – if only rifles grew on tree branches!

The sun went down in a sea of blood, promising another hot and windless day on the morrow. The bull wandered away, pretending to forget us – but he did not wander far enough nor did he cease to watch us for a moment. A willy wagtail fluttered down to dance on the upturned riding saddle.

The next instant, before I could restrain her, Tum-tum slid down the tree stern first, and began to stalk the bird. I watched with interest.

The Intelligent Bull just as interestedly watched the bird and the stalking cat. He permitted the cat to make its fruitless spring before coming again into action, and when she had recovered from her disappointment he was only ten yards from her. And, perched like an ancient featherless galah, I was unable to render her any assistance when in wild panic, instead of running for my tree, she sped for safety to the cabbage-tree grove, with the bull hard on her heels, momentarily forgetful of me – a tiny little fugitive followed by a terrific Juggernaut.

Such was my haste that I fell out of the tree. I rushed to the saddle, I had only just unstrapped my rifle, when the furious bull was well on its way back. Made heroic by thirst, a worm turned at last, I rushed to the protection of the tree, and round its trunk I pointed the rifle; then I pulled the trigger.

Malignant to the very last, the Intelligent Bull pulled up short, staggered towards the stretcher – AND DELIBERATELY LAID DOWN ON IT EVEN WITH THE BULLET IN HIS BRAIN. It was impossible to drag from beneath 900 pounds of beef either ruined stretcher or blankets!

It was impossible, too, to sleep on the bare ground of that ant-infested country, even had water been abundant.

Having made and drank tea with Tum-tum riding on my shoulder, I trudged the twenty weary, dusty miles to the homestead – for a new camping outfit. The Bull, it seemed to me, must have had a thoroughly enjoyable afternoon, even to his crowning death-bed joke. Of course, I had the last laugh – but there was precious little of it left when at last those miles were over!

The Yandama Dragon

When I was young, I heard many stories of the Yandama Dragon who roamed the country in the far north-west of New South Wales. He was a bull camel that had been abandoned by his Afghan owner, and in due course he became a tiger, a lion, and then a dragon, charging here and there and smashing down fences, killing fence riders' camels, chasing stockmen and the few aborigines, and keeping women and children to their camps and houses.

On five occasions rifles had been brought into action against him, but he was impervious to bullets, even when directed by expert shots. He was reported to be at places eighty miles apart in one week. He was fearless, audacious, as cunning as a crow. The local Saint Georges fell down on the job of slaying him, and they assiduously built up his reputation to cover their own failures.

Consequently this fearsome creature was more legendary than real at the time I took over three camels and gear and began the patrol of twenty-one miles of the South Australian-New South Wales Border Fence well in the country of the Yandama Dragon.

The inspector assured me that the Yandama Dragon had not been seen nor tracked for three months, and that it was generally thought it had gone into South Australia when a brainless dogger had left open one of the few gates in the famous netted barrier.

At this time I had not had over-much experience with camels, but the three Government-owned beasts I took over and signed for were quiet and reasonable. The riding camel was a bullock of uncertain age, while the two pack camels were females long past the kittenish phase of life. Having been on the section for many years, they were good and contented campers and, save for the weekly sandstorm and the flies and the soda bore water, life was pleasant enough – for a common working man.

I had been on the section a little over three weeks when I met the first man, and he was the inspector. Fortunately I had then done a little work – clearing wind-driven buckbush off the fence for a mile or two and burning it, and slicing away the tops of several sandhills which threatened to bury the fence. The inspector said:

“I get two sorts of men here: the man who won’t work unless I am looking at him; and the man who won’t work when I am looking at him.”

At that I promptly sat down until he went on.

A month later I met the second human being. He was Good King Wenceslaus, an aboriginal chief who wore suspended from his neck a brass plate, on which were inscribed his name, rank, and vices. He rode a mule and was escorted by four gins who were on foot, and he was looking for dog tracks. I pointed out dog tracks that a breakfast plate would barely cover, and he became at once thoughtful.

“It looks like at ole Yandama Dragon feller he come back into Noo South,” he said slowly. When I reminded him that these were dog tracks, he went on to explain:

“You see, that there wild feller dog he go where Yandama Dragon go. You see, Yandama Dragon he kill camel, sometimes he kill little feller steer, and that there wild dog feller he stand by and eatem up. You see that feller Yandama Dragon you run for tree quick. Him eyes beeg as so so” – and he held his two hands about a foot apart – “and him have two tree firesticks down him throat.”

After this visitation, I enjoyed two weeks of restful peace when it was unnecessary to agree six times every day that the weather would continue fine for at least three years. Came then the evening when I camped among a bunch of mulgas at the edge of a large lake. The fence crossed this depression in under two miles. Being an Australian lake, there was no water in it, but on it at this time were patches of green pigweed for which camels have a passion. My three companions at once hobbled down to the lake bed to feed off this pigweed.

As is to be expected in December, the night was clear and silent and warm. When tents are seldom erected and houses are places of torture, a man prefers to sleep under a tree.

During the night I was awakened twice by the snapping of dry sticks, and for the last three hours of darkness I sat on the stretcher and nursed a rifle, while watching for fire which would give me the position of the dragon’s mouth, and trying to decide which of the trees would be the easiest to climb.

The new day revealed the three camels feeding midway across the lake. I visually searched its many acres as well as the curving line of scrub bordering it, but the Yandama Dragon was either asleep or gone on a long journey for I could not spot him. I did find, however, the tracks of the Dragon's companion, which were all round the camp. It must have been an enormous dog, and never before or since have I known a wild dog incautiously tread on dead sticks. This brute evidently feared nothing.

Having eaten breakfast, and packed and set out the pack loads, I took the three noselines, and set off for the camels. It should be understood that a camel's noseline is a length of light rope, to one end of which is attached a loop of twine, to slip round the wooden plug drawn through the camel's nostril.

With these noselines looped over an arm, I approached my beasts, who came to stand motionless, and to gaze at me with singular fixity. I was about midway between them and the lake shore, and a good thousand yards from the fence, when from behind I heard the bellowing roar of the Yandama Dragon.

There was this dragon charging at fifty miles an hour, his four legs splayed like those of a beetle, white foam being flecked back on to his shoulders and hump, his red mouth bladder blown with wind, and as large as a soccer bell. There was not even a rabbit burrow offering escape.

To run was useless. I would have been caught and trampled to jelly long before I could reach the fence. I could see the fire in his eyes, while the distended mouth-bladder looked like a flame and the foam from his mouth was like steam.

And now came a remarkable exhibition of the sub-conscious mind over the conscious mind. It compelled me to stand quite still and shout without cease the language of the bullocky, which as everyone knows, contains many Afghan words.

The Yandama Dragon duly arrived. He thrust close to my face his great and noble head, and, when he sidled round and round, my subconscious ego forced me to turn round, too. He blew clouds of "steam" into my face, and I could have lit a pipe at one of his eyes. He bellowed and roared.

His scarlet mouth-bladder touched me more than once. His eyes expressed awful triumph. I saw that through his left nostril still was drawn the wooden plug fixed there by his one-time Afghan master. All this I saw between clouds of steam and, controlled by my subconscious ego, the fingers of my left hand parted the loop of twine at the end of one of the noselines, and my right hand flashed upward and gripped the Dragon by his snout.

The next instant he was noselined.

Sound stopped. Steam was cut off. We regarded each other with dumb astonishment, wondering which of us looked the more stupid. From a dragon the beast was become a gentle lamb.

I took him with the others back to camp, and there I put on him one of the cows' saddles and loaded him with gear.

All that the Yandama Dragon wanted was a little human attention. He was tired of being so neglected. His reputation, after all, was one vile slander.

A Real Life Drama

The course of true drama should convey to the audience a mastering sense of inevitability. Modern plays and novels lack this trait for the reason that authors and playwrights have to pander to their publics, if they would eat, and provide happy endings. Which is why the ancient Greek dramas have seldom been surpassed.

The life story of Ray Mac would have provided a Greek playwright with a masterpiece, for, from its promising beginning, its tragic end was as inevitable as death which concludes all life, governed as it was by natural laws beyond human power to frustrate.

Ray Mac was the son of a once wealthy squatter. In exceptionally favourable circumstances he began life in a palatial homestead, growing up into a handsome youth, doted on by his father, receiving his primary education from tutors and his finishing off at a famous Sydney school. All that was wanted to make his life completely happy was the love of his mother, but Mrs. MacGinnis had died when he was a small child.

Old MacGinnis died when the lad was on the point of taking up medical studies, and when it was found that the old man's estate would have to go to Carey Street, Ray Mac gave up the idea of being a doctor and instead became a jackeroo on Wednesday Station. That was where he had been a year when I met him in 1922 when he was nineteen years old.

Dark in colouring, slim and active and good looking, he appeared to be more Spanish than Scotch-Australian. He danced well, rode better than he danced, conversed well on subjects other than sheep and wool, and was madly in love with the governess to his employer's children.

But the laws of nature are immutable. You can deceive yourself that they can be put aside, crushed, ignored, but they govern life, all life, as they govern the courses of the stars.

One afternoon Ray Mac came to me with the request to accompany him to the shearing shed, in his eyes fear and doubt, his face and hands indicating great nervous strain. Within the shed was a small room used by the shearing contractor, and in that shed he divested himself of his upper garments to reveal a beautiful torso and unblemished skin.

"Now, what do you make of this?" he asked, when feverishly slipping down his slacks. From the toes to above the knee, the skin of both legs was distinctly dark, as though he had habitually worn shorts, which I knew he never did.

"What do you make of it?" he almost screamed, so terribly that the sound sent a shiver through my body.

"Dress, Ray, and take it easy," was all I could then say.

A few minutes later we were walking down the dry creek bed, the shock of the tragedy weighing more heavily on me, for he was wildly hoping that a certain thing was not.

Your anthropologist may ignore significant facts, and your philosopher may vociferously claim that man is the master of his own destiny; that he can move mountains with faith. Of some matters, your common man has clearer understanding and at this point many will guess what were the immutable laws of nature working within poor Ray Mac.

"What do you think?" he asked, after we had become seated on a flood-washed tree trunk.

"I don't see how it can be, knowing your history as you have related it," I replied, speaking slowly, to add, in order to give him comfort: "Never accept a thing as fact until it is proved."

"It's proved all right, Hampshire. I'm going black," he said dully.

"Do you remember your mother?"

"Yes. I retain dim memories of her, of her playing with me in a garden and on the verandah of my father's homestead. But she was white. I know she was white."

To prevaricate, to raise false hopes in Ray Mac at this crisis appeared to me as unwise, and there are moments when verbal brutality is to be preferred.

"Proof!" I said gently. "You will have to prove that without delay in order to set you mind at rest. Remember that thoroughbred kelpie's litter of pups and the one which was a distinct throw-back. What of your mother's people? Where are they?"

"In Scotland. My mother was born and bred in Scotland. I tell you, she was white. You – you insult my mother."

He gripped my arm in a frenzy of rage, making me feel wholly a cad. That gave me a space to think, and, when he had calmed a little, I suggested that, as he had no living relatives in Australia, it might be possible to find the bookkeeper who at birth served his father, or even the doctor who attended his mother. Find them, and they might be able to say something. Meanwhile, to think the worst was futile until the thing was proved. And because Mrs. MacGinnis was Scotch, a race not living contiguously with a black race, in my mind what Ray had to prove was if she was actually his mother.

A month went by, during which Ray Mac bravely shut out from his eyes the haunting terror eating into his soul. Towards the end of that month he received a letter from his father's bookkeeper, then living in retirement in Adelaide, and at once left to interview him. Whilst he was away, I again answered the voice which calls from beyond the mirage, and his subsequent life I have pieced together from his letters and others.

To the old bookkeeper he showed his legs, and that old servant had the grit to break his oath and state that Ray's mother was an aboriginal, and that his father was unknown. Owing to the wit of a Scotch woman passionately desiring the baby nature denied her, and to the tolerant assistance of her husband, as well as to the loyalty of the bookkeeper, the secret of Ray Mac's birth was successfully kept. The baby being born whiter than the majority of half-castes, those three believed he would always remain white.

On his return to the homestead, Ray Mac courageously revealed the circumstances of his birth to the girl he adored, and he it was who demanded release from his vows. His employer, knowing the pressure nature would continue to exert, persuaded the young man to accept a position with a firm of wool brokers in Melbourne, but he did not rightly estimate the power of that pressure; and, as it had to be, Ray Mac returned to the bush within a year when the stain was beginning to show in his face and hands.

Some five years after that return, I passed through Wednesday Station to find Ray Mac almost black. He had lost the public school polish, he laughed too easily, and, instead of the dressed youth I had known, this man loved colour in his clothes. No longer was he interested in subjects other than those concerning the bush. He said that he had long recovered from the break from the pretty governess, was quite resigned to his fate, and was content with life.

There is a further fact which appears not to be appreciated by the learned – the power that the real Australia exerts on all human beings. I have yet to meet the man or the woman who has lived more than four years in the outback candidly say that he or she hates it. As with others, so with me – it attracts, draws, for ever pulls at the heart of the absentee, enslaves one so that outside it one can never feel the contentment and happiness one feels within it.

How much stronger must that power be to men like Ray Mac in whom flows the blood of nomadic ancestors? Stronger still must it influence the aborigines themselves. I guessed rightly that Ray Mac would not long remain in Melbourne. I was sure he would not be able to resist the pull of the bush. I knew another thing, too. I knew that the inherent desire to "go on walkabout" would conquer him with far more certainty than it has conquered me and hundreds of white men with me.

So it did. When Ray Mac had risen to be the under-manager, without warning he went bush with a half-caste girl. Later he was married by a police sergeant. For a period of seven months, he worked as boss stockman on another run, when the walkabout demon seized him again, and this time he and his wife went off with the full bloods.

I heard of him only the other day from a bushman who came to see me and discuss old times. Ray Mac now lives with the tribe. He will not work, never shaves, wears old and tattered clothes. His descent was the more rapid, perhaps, because for so many years he had thought himself to be pure white.

So you see that a loving woman, a doting man, a loyal bookkeeper, a succession of school masters, and an adoring girl, singly or collectively, could not have made this real life drama end happily.

The Strike Leader

Have you ever met a man or a woman whose chief occupation is making bullets for someone else to fire? They are to be found in any community, even in many families. One of my brothers was an adept.

Below my father's business house were huge cellars. I can remember when one of them always contained several hogsheads of beer from which four glass jugs were filled for every meal and placed on the male assistants' table. There was a strict rule that the person who drew the beer had to sing or whistle all the time he was in that cellar. Eventually the custom of drinking beer was followed by the vice of sipping tea.

In the other cellars, my grandfather – and my father after him – stored stocks of manchester goods and floor coverings, that one under the shop front being lighted by fanlights extending from the pavement to the bottom of the shop windows. They opened inwards, and, standing on a packing case, we boys could look through across the pavement to the far side of the street.

My brother made a bullet in the suggestion of opening one of the fanlights and, with a catapult, firing duck-shot at the ankles of passing ladies. Not particularly cautious, I saw, however, that such action would be followed by inevitable retribution, and having pointing this out to the ammunition maker, he offered another bullet in the suggestion of making targets of leash-led poodles on the further pavement.

Unfortunately, I prided myself on accurate catapult shooting, and shortly afterwards the first victim yelped and bit at the imaginary wasp sting, then to be picked up by the alarmed lady owner and rushed to the chemist on the next corner. That morning I introduced to the chemist four hideous cannine monstrosities. Said the armament maker, offering the third bullet:

"What about going along to the chemist and asking for a little commission?"

That appearing to be reasonable, I approached the chemist with this business proposition and secured his promise to consider it. On my way home he most unsportingly rang up my father to relate a good joke, and I need add nothing further than to remind you that that generation of fathers knew how to deal with their sons. For much less, a modern boy may be sent to a reformatory and machine-made into an habitual criminal.

Always beware of bullet makers. Never, however, be so blindly foolish as to make the bullet you are destined to fire, as I was, when in my youth I worked on a station out of Cunnamulla, Queensland.

For something like three months our ration list was minus potatoes. We then were on the usual weekly ten, two and a quarter – otherwise 10lb flour, 2lb yeast, and ¼lb of tea, plus a bottle of sauce and a handful of raisins. When a peculiar form of dust, alleged to be dried potatoes, gave out, the men began to grumble. More than once the manager said that rations were on the way by bullock waggon, but they never seemed to arrive.

In those days, some of the squatters made much money by never ordering rations until the supplies in the station store had almost vanished, so for three, and sometimes five, weeks, the hands would be on short commons. It is surprising how many ways there are of killing a crow.

At last, when bare ten, two, and a quarter were reached, even the cook growled and his inventive genius waned. Every meal time he, Old Humpy, Fly-by-night, Blue Evans, and the others talked about the great strike of '98, and of how the wool sheds were burned to the ground and many of the river wool-boats sank.

To me it appeared absurd to growl constantly among ourselves, for, singly or collectively, we had no power to hasten the arrival of fresh supplies. That was entirely the manager's business. In an unguarded moment, I suggested that we go out on strike until the "spuds" did arrive; further that the strike should take place the following morning, after we had eaten heartily of the usual bread and mutton chops.

It was an idea that came to be regarded by the others as a gem of originality. Yes, that was the idea! Strike till the spuds arrived! Not one would turn out for work after breakfast the next day.

"Wot we want, boys, is an organiser," pointed out the cook.

"That's so," whined Fly-by-night. "We can't go on strike without organisation. Wot are we gonna do about it?"

"I votes we appoints Hampshire as leader and organiser?"

Humpy puts forward – and the vote was carried.

Instead of realising I had made the bullet I was to fire, I felt proud in my position as labour leader. I had visions of becoming a great leader of men, the clarion spokesman of the submerged nine-tenth, a great leader of men wielding vast power, dictating to the accursed bosses, finally grasping the Prime Ministership.

"What we will do," I laid down impressively, "is this. After breakfast we will pocket all the cooked food we cannot eat. As usual, we will go along to the office at seven-thirty for orders, but this time I will inform the boss that we will not labour until he gets us spuds from town. The mail coach will be leaving Cunnamulla at ten tomorrow morning, and he will have time to ring up and arrange the transport of several bags. How's that?"

"Good!" exclaimed the strikers.

That evening I wrote and memorised a 300-word speech which I recited to my excited and approving followers.

"Put a little fire into it, and she'll do," the cook said in final judgment.

Accordingly, the next morning seven men waited for orders outside the station office; and, as usual, the manager came out of the office rubbing his eyes, to walk along to us to give his orders before returning for breakfast. He was a short, tubby, red-faced, grey-haired man of about sixty, with piercing dark eyes, a black, bristling moustache, and a mottled complexion. Not an easy antagonist for a new chum strike leader.

The strike leader stepped forward, but the strike leader forgot his lines, and what he said was, in effect:

"We have decided to go on strike till you get us some spuds. The coach leaves town at ten, and you will have plenty of time to see that a couple of bags are put on board. In fact, if you will promise to do that we will, I think, carry on our labours."

The manager's eyes opened wide. His moustache bristled more than ever. His face became suffused with blood. Ignoring me, he addressed the men.

"Oh! So you have, have you?" he said in steely tones. When I turned to them I noted that the cook was not of their number.

"You are not striking, Humpy, surely?" the manager said directly to the old man.

"Well, mister, not exactly on strike, but a man must have spuds now and then."

"Well, what about you, Searle?" This to Fly-by-night.

"Oh, I don't want to upset things," whined Fly-by-night, shuffling on his feet.

To each of the others the manager craftily put the same direct question, being sufficiently a psychologist to know that he could the more easily deal with men singly than collectively under the leadership of one man. Insufficiently experienced, I dumbly permitted this. Still only Humpy and Fly-by-night and the sneaking-off cook were found wanting. The manager gave his decision.

"The ration teams are due tomorrow night," he said. "I will not have spuds brought out by the coach, so don't make me hurt myself laughing by going on strike for one day."

Obviously he could not concede more than that, and the men accepted their orders. To me he spoke last, saying: "You can come to the office with me."

Arrived there he instructed the bookkeeper to make up my account and draw my cheque when he had had his breakfast.

"I am putting you off," he said, "not for leading a strike, but for being a fool. No strike succeeds unless the strikers stick together. You would never receive support from men like Old Humpy and Fly-by-night, and Bill, who have been so long on a station that they think they own the top wires in all the fences. Only an idiot pulls chestnuts out of a fire for other people, and only an idiot fires bullets made by other people, too. Let this be a lesson to you. You can start again in the morning.

I did not explain that the bullet I fired was of my own making, and I did not accept his offer of re-employment. I was too hurt by that man's common sense and my own stupidity. It requires much more than self-confidence to become a Prime Minister.

Some time afterwards I heard that the manager found excuses within a week for sacking the cook, Old Humpy and Fly-by-night.

The Man Who Laughed Last

Old Angus MacMurphy had many points in his favour. He neither drank nor smoked, and he never used bad language. He was a good boss. He was a good sheepman save in one respect. He paid his due when he had to; and he was a kind husband and an indulgent father.

MacMurphy owned a fair-sized station out from Wanaaring, and, because he had risen from a bullock driver to a pastoralist, and a Justice of the Peace, he was held in great esteem despite his peculiarities. How he ever managed to drive a team of bullocks drawing one of the huge tabletop waggons was the Mystery of The Corner, for there were old identities who stoutly maintained that never in all his life had he uttered a swear-word!

Consequently, as a bullock driver, Old Angus MacMurphy was unique. As a Justice of the Peace he was unique, too. His homestead being but four miles out of town, the police sergeant could always rely on his services when there were any drunks and disorderlies to be arraigned.

Old Angus would take his seat on the bench like a man whose mind is made up to have a pleasant morning. He would glare over the top of his spectacles at the succession of unfortunate prisoners produced by the sergeant; and he would tap a pencil on the little, raised desk with fierce impatience to pronounce doom.

The sentence was always the maximum permitted.

At the beginning of one October he had 3,000 prime wethers to drove to Cockburn, South Australia, for trucking to Adelaide. The job normally should have fallen to his sons, but there was a pretty barmaid at White Cliffs and they were not available. Old Angus, assisted by a cockney whose thirty years of bush life had not converted him, had left with the sheep when I happened along just as Mrs MacMurphy was about to drive after them with the buckboard.

On her offer of the job, I transferred my swag from bicycle to outfit, parked the machine in the poison house, and took the reins. The old lady would have gone, too, despite her seventy years. Had she not offsided to her husband when he drove bullocks back in '69?

I caught up with the sheep about ten o'clock. When I explained the transfer to Old Angus he blinked his blue eyes and waggled his close-cropped white beard, and made no comment.

And after the first day – the season being good – we adopted a general routine. Before dawn I got up to cook the breakfast, and Cockney went off to bring in the hobbled horses. After the sheep had got away, I would take down the hessian yard, roll up the hessian and collect the stakes to which it had been fastened, and pack everything up on the buckboard. During most of the day, I would drive this turnout behind the sheep, with Old Angus riding on the left flank, and Cockney on the right.

Now Angus, although a good sheepman and a good bullock driver, was a poor drover. Perhaps that was due to his bullock driving, when a man has to walk close on their near side in order to swing his whip over and against the far side of the offside bullocks.

Always on this trip did he take the left or near side wing; and, because he rode too close, the flock were constantly pressing to the right and giving Cockney much more work than was necessary.

For some time Cockney stood it in silence. The he made a great show of pushing the sheep back to Old Angus. When that failed to relieve the pressure, he gave hints of his displeasure by roundly cursing his dog. That, too, failing, he relapsed into moody silence for a whole day. The following day he lost his temper and roundly cursed Old Angus.

The old man, waiting for him to finish, sent across the backs of the sheep his famous magisterial glare. Then:

"I'll no ha'e sich languidge," he roared. "Stop it, mahn! The Gyptians did na raise the Pyramids wiv curses. I'll no ha'e it, I tell ye. Silence!"

"Well, you stop pushing the adjectival sheep across to me," Cockney roared back.

For ten minutes the argument continued; but after the first three minutes, the sheep became accustomed to it, and gave their attention to the ground feed.

Still did Old Angus unconsciously keep pushing the sheep over to Cockney. Of course, climax had to come sooner or later.

Cockney dropped his reins to his horse's neck. Raising his arms, he beat one hand against the other, and loudly clicked his fingers.

"Wot's the matter wiv the mahn now?" yelled Old Angus.

In a flash, back went Cockney's answer: "That's the deaf and dumb signs for 'Dash and blank, and blacky blank you, sir.'"

It was so unexpected that I leaned back on the high seat of the buckboard and roared with laughter. From Cockney, Old Angus transferred his magisterial glare to me. He never said a word.

That night in camp, every time I looked at Cockney I was compelled to chuckle again. Now and then the boss would look up from his pastoral journal and glare.

Two years slipped by, and November found me patrolling an eighty-miles section of rabbit fence in the Wanaaring district.

This particular November was humid and thundery, and despite all care the meat went bad after only one week out from the homestead.

I don't know how the vegetarians get along. I do know that it is impossible for me to live without common salt – and that one cannot long work hard on damper and jam. And after four days without meat, I tried rabbit – and any bushman knows what that means.

Then I tried a white cockatoo; but, although I boiled it on and off for three days, nothing happened. He must have been over fifty years old. And then, coming to the edge of a big, natural clearing, I found half a dozen kangaroos feeding on it.

The clearing was twenty-nine miles from the homestead, and, at the shortest, seventeen miles from any track. I walked boldly up wind. Five minutes later I was skinning the 'roo – and congratulating myself on having secured a well-conditioned beast when, behind me, a stern voice said: "Don't you know that kangaroos are protected?"

The involuntary start was not the act of a guilty man, but of one surprised by the proximity of a human being where one was least expected. From the hard grey eyes boring into me, mine swept down the uniform of a mounted constable. When I explained that I had been out of meat for more than a week, he said: "That makes no difference. What's your name?"

Having obliged him with the information, I induced him to

accompany me back to the pack camels, where I showed him the empty meat bag. That appeared to satisfy him; and, when he rode away, I raced back to the "kill" to beat the blowflies.

Now, it is the unwritten law in the outback, of course, that if a traveller is out of meat, and if a squatter will neither give him or sell him meat, he may kill a sheep, provided that he hangs the skin over a fence or rail and takes no more of the carcass than he can eat at one meal.

When I shot the kangaroo I was not actually starving, but I was bordering on it; and nothing would have been said by the squatter for whom I was working if I had shot one of his sheep – had there been any sheep on that part of the run. Judge my amazement, therefore, when, on my arrival at the homestead, I was served with a summons to appear at the Wanaaring Court on the charge of having killed a protected animal. And when, eventually, I stepped into the dock – there, glaring at me over his spectacles, was Old Angus!

The sergeant read the charge. The trooper gave his evidence. I managed to delay my doom being pronounced by Old Angus by asking the Trooper if I had not shown him the empty meat bag. Like a sport, he admitted it without hesitation. I harangued the court, drawing vivid word pictures of my meat hunger and physical stress.

The sergeant looked glum. Old Angus looked really happy. Then he said: "Five pounds."

"Eh!" I gasped, so great was my astonishment.

"Five pounds or seven days," said Old Angus curtly. "Next case, sergeant."

The sergeant smiled. For ten seconds I stared at the beak. I saw his eyes twinkling, and his beard waggle. He was the man who laughed last! And I was hustled out of the dock.

The following month, when I returned from a fence trip, among my letters I found one addressed in printed characters. The envelope contained nothing – except five one pound notes! For twenty years I have been wondering if it was old Mrs MacMurphy who sent them to me – or whether it was old Angus himself.

He may have had a sense of humour – and of justice!

Fur Fever

A man on gold never watches the clock. To him Time does not exist; even food is ignored until the body grows weak from the lack of it. The energy of his mind is consumed by the magic of golden dreams from which he is recalled only by waning daylight. Yet there is no excuse for the prospector on gold working over-long hours and starving himself, for the gold, having been hidden in the ground for countless ages, will not run away.

To the fur-getter Time is very real, ever present at his elbow to nudge him on to ceaseless labour. Instead of watching and anxiously waiting for Time to relieve him of labour, he finds Time always at his heels, always trying to catch up to him, in his mind the ever-present dread that a climatic change will occur to stop the flow of fur he is turning into gold.

Moss Brown's motto was: Make hay while the sun shines; loaf when it rains. He liked taking Government fencing contracts when in his dictionary there was not to be found the word "stop." He came out from Broken Hill in a one-part Ford truck, the first Ford car to reach Broken Hill, eventually to be converted into a truck. It used to go with leaps and bounds, but I would cross Australia on it today because, despite the leaps and bounds, it always got to one's destination.

Seeing the countless grains of gold, he asked for a partner. I became it. I say "it" advisedly, because for months and months I was an inhuman machine which knew not leisure, and precious little sleep.

It was February when we started work on one of the great surface dams east of Victoria Lake in the western division of New South Wales. We netted the dam water and built trap-yards one day when even the crows refused to leave the shade, and the evening of that day found us at opposite corners of the dam, each with a shot gun and cartridges with which to keep off the kangaroos from breaking the flimsy netting fence and releasing our catch of golden grains.

The surrounding country was a Sahara, made so by the passage of sheep and countless animals daily converging upon the water. The sheep now had been moved, for there was but a foot of water remaining, and that foot might be sucked up by the sun in any one hour.

Dusk was falling when the first rabbit slipped over the dam bank without pausing, with terrible determination to reach the water. Another appeared, then two, then four, then a countless procession. We could hear the faint rustling noise of their passage. One I easily caught when it passed me, and it squealed seemingly less from fright than from anger at being delayed. When released it continued its journey as though oblivious to the fact that a human hand had snatched it up.

The fence round the square sheet of water was erected about one yard from its edge. Twice on each of the four sides the fence was fashioned into a V, the point of the V six inches from the water, and at the point of the V a small hole cut large enough to permit a rabbit to squeeze through. At opposite angles a V in the fence, pointing outward from the water, led into a large, strongly built netted trap-yard.

Frantically searching a way through to the water, a rabbit would enter one of the V's, reach its point, poke it's head through the hole when its twitching nose would be within a few inches of the water it must drink. Thirst burning away suspicion, it would edge further through the hole and drink with half its body beyond the hole. Another rabbit coming behind it, hearing it drinking, would nip it on the rump, whereupon the first rabbit would worm the whole of its body through the V, and, in order not to wet its feet, it would move to one side of the V where it would have room, and then be imprisoned between the water and the fence.

From then on rabbits trickled through the V's like golden drops of rain falling through an hour-glass, and their thirst quenched, their bodies distended with water, there was no going back the way they had entered save through one of the larger holes in a V leading into a trap-yard.

I know of no greater drama that that which is enacted in the pit of an almost dry dam at the end of a red hot day where thousands of animals – rabbits, foxes, kangaroos and wild dogs – meet and mix without fear of each other, quenching a thirst which has tormented them for hours, whilst they crouched in the shade cast by surrounding scrub, waiting, watching the sun which seemingly never, never would set.

From our fence, masked by the darkness, would reach our ears the ceaseless murmur of scurrying rabbits. The light of a hurricane lamp would show them packed in long lines drinking at the water's edge, blocking the V's in maddened effort to get through, running along the outside of the fence in thousands, close packed already in the trap-yards where by morning there would be a thousand in each.

Stationed a little below the summit of the dam bank in order to obtain a skyline against the stars, we would observe rising above it, strange monstrous shapes against the dark sky, shapes unimagined, like a cross between a giant spider and a crab. Kangaroos ungainly creeping silently towards the water, unlike the rabbits, their suspicion not swamped by thirst, knowing that man was there, fearing those loud reports of guns, warned by sentinel 'roos. In the dark unable to see the gun sight, we shot them or frightened them off, fearing to move from our positions to dispatch the wounded animals in case the other might mistake one for a 'roo and shoot – which has been done more than once.

Foxes and dogs would cross our skyline too quickly for action. In any case, they were not a menace to the fence, over which they would lightly leap, and lap noisily as though they would never stop. Perhaps on their way out they would fancy a rabbit, when there would come up out of the pit a roar of scampering feet when thousands of rodents would rush to escape.

One night, after Moss Brown had fired from his position at the opposite corner of the dam, he began yelling, which gave me cause to think he had shot himself. When I called out he pantingly replied: "I shot and wounded a 'roo on the top of the bank, and he rolled down to me, and now he's trying to get into bed with me. He's all hind feet and front claws and teeth."

At that time rabbits fetched £2 a hundred in the Sydney auction sales. The Americans and the Belgians were keen buyers and rabbit skins and carcasses were fifth on Australia's export list. In the old countries the skins were made into beautiful Arctic fox and minx furs and coats, and as such were worn by the great ladies of Europe and America, little dreaming that on their backs and round their lovely necks nestled the good old Australian rabbit.

When we moved to Victoria Lake, then as dry as a dog's buried bone, there was no necessity to use traps of any description. We used to drive the rabbits into the burrows, select a surface warren on soft ground, and block up all the exits. Every runway would be choked with rodents, so that at most of the holes would be seen the hind quarters of rabbits unable further to get in. Starting from one exit, I would drag them out and kill them as fast as Moss could skin, with a forearm easily breaking the surface crust. Here and there would be an underground chamber, crammed with rabbits, from which other runways would lead out like the spokes of a cart wheel. In this way we would catch and skin 500 rabbits in a morning.

April came, and with April the autumn rains. The rabbits scattered over the country, cleaned out old warrens, and set to work breeding. Moss found another partner, and I bought a truck and equipment of my own and set to work gin-trapping early in May. The fur fever burned and burned. Skin prices soared to an average of eighty pence a pound. Eight skins to a pound; averaging ten pence a skin. That winter, for several pounds of beautiful fawn skins I received 116 pence a pound. Seven went to the pound – averaging one shilling and 4½ pence a skin.

I thought of selling my stretcher and blankets. What was the use of a bunk, anyway?

By noon every day I had moved sixty gin-traps to fresh ground and had set them. Then back to camp for a hasty meal, and to stretch the skins obtained the day before. At two o'clock, the first visit to the trap-line to take out thirty shillings. Back to camp to prepare fox baits of fat balls dipped in strychnine crystals. Then to cook food, and, if time remained, inspect and plan other trap-lines.

At sundown, a hasty meal. When darkness was falling, dragging a sheep's head over the ground to make an easily followed fox trail, and, along that trail at fifty-yard intervals, laying two baits – two, because a fox would have to swallow one to pick up a second.

Then out again on the trap-line. Walk, walk, walk. I had been walking at top speed all day. Now with a hurricane lamp to take more tenpences out of the traps. Nine o'clock that would be, and at ten o'clock, one would be at the far end of the trap-line lounging beside a roaring fire, and walking round it if sleep threatened to conquer the mind. The trap-line again, and back at camp at midnight. Into the blankets for four hours, the alarm clock lashed to one's neck, because if set on a box beside the bed it would fail to rouse.

Four o'clock in the morning and bitter cold. A drink of strong coffee laced with brandy, a bite to eat, and a cigarette before the dawn lightened the sky. In the half light of daybreak, ready at the home end of the fox trail, carrying chaff bags to cover fox carcasses from the crows; there at that hour to beat the crows finding the baits and causing waste of time looking for foxes supposed to have taken them.

Here a splash of brown. Over there another. There must be at least four others. Somewhere they are among the short bushes. Walk, walk, walk, quartering the country to pick up ten-shilling notes.

Ah! Not so bad. Fox skins to the value of £3. Again on the trap-line, picking up the traps and carrying them in bundles to fresh ground; taking out seventy-one rabbits in those twenty-four hours. Say £6. Not so good as the day before, but a littler better than the day before that.

It is noon again and the traps are all set on new ground. Confound the sun. Why cannot it stop still for a little while and give a fellow a chance to get his breath? There are those skins to slip on wire bows and the fox skins to peg out on a clay-pan, fur down. At the end of the first three weeks I was weak enough to lie down on the bed just for five minutes – and slept for fifty hours. Henceforth, I rigidly kept the Lord's Day, and, as a result, worked faster during the week.

The new grass came up. Countless baby rabbits filled the traps, stopping the flow of gold. At the end of June, the foxes' mating season started, when the foxes will not eat meat no matter how carefully served up to them. The problem arose – what did they eat? Solve that, and it would be possible to gather ten-shilling notes up to mid-September. I shot a fox and held a post-mortem examination to find that it had lived on scorpions and centipedes, and because I was a dud in catching those hibernating pleasantries, I went back to stock work.

But I watched the rabbits with lustful eyes, and followed the skin market reports as eagerly as a lover reading his love's letters. Drought set in, and at the end of two years the skin game was finished. A man said to me: "Let's go to the West. Over there, if the rabbits fail, we can go dry-blowing for gold."

That very hour we packed up camp and started off for Perth, a journey of 2,500 miles.

The decision finally produced the novel, "The Sands of Windee," the plot of which cost three men their lives, and dragged me into the greatest murder case in the history of Western Australia.

THE MURCHISON MURDERS

To give a clear picture of the country, and to clothe in words the personalities in the most sensational murder drama that ever took place in Australia, is essential to the proper appreciation of a case containing, as it does, several features believed to be unique.

In the bush proper of Western Australia three men disappeared from human ken between December 8, 1929, and May 18, 1930, and it was not until the following February that the relatives of one, making inquiries from New Zealand, first called the attention of the police to those disappearances and started investigations that occupied many months, and entailed thousands of miles of travel, and the compilation of volumes of reports and statements.

All caused through a novelist's search for a plot to be used in a murder-mystery story.

Government Camel Station

The Government Camel Station is 163 miles north of the wheat town of Burracoppin, and about 75 south of the gold-mining town of Paynesville.

The homestead is a four-rooms-and-kitchen stone building, situated about 100 yards west of the vermin fence, which, from the south to the northwest coast, is some 1130 miles long – undoubtedly the longest netted fence in the world. Standing at the homestead front door, one faces east, able to see the fence and the wall of mulga scrub beyond the fence track. From the back door a few scattered acacias are the only obstructions to the view. About half a mile north-westward a double-summited hill rises from a roughly circular plain, the two summits forming the rounded humps of the animal after which the place is named – Dromedary Hill.

One familiar with the locality knows that northward along the fence at the edge of the scrub timber, there is a hut and a well named Watson's Well; that southward along the fence there is nothing until Campian is reached, 138 miles distant; that by following a westward track for 10 miles one will reach The

Fountain, a stockman's hut, and, after a further ten miles, the homestead of Narndee Station to which the stockman's hut belongs.

As for people and traffic, one might wait a week, two weeks, to see a human face or a dust-coated car pass along the fence track; and only rarely did a Narndee man call when on his way to that station's paddocks east of the Camel Station.

Dry, parched, heated land in summer; brilliant, bracing, beautiful in winter.

At the Camel Station lived George Ritchie. To the Camel Station once every month came two Government boundary riders: Lance Maddison from the north, Arthur Upfield from the south. From the west at irregular intervals came a station contractor named James Ryan, and a stockman named "Snowy" Rowles. These were the men destined to play important roles in a terrific drama.

Enter "Snowy" Rowles

I first met Rowles at the Narndee outcamp, The Fountain, where he was stationed. He was then twenty-five years old; a man well-proportioned, fair-haired, blue-eyed, clean-shaven, neat in dress, and, from the feminine standpoint, better-looking than the average.

Looking backward, I can find no excuse for any one on the Murchison not liking Snowy Rowles. His appearance at a bush camp at once vanquished depression. He arrived at the Camel Station one day, late in '28, on a motor-cycle, looking for a job. It happened that the owner of Narndee had bought a bunch of mules from the Government and they were being handled by a breaker in the Dromedary Hill yards, preparatory to being taken to Narndee. Rowles offered to ride his worst mules – for exercise.

There was left no doubt in the mind of any who saw him, that he rode as well as the best in the great North-west of the State. He was offered work on Narndee, which he accepted.

His horse-riding was point No. 1 in favour of this newly-arrived stranger. The second point was an equable temper; the third a most engaging disposition; the fourth a willingness to oblige. As a fifth point, he was a good bettor and a good loser. And the sixth and most important point was a ready sense of humour.

On his arrival one day at Dromedary Hill we asked him if he'd brought any meat, as we had to eat either tinned "dog" or kangaroo. No; he hadn't. Then he had better go back to his camp (10 miles) and get some.

"Righto! You scour out the fry-pan", he urged, laughing; and away he went on his motor bike in a cloud of dust.

Expecting a fore-quarter of mutton at least, we got busy with fire and fry-pan. In half an hour he was seen dodging this way and that over the plain between the house and the hill; a spurt of dust as big as a cloud in front of his machine.

"What the devil is he doing?" demanded my companion.

"I always did think that what one wants in these parts is a pair of binoculars", I rejoined. "He'll break his neck among those rabbit burrows and rocks."

It was country over which I would not gallop a horse.

Instead of bringing back a fore-quarter of mutton Snowy Rowles mustered into the back yard a"boomer" kangaroo that he had rounded up; tailing it home like a sheep being brought in by a man on horseback.

Plots – and a Plot

In a proper review of the Snowy Rowles case, it is impossible to disregard my work as a novelist; because, although I did not provide Rowles with a motive, and was in no way an accessory before or after the fact, the Crown alleged that I did provide him with a method of destroying the bodies of his victims.

It is the ambition of many novelists who are free from the obsession of sex, to discover an original plot, or at least an original variation of an old one. Fiction plots are like nuggets of gold dug out of a unique mine. A hundred years ago this mine contained much gold; to-day nuggets are scarce, and much digging is necessary to unearth them.

Notable nuggets were discovered by: Anthony Hope in The Prisoner of Zenda; Burroughs in his Tarzan of the Apes; Rudd in his On Our Selection. They were golden nuggets literally as well as figuratively.

During a several weeks' stay at the Camel Station in the early winter of 1929, I thought much of the type of story to follow a psychological study – then nearing completion – of a lonely man on a desolate beach. Day by day Ritchie and I followed a simple work routine. In the morning one of us brought in the two camels on which we were working, and these were harnessed to a heavy buckboard and taught to pull it, to walk, to trot, to stop quietly at gates, and, above all, to stand still.

To us the constant driving quickly became automatic, and when labour becomes automatic one's mind is free to rove. One bitterly cold day, whilst we drove round and round Dromedary Hill, I recalled that Wilkie Collins dug up the murder-mystery nugget from the mine of golden plots. Nuggets of variation have been unearthed by such masters as Edgar Allen Poe and Sir Arthur Conan Doyle; but it appeared to me that these and lesser diggers in that field were bound by a single cast-iron set of rules. The body of a murdered person is found – formerly on the library floor; latterly on the top of a bus, beneath a lift, or other unlikely place – and then the detective has a look at the corpse, and his investigation leads inevitably to the arrest of the murderer.

Questions demanded an answer. Why a corpse? Why be satisfied with what satisfied our grandfathers? Why continue littering the pages of a novel with blood? Here, then, was a new nugget, a beautiful theme nugget, waiting to be discovered. Instead of having the same old corpse in the first chapter, as the Masters and their sheep-like followers always did, why not date a fictional murder two months before the story opens? Why not write a murder-mystery without a corpse at all? In short, why not completely destroy the body of a victim of homicide, and then permit my fictional Detective-Inspector Napoleon Bonaparte to prove, first, that a murder had been committed, secondly, how it had been committed, and, thirdly, who committed it? I could make him begin his investigation two months after the corpse had been destroyed without trace.

Difficulties

The idea was attractive, but clothing the idea with life quickly presented difficulties.

How many murderers in real life – including doctors and other intelligent persons – have failed to dispose of the bodies of their victims, despite all their ingenuity! Crippen, Landru, and Mahon come easily to mind; and Deeming's fate was inevitable. Each of them cut up their victims, and then were unable to destroy the parts. Of all killers, perhaps the Paris Bluebeard came nearest to success.

I was faced with what I may term Problem Number One. With appliances that the average person could obtain, how could a human body be so utterly destroyed that no trace of its existence should remain to damn a murderer? A crematorium, or a bath of corrosive acid, are not within the reach of ordinary people desirous of cheating justice. Putting a body down a well, even dropping it down an abandoned mine shaft and exploding tons of earth on it, would not destroy it. Although concealed, it would still exist, still menace the security of the murderer.

The Nugget is Suggested

I had decided upon the locality of the story to be written. I had gathered around me the cast of characters, had even planned a rough chart of the action; but I could not start the story because I was unable to invent a simple and effective method of destroying my intended corpse.

Whilst playing poker one night, with a cold south wind rumbling round the chimney above the roaring wood fire, I said to Ritchie:

"Can you tell me of a good way of getting rid of a man, assuming I killed him on paper? I want a method of completely destroying a human body, so that there will be no slightest trace left for Bony to find."

"What! Are you going to start another book?"

"Yes, I am. I want to write another Bony yarn, in which he gets a job of work worthy of his brains and his bush craft. I want to give him the case of his life, if I can nut out a simple way of getting rid of the eternal hackneyed corpse."

"Well, all right. Suppose I wanted to do you in. I'd kid you into the bush, and when your back was turned I'd shoot you stone dead. Then I'd gather wood and lay you on it, clothes, boots and all, pile wood over you, and burn you. In a couple of days I'd come back with a sieve, and I'd go through all the ashes with the sieve, and get out every metal object, and every piece of bone that wasn't burned up by the fire. The metal objects could be thrown down a well, and the bones I'd dolly-pot to dust. So that no chance passer would wonder what the fire really was for, I'd shoot a couple of kangaroos and burn 'em over the same place."

I went outside and looked up at the chilly stars. The very kernel of my Problem Number One was a dolly-pot to deal with the bones that an ordinary fire would not destroy. Why had I not thought of a dolly-pot? It is a common object on the Murchison, as in other parts of Australia. Anyone could possess a dolly-pot. There was one in the blacksmith's shop at the Dromedary Hill homestead.

Problem Number Two

The plot of the new novel was rushing into shape. My murderer should destroy the body of his victim in the way given; and then Bony should get to 'work, and prove – ! But what could he prove? What could he prove if there was not a particle of the body remaining for him to exhibit before a judge and jury, who require the production of a body, or identifiable parts of a body, before they will listen to a charge of murder. If my murderer carried out Ritchie's astoundingly simple method, how could my detective build up his case, though he possess superhuman intelligence? Obviously, my murderer must make one mistake in his perfect murder, because unless he did so no detective in real life, or even in fiction, could prove murder against him.

Appreciating the fact that Ritchie had supplied me with a gold nugget, I offered him a pound if he could find a flaw in it. I believe he thought that pound was going to be easy money.

The problem was compressed into a simple question. If a man did such and such and such, how could he make a fatal error? Thresh at it, argue how we would, we could not discover a flaw. It became a tantalising but intriguing conundrum: I could not solve it, nor could my friends on the Fence, at Burracoppin and at Perth.

His mind on the pound, riding a fresh horse, hatless and unshaved, and carrying a .22 bore rifle, Ritchie one day met Snowy Rowles coming to the Camel Station on his motor-cycle. Without preamble of any kind, Ritchie said:

"Hey, Snow! If I was to shoot you stone dead, drag your body over to that dead scrub, burn it thoroughly, then come hack tomorrow with a sieve and go through the ashes for the bones and the metal objects on your clothes, dump the metal objects down a well, and dolly your bones to dust, how could my crime be discovered?"

Rowles subsequently admitted that he thought Ritchie had gone mad. Muttering something about being in a hurry, he skidded away on a roaring machine, expecting at any second to feel the bite of a bullet in his back.

Ritchie remained on his horse, looking after him in astonishment. Not until several hours later did he realise that the joke was against himself.

The Solution

The weeks passed.

I went back to my fence section; using two camels drawing a heavy hooded cart tandem fashion. 163 miles was that section; and at the completion of the first trip I had not worked out the solution of my problem, and I had practically given up the idea of ever finding that beautiful fiction nugget. Ritchie failed to earn the pound; Maddison was no help; Rowles did not succeed.

Then one morning, when most certainly I was not thinking about murder problems, but was gazing down my shaft camel's gaping throat whilst I struggled to put on him a pair of winkers, the solution flashed through my mind like the stab of a searchlight. My murderer could carry out Ritchie's method in every detail and yet leave a clue for Bony to find, follow up, and convict him. Where he could make, his fatal slip was in his lack of knowledge of his victim's war record. Within three seconds, whilst I gazed stupidly at Curley, the camel, I saw placed in position the last piece of a jigsaw puzzle.

The plot of the new novel was complete to its last detail.

Further weeks passed in another trip to Burracoppin and back. Then the Inspector reversed the positions held by Ritchie and myself, and from the interior of a boundary rider's cart I transferred my writing to the comfortable stone-built house, where night after night I wrote, aided by the blessed peacefulness of the bush.

October 5, 1929, was a Sunday. According to my diary for that evening there were present in the Camel Station homestead "drawing-room" Ritchie, Rowles, the Inspector's son, the north boundary-rider, and myself.

Those others remember that night particularly, for a reason I do not propose to state; I remember it particularly because it was the last opportunity I had to discuss my Problem Number Two, which was to locate a weak spot in Problem Number One. It was not then discussed with intense interest, because every one at this time was fully conversant with these two problems, but it was an incidence which was used by the Crown to establish through several witnesses that Snowy Rowles was conversant with the method of body destruction used in my novel The Sands of Windee published eighteen months later.

Ryan and Lloyd

Rowles left his employment on Narndee Station on October 30 of the same year, and took up the work of fox poisoning for a living; he being now the owner of an old but serviceable motor-car. Operating in the locality, he camped with me several nights on various dates, and if I had had no domestic ties it is likely that I should have joined him, for by this time I was becoming sick of the Vermin Fence, and wanted to have a look at the far north. Rowles was always welcome. He was an excellent guest, willing to do his share of the chores, and anxious to put in his share of the rations when his stay was extended.

About November 24 a contractor named James Ryan arrived at my homestead on his way to Burracoppin. About forty years old, he was what he looked, a naval man. He drove his own newly-purchased Dodge runabout car, and on his departure he promised to bring back for me rations and mail, neither of which I had received for some five or six weeks.

About the first day of December Rowles arrived from the direction of Youanmi. He wanted to know if Ryan had returned, and told me that he hoped, when Ryan did return, to join him on a trip to the far north-west. I did not know that Ryan intended pulling out from Narndee and was not interested, since neither Rowles nor Ryan was working for the Department; therefore they did not concern me, particularly as I had heard that the owner of Narndee was slackening hands.

Rowles appeared anxious for Ryan's return, and left me to run south to meet him. He did so at the 96-mile rainshed, and as his car had broken down, he returned with Ryan, who had brought with him as a mate a young athletic man named George Lloyd.

The party stayed with me that night, but it did not seem certain that Rowles would accompany Ryan and Lloyd to the former's camp until the next morning. During the evening Ryan sang songs in a really fine voice, accompanied by Lloyd on a brand new accordion.

Early the next morning the three departed, and either that afternoon or the next Rowles and Lloyd passed through the Camel Station on their way to the 100-peg where Rowles's old car had broken down. They brought the car back, and left it in a shed.

That was the last I saw of either Lloyd or Ryan.

The Inspector arrived from Burracoppin on December 10; Ritchie on the day previous. The day after the Inspector left for the north, Ritchie went up the Fence to Watson's Well, where a prospector named James Yates was camped. On his return he brought the information that Rowles, Ryan and Lloyd, instead of coming past the Camel Station homestead to reach the north track, had travelled along the north boundary of the hill paddock, round the back of the hill, and had passed through the rabbit fence at Watson's Well to get to that north track.

There was nothing significant about this. Ritchie did not make it clear to me – I was not that interested, anyway – that Yates had seen only Rowles, who told him that Ryan and Lloyd were walking through the scrub looking for timber with which to build a sheep-yard. To me, it appeared as Rowles had said. Ryan had pulled out from a bad contract, and he was with him on the long trip to the north-west. He had laid his plans rather well.

Christmas 1929

Late in the afternoon of Christmas Eve the north boundary-rider and I left for Youanmi to buy a sucking pig and a bottle of beer, and there on the steps of the Youanmi Hotel stood Snowy Rowles.

"Hello? What are you doing here?" I asked. "Thought you were in the north-west with Ryan and Lloyd."

"Oh! We got as far as Mount Magnet," Rowles replied. "Ryan stays put, so I borrowed his truck to come over here for Christmas."

It came out later that he told my companion he had bought the truck from Ryan for £80.

Now there was nothing extraordinary in this story. Long before then Rowles had told us that his grandfather had come to his rescue with money on a former occasion, and that he was thinking of applying for a loan with which to purchase a good second-hand truck. And, too, Ryan was one of those unfortunate men who are fascinated by hotels, and who sometimes will attempt to sell their shirts, let alone a runabout truck, to buy a few more drinks. It was easy to picture Ryan, semi-intoxicated, generously granting Rowles permission to take his truck, with Lloyd, who did not drink, in the offing earnestly waiting to get his mate out of town.

Not the slightest suspicion that anything was wrong entered our minds. No one of the three was a close friend of ours.

Shocks

Meanwhile the depression had fallen like a blight, the staff had been reduced, and my section of fence had been altered to run 100 miles north, and 100 miles south of Burracoppin.

It was at the 78-mile peg south of the Department's headquarters' town that the Inspector came along, to say:

"You remember Jack Lemon, who works on Narndee"

I did. Lemon had taken Snowy Rowles's place. I remembered Lemon telling me a few months before how he had come from the East and had "palled up" with a man on the boat; how they had tramped to the Murchison from Perth; and how his pal had got a job on Wydgee Station, and himself one on Narndee; these two stations adjoining.

The Inspector went on to explain to me that Carron, Lemon's friend, resigned his employment or was paid off, and had left Wydgee Station in company with Rowles, some time in May, 1930. It was also known that Rowles had cashed Carron's pay cheque, and had bought beer out of the money at Paynesville, a mining town east of Mount Magnet. It appeared that Lemon had sent a reply-paid telegram to Rowles at Youanmi asking for information regarding his friend, and Rowles had not replied either by telegram or letter.

"It is likely that Louis Carron's disappearance would never have been remarked had he not been a confirmed letter-writer. Up to the time he left Wydgee Station he had written regularly to friends in New Zealand and to his pal, John Lemon, at Narndee.

All this the Inspector learned during his trip north – his section extended to the 421-mile peg – in February, 1931, ten months after Carron and Rowles had driven away from The Fountain in Ryan's truck. Jack Lemon was the last man to see Carron, who promised to write and tell him how he got on in his search for a new job.

My untrained imagination jumped at a solution of this little mystery. Carron, paid off with a cheque, goes with Snowy, and they decide to purchase a case of beer and have a peaceful or private carousal in the bush – much cheaper than drinking at an hotel. Naturally, in possession of a case of beer, they both become stung. A quarrel arises, there is a fight, and Carron gets killed.

"That might be how it happened," the Inspector agreed. "Anyway, the detectives are scouring the whole country in a search for Carron's body. It looks pretty black against Snowy."

"Have they arrested him?"

"No, not yet. He's working now on a station called Hill View, a couple of hundred miles or so north of Youanmi."

"Then it mightn't be Snowy," I objected.

"But they know that Carron left the Fountain with Rowles. They know that Rowles cashed Carron's cheque at the Paynesville hotel. And they know that Rowles never answered Lemon's telegram."

Three weeks after this conversation the Inspector returned again from a north trip. He said grimly:

"Ryan and Lloyd are missing now. They haven't been seen since they left the Camel Station in December, 1929."

I must have looked a half-wit, standing with my mouth open in utter astonishment. And whilst thus standing came the next shock.

"And they've found Carron's charred remains near the one-eight-three mile hut – a ring, false teeth, a dental plate, bones.

"Go on?" I urged desperately.

"And when they went to arrest Snowy Rowles they recognised him as a man who escaped from the Dalwallinu lock-up after having been convicted for burglary in 1928. They haven't arrested him for murder but for gaol escape, so that the detectives will have whips of time to complete their investigations into the disappearances of Carron, Ryan and Lloyd."

It was all so incredible that for several minutes my mind refused to accept it. I found it harder to believe that Rowles was a burglar than a suspected murderer. No man was less like even my modern conception of a burglar. He had never stolen anything from me, or so little as a piece of hoop-iron from the Government Station. He might have killed Carron during a drunken brawl; but . . . a common burglar!

"Looks like he put that book lot of yours into practice," said a man with the Inspector.

"Seems that you and Ritchie were the last people to see Ryan and Lloyd alive in the company of Snowy Rowles," added the Inspector. "If you take my advice you'll write out a statement to the police. They know all about you, and all about your hunt for a murder-plot."

Bush Psychology

There are many points in this case which are sure to perplex a reader unfamiliar with the psychology and habits of the bushman. During the trial several witnesses were obliged to interrupt their evidence to explain why something was done, or how something else came about. When preparing his case, Mr. Gibson, the Crown Prosecutor, had the assistance of Detective-Sergeant Harry Manning, who conducted the police investigation – assistance of great value, because Manning is an experienced bushman. On the other side, Mr. Curran, defending Rowles, seemed not to have the same assistance, even from Rowles, who was a superb bushman.

Here is one illustration: At the inquest Mr. Curran said to witness Lance Maddison:

"There are hundreds of square miles of dense scrub around the hut (the hut near the bore about where the remains of Carron were found); don't you think it would be foolish for a man to try to burn evidence of a crime around the hut?"

"I can't say," replied the cautious witness.

To a city dweller, Mr. Curran's question would have appeared quite logical. In point of fact, that hut was an ideal locality, as will be explained a little later. To the city-dweller, also, the most astonishing feature of the disappearance or the three men is that no one missed them, or thought to inquire for them, until nearly twelve months had elapsed. Yet to the bushman there is nothing singular about that, mainly because a large part of the population of Central Australia is a floating population, to which all three missing men belonged.

The Hounds of the Law

In early January, 1931, John Lemon interviewed Constable Hearn, of Mount Magnet, and reported the fact that his friend, Louis Carron, had not written to him since he had left his camp on Narndee Station – that formerly occupied by Snowy Rowles, named The Fountain. At this time Hearn had already received a letter from a Mr. Jackson, of Dunedin, N.Z., making inquiries for Carron. But not until February 17 did he, accompanied by a veteran bushman, Constable McArthur, set out from Mount Magnet to make inquiries.

Because John Lemon understood from his friend and Rowles on their departure from his camp that they were going to Wiluna in search of employment, Constables Hearn and McArthur started their inquiries from that town – 200 north of west. Drawing a blank at Wiluna, they came back to the Vermin Fence and then south to the Camel Station, which they made their headquarters; approximately another 200 miles.

Such is the peculiar nature of the soil on the Murchison that tracks made by carts and waggons remain visible for years. Up and down the Fence, and off every cross road, there are in evidence to-day seldom used tracks originally made by the waggon carting the Fence posts, and drays bringing out of the bush their loads of sandalwood. And over all those tracks might be driven a car.

On this huge area of country, to find the remains of a man which might have been burned or buried ten months before, seemed to be closely allied to the problem of finding the needle in the haystack. And yet in a remarkably short space of time the hounds of the law found evidences of a large fire in the vicinity of a bore at the 183-mile peg – twenty miles north from the Camel Station, on the No. 1 Vermin Fence.

At this point the Fence track passes through dense narrow-leafed mulga. Here there is a little-used gate; and should the curious pass through this gate and follow the little-used track for half a mile he would arrive at a small iron hut set amidst the dense scrub, which hides it entirely from the traveller on the Fence track. There was no water at this place, and the section rider, Lance Maddison, had occasion to go there only about twice a year to report on the condition of the hut. 300 yards farther west, the police came to a bore, quite out of order and, therefore, useless; and in the vicinity of this bore they found the site of a large fire. Slight trails of ashes led them still deeper into the bush, where they discovered two more heaps of ashes. Examination of these showed that the heaps had been made with ashes carried from the main fire, for beneath the heaps the grass was unburned, proving that the ashes had been dumped there when cold.

Among the ashes they found what were thought to be pieces of skull-bone, human bones, animal bones, charred woollen material, and a bone button. They found, too, among the ashes of the smaller heaps, artificial teeth, gold clips from a dental plate, metal eyelets from boots or shoes, a wedding ring, several strange wire stitches, etc.

These exhibits, with their report, were forwarded to police headquarters. It was thereupon decided to send Detective-Sergeant Manning north to take charge of the case.

Murder in Fact and Fiction

The fictional murder case that engaged the attention of Inspector Bonaparte in The Sands of Windee was paralleled to an extraordinary extent by the actual murder case investigated by Detective-Sergeant Manning. Manning's task was both greater and less than that presented to Bonaparte; and, the following points of similarity seem worthy of note, as indicating why the Crown suggested that Rowles adopted the book method of body destruction in part, in the case of Louis Carron.

MANNING	BONAPARTE
Police examined ashes of a large fire 10 months after Carron disappeared.	Bony examined ashes of a large fire two months after Marks was reported missing.
Police found in ashes human bones, false teeth, dental plate	Bony found in ashes one boot-sprig. Also a silver disc in the

fasteners, a wedding ring, etc.	fork of a tree some distance from the scene of the murder.
Police found in ashes a piece of melted lead of equal weight to an 0.32 bore bullet.	Bony found in ashes three pieces of melted lead, each of equal weight to an 0.44 bore bullet.
Police found in ashes, besides human hones, plenty of animal bones.	Bony found in ashes no human bones, but plenty of animal bones.
Police found an iron camp-oven which, it was assumed, was used to smash up the bones of Carron.	Bony found that a prospector's iron dolly-pot had been used to pound to dust the bones of Marks.
Manning investigated a careless attempt to destroy a human body.	Bony investigated the almost perfect murder, the body of Marks having been most efficiently destroyed.
Manning found in one ash heap bones which he took for human finger hones.	Bony found in the ashes bones which he sent to his headquarters to determine if they were human finger bones or kangaroo paw bones.
Manning had to convince a real life judge and jury that Carron had been murdered by Rowles.	Bony was diverted from bringing his case to a judge and jury because logically he would have failed to convince them.
Manning is par excellence a bushman.	Bony, having the tracking powers of his aboriginal mother and the reason-powers of his white father, was a super-bushman.

Step by Step

On leaving Perth Sergeant Manning proceeded to Mount Magnet, where he conferred with Constables McArthur and Hearn. It happened that when Mr. Jackson's letter was received Constable Hearn was due for annual leave, but he requested that his leave might be postponed that he might ascertain Carron's fate. Constable McArthur was sent to relieve him; and, therefore, when Manning set out for the scene of the assumed murder, he was accompanied by Constable Hearn.

A second and more careful examination, made with a sieve, brought lo light a burned human molar tooth having a cavity on the biting surface which might have been filled by an amalgam. The camp-oven was found near the main fire, and Manning saw that ash still adhered to the outside. It seemed probable that it had been used to transport some of the ashes and bones to those other heaps, because the grass beneath the smaller heaps had been dumped in those several places when cold, as I have already stated.

Manning measured the area of the main fire-site and found it to be eight feet by six. Evidence of the heat was provided by a coffee-tin that lay on the ground several feet from the ashes. The side of the tin facing the fire was badly burned. He ascertained from tracks made by a set of motor or truck tyres that a vehicle had been driven from the direction of the fence gate, and, after passing near the site of the fire, had turned and gone back.

Routine Work

Began then for Sergeant Manning that part of a detective's work which is seldom made much of in crime fiction – the taking of statements. Obviously, the first man to approach was John Lemon, Carron's friend. Already Manning had a description of Carron, supplied by Mr. Jackson. Carron was about 27 years of age, of medium build and erect carriage, with a sandy complexion, and an abrupt manner of speaking. Manning wanted to know from Lemon if Carron had false teeth; to which Lemon said: "Yes"; since he had often seen his friend cleaning them. He did not know where those teeth had been made, or by whom. And thus a line of inquiry started out from Western Australia to Hamilton, New Zealand, which resulted in a dentist named Sims being found who had made Carron a complete lower denture, consisting of diatoric teeth, and an upper partial denture being fixed to Carron's sound teeth by two gold clips.

And thirteen diatoric teeth, four pin teeth, and two gold clips had been found in the various ash heaps.

"Did Carron wear a wedding ring?"

"Yes," replied Lemon. "He wore a ring so tightly fitting that he once said he would have to have it filed off."

A second line of inquiry began, this time towards Carron's wife, Mrs. Brown, in New Zealand. (It should be explained that "Carron" had assumed this name in order to overcome the objection of his wife to his leaving New Zealand.) She remembered the ring, remembered when it was bought and at which shop in Auckland, N.Z. Eventually, Mr. A. T. Long examined the ring. He had sold it to Mrs. Brown in December, 1925. He knew the ring because of its markings, it N.Z. patents number; and he also knew that a workman in his shop had altered the size in an inexperienced manner.

From John Lemon, Sergeant Manning worked back toward Wydgee Station, via Wheelock, a prospector, Worth, a bookkeeper, and Beasley, the manager. The date on which Mr. Worth made out and Mr. Beasley signed Carron's pay cheque for £25/0/07 was ascertained. On Wydgee it was further learned that Carron had sent to a Perth jeweller's two watches for repair, and these watches had been returned, each in a separate box. Yes, the boxes contained wire stitches similar to those found in the ashes.

Out went another line of inquiry. The jewellers said that a Mr. Stone, a box manufacturer, made the boxes for them. And Mr. Stone recognised the wire stitches as those made by one of his machines which had a slight defect causing the defect in the stitches found among the ashes. Back again to the jewellers, who stated that the same watches they had repaired for Carron had been sent them for further repairs from Messrs. Fleming & Co., at Mount Magnet. A Mr. Male, of Fleming & Co., recalled having sent the watches to the Perth jewellers, and described the man who brought them to him – a man he knew as "Snowy" Rowles.

Lemon had said that his friend and Rowles left him for Wiluna in search of work. Constable Hearn could not hear anything of either man when he made inquiries in Wiluna. Manning now followed the trail. He camped at the Camel Station homestead, he travelled north along the fence to the gate at the 206-mile, and eastward then for eighteen miles to Youanmi. And at Youanmi he found that Rowles was well known.

The detective went through the books of Mr. Jones, the licensee of the. Youanmi Hotel, tracing various cheques cashed, and dates on which Rowles had booked in. Then to Paynesville, miles westward, to gain information about a cheque made out by Mr. Edward Moses, when he learned of the transaction regarding the tender of tender of Carron's Wydgee cheque for £25/0/7. And then back again to Narndee Station, where further information was obtained from the station books.

Hundreds of miles were traversed in a motor car, filling books with place-names, distances, dates, and names of persons. Eventually the detective had the name of every man working in the district at the time Carron disappeared. Precisely as did Bony in Windee, he made out his list of "fish," among which might be the "sting- ray." He had gathered that a man named Upfield, who wrote novels, was in charge of the Camel Station a few months prior to the disappearance of Carron. He learned from a man named Ritchie of Upfield's search for an effective method of corpse destruction. He knew that the man last seen with Carron was called "Snowy" Rowles, who since then had become employed on Hill View Station; and that Rowles had an excellent character, was a fine bushman, and owned his own runabout truck.

Yes, he had bought the truck from a man named Ryan. Where was Ryan? Oh! he had left the district with a man named Lloyd. He had taken with him a valuable compass and other things belonging to Narndee Station.

Strange!

And now information began to pour in regarding Ryan and Lloyd. Circumstances in connection with them had taken on a sinister light in view of the discovery of Carron's remains.

The detective's interest in Ryan and Lloyd was fully aroused. Where was Ryan? Last heard of at Mount Magnet, and, on Manning's reaching Mount Magnet, he found that nothing was known of Ryan, or of Lloyd, his mate: and certainly they had not stayed there during the Christmas of 1929.

Returning to Narndee later, Manning, with Constable Hearn, Mr. Bogle, part-owner and manager of Narndee, and Douglas Bell, a half-caste who had worked for Ryan before Ryan left for

Burracoppin, motored down to Challi Bore, Ryan's camp, and there discovered eight sites of fires similar to that at the 183-mile Rabbit Department Reserve, among the ashes of which were found eyelets of boots or shoes, metal parts of an accordion (Lloyd had owned one), and a quantity of bones burned and broken up so small as to defy any expert to say if they were human or animal remains.

Now there were three men of whom nothing could be learned after they had been last seen in the company of this "Snowy" Rowles. To Manning, as to any other reasoning man, it now appeared that among the facts he had gleaned were those that strongly supported the assumption that Rowles was a murderer thrice over. Motive was evident – the motive of gain. Rowles owned a truck possessed formerly by one of two mates, and he had cashed a cheque made out for wages paid to a third man. Certain relics had been found at the 183-mile Rabbit Department Reserve among the ashes of a big fire, and at Challi Bore eight big fires had consumed at the least boots and or shoes and an accordion.

It admits of little doubt that sergeant Manning and the two constables were convinced that Louis Carron's body had been destroyed at the 183-mile Government Reserve and that Ryan and Lloyd had been similarly destroyed at Challi Bore. Being bushmen they arrived at certain facts:

Three men had disappeared.

Each of the three when last seen alive was in the company of Rowles.

At Ryan's camp near Challi Bore were the sites of eight large fires, and the very first question which arose was: What had been burned in those eight fires? Answer: Boots, clothing and an accordion. Assuming that Ryan and Lloyd decided, preparatory to leaving, to jettison worn boots and clothes, and that the accordion having in some manner been broken, it was also discarded, still, as bushmen leaving a temporary camp they most certainly would not have gone to the trouble of burning those articles. They would have dropped them to the ground, packed up the necessary gear, and left. Only one construction could be put upon the action of the man who lit those fires. He wished to destroy something of vital import, something that would prove that Ryan and Lloyd no longer lived, o longer required boots and clothes and an accordion.

(This contrary to Mr. Curran's remarks at the inquest that no man wishing to destroy evidence of a crime would do so in the vicinity of a hut.) The locality of the 183-mile Reserve was an ideal one for the purpose. Lance Maddison, the boundary rider, stated that he never camped there. There was no fresh water. The hut was half a mile west of the fence, and bushmen do not travel one full mile without necessity. His duty compelled him to visit the hut – but not the bore – twice every year to effect repairs. None but Maddison went there.

A Bush Detective's Conclusions

Manning's probable reasoning might be put thus:

"Assuming that a man intended to copy the details of Upfield's murder plot, and that he burned the body of his victim in the open bush, the first stockman who chanced to pass the site of the fire would examine the ashes, and would logically ask himself: 'What fool went to the trouble of burning a kangaroo here?'

"In Central Australia kangaroo-shooters would not earn tobacco money if they spent time burning the carcases of kangaroos in the open bush; but they most certainly would burn carcases of animals they shot near a dwelling or a water-dam to destroy pollution.

"Whoever burned Carron's body near the hut and bore at the 183-mile Reserve knew the plot of Upfield's book, and appreciated the value – to himself – of allaying suspicion regarding a fire site. Wherever he destroyed Carron's body, he had to create a false reason as to the purpose of the fire, besides providing a superficial reason for the situation of the fire.

"That Government Reserve is an excellent place in two respects. Those respects are applicable also to Challi Bore. Maddison at the hut, and Ryan at his camp, would assuredly burn carcases from time to time: Maddison from duly, Ryan for his own health. Maddison would burn carcases of kangaroos that had lingered at the bore – smelling the water – till they died; and Ryan would burn the carcases of kangaroos he shot during his work and took into his camp for meat; mutton from Narndee not being regularly purchased. At both places would be a quantity of animal bones, and at both places the burning of animal bones would be a normal task.

"To sum up: Whoever destroyed those three men had first to find a place where a fire would not arouse suspicion, and had then to avert suspicion of the real reason of the fires by providing evidence that kangaroo carcases had been burned for a normal reason. Both at Challi Bore and the Reserve a chance visitor would remark that at the former Ryan had left a clean camp, and at the letter the boundary-rider had recently done his work.

"It remains to be explained, if only animal carcases were destroyed, why the burned bones should further have been broken up small."

By this, or an almost similar chain of reasoning, Sergeant Manning would be entitled to argue that the man calling himself "Snowy" Rowles either had killed the three men for their small property effect, or knew what had become of them. If Rowles had indeed killed those three, he must have planned to do so. It was highly improbable that he would be roused to three separate killings by passion or on abnormal impulse. It the first assumption was correct, Rowles must be thoroughly cold blooded and callous – a cunning and highly dangerous personality.

Rounding Up Rowles

So it came about that Sergeant Manning and Constables Hearn and Penn travelled to Hill View Station, dressed in worn bushmen's clothing. There they learned that Rowles was stationed at the outcamp several miles from the homestead: and, instead of travelling direct to the outcamp, they made a wide detour, planning to reach the outcamp from the opposite direction and at a time when Rowles would be out on his work. Had Rowles been at home he would have thought the police officers were merely kangaroo shooters, or prospectors.

But Rowles was not at his hut when the police arrived, and it was not until 2.30 on the following afternoon that he drove up in a sulky. Manning then was a little distance away in the bush; but the other two policemen were nearby their car. Rowles began to unharness his horse from the sulky, and whilst he led it away Constable Hearn took from the back of the sulky a 0.22 bore rifle. Having let the horse go, Rowles returned to the sulky, where

Hearn was casually examining the rifle, and Penn and Manning converged upon him.

Manning then recognised Rowles as a man wanted for gaol-breaking, whose name was John Thomas Smith, Manning said:

"How long have you been known as Rowles?"

To which Rowles replied: "You know very well who I am, and if I had known who you were, you wouldn't have got me so easily."

Manning said that, they were looking for a man named Carron, who was last seen in his, Rowles's, company. They were also looking for James Ryan and George Lloyd.

"What are you trying to put over me now, Manning?" Rowles demanded.

To which the Detective-Sergeant counter-questioned:

"Where did you get the utility truck over in the shed?"

"I bought it from Ryan," Rowels said. "I can soon satisfy you on that point."

It appears that there was a small box nailed to the door of the hut, in which the key was left; and when the door had been opened they all entered the hut, where Manning and Hearn each picked up a 0.32-bore rifle, both weapons proving to be loaded. Manning asked Rowles if everything in the hut was his property, and Rowles said it was, excepting the rifles, a sewing machine, and a gramophone.

Permission then was given the suspect to cook for himself a meal, and whilst he was doing this the police began searching the hut. A pair of hair-clippers found in a drawer of the sewing-machine (a most unusual object to be found in a stockman's hut) Rowles said he had bought from one Sher Ali for 12/6. On a high shelf was a parcel wrapped in newspaper. When one of the policemen reached for it, Rowles said:

"Where the hell did you get that? I know nothing about it."

The parcel contained a wrist-watch, three shirts, a razor marked as being made expressly for a firm in New Zealand, a watch-chain, and a pair of scissors.

Later the police went to the utility truck with Rowles, and found set in the dashboard an open-faced watch that Rowles said was there when he bought the truck from Ryan.

Without doubt these two watches furnished the most damning

evidence against Rowles. Both bore marks that Manning traced to the Perth jewellers, Levinson & Sons. The marks made on each watch tallied with record cards that proved that the firm had received the watches from Louis J. Carron, Wydgee Station, on April 11, 1930, and that, as was the custom, the watches had been returned to Carron in particular boxes, held by certain wire stitches.

At a later date, it transpired, Rowles himself sent the watches to Fleming & Co., of Mount Magnet, who dispatched them to Levinson & Sons. There could be no argument, therefore, that Rowles did not know what the parcel he disowned contained.

After Rowles had eaten a meal he asked to be allowed to change his moleskin trousers and flannel into a blue serge suit. Detective-Sergeant Manning pointed out that it was hardly necessary, for he had a long dusty ride ahead; but Rowles persisted, and was allowed to change before the car journey to Meekathara was started, a distance of approximately 80 miles.

Statements and Admissions

The following morning Detective-Sergeant Manning visited Snowy Rowles in the Meekathara gaol and obtained a statement from him regarding his association with Louis J. Carron, and a second statement regarding his association with James Ryan and George Lloyd. When Rowles had signed these two long documents, he said:

"What are you going to do with the truck?" Then: "A man must have a kink to do this sort of thing. I am sorry I did not take my old lady's advice." (This sounds genuine, since Rowles always referred to his mother as "my old lady.") "She wanted me to give myself up when I escaped from Dalwallinu, and if I'd taken her advice I would have had that all over by now, and would not have had this other thing to face.

"What other thing are you referring to?" Manning asked, for Rowles had not then been charged with murder but with goal-breaking.

"Oh," replied Rowles; "the less said about that, the better."

Subsequently Rowles was taken to Perth and charged with breaking and entering, and sentenced to three years' imprisonment. Had Rowles not committed burglary, the Crown doubtless would have been obliged to arraign him on a capital charge at the June Criminal Sessions, 1930, when time would not have permitted the attendance of three important New Zealand witnesses.

Where Rowles Failed

Months of hard work followed the arrest of Snowy Rowles for breaking gaol at Dalwallinu. The correspondence with the New Zealand police regarding identification of the teeth and the ring found among the ashes near a lonely bush hut was enormous. Since the witnesses, Mrs. Brown (Carron's wife), Mr. Sims, the dentist, and Mr. Long, the jeweller, could not be extradited, they could but be persuaded to travel to Western Australia in the interests of justice. Their expenses and remuneration for loss of time in their businesses cost the State £1,000.

Eminent pathologists studied the bones Sergeant Manning had brought down from the Murchison. The Government Pathologist would not say if the pieces of skull bone belonged once to the head of a white man or a blackfellow, but after further study Dr. McKenzie gave it as his opinion that the hones belonged to the skull of a while man.

And those few bones that were fitted together into larger pieces were the only human bones identifiable from the remains of three men. Had the slayer of Louis J. Carron further broken up the pieces of skull – as it can pardonably he assumed that he did in the case of the bones of Ryan and Lloyd – it could not have been proved that a human body had been destroyed at the 183-mile reserve. Had the slayer of Carron sieved the ashes for those metal objects he would have escaped the net Manning drew around him with quiet persistence; for the Crown had to prove that Carron's remains were among the ashes before it could hope to prove that Rowles had killed him.

That Rowles did not smash into smaller pieces those few portions of a human skull, that he did not carefully through the ashes for metal objects, can only be attributed to his belief that that those three men from Central Australia's floating population would never be missed; and that, after all, the care with which he destroyed Ryan and Lloyd was not necessary with regard to Carron.

Pre-Trial Impressions

The most sensational murder trial in the history of West Australia came before Mr. Justice Draper and a jury on Thursday, March 10, and continued until late on the following Saturday week. An unusual feature of the case was that Rowles's defence was being kept a close secret, despite the efforts of keen pressmen to get a "line" on it. Public interest was enormous, and public opinion – created by the inquest – was heavily against the accused man, even in the botanical gardens surrounding the Court, where I waited my call as one of the many witnesses.

Sitting on a seat beneath an English oak from which the acorns were falling, with the cooing of a dove, the twittering of several pigeons and numerous small birds in my ears, my mind was oppressed by a sense of unreality – as though I dreamed an ill dream, yet was fully conscious I was dreaming. Sometimes that glimpse of the interior of the court, revealing to me the tense faces of the jurymen, indicated that there was being staged a theatrical drama, for which all the actors had been released, and myself one of them; that it was a play within a play; and that presently it would be over, and we all would then realise how great a play it had been.

But, the ever-present dread lurking at the back of the mind, like the knowledge that one is only dreaming, produced a kind of stunning horror that banished from the play-goer the gay mood of the play.

The sense of unreality was combined with a depressing sense of inevitability. I was like the man to whom the future has been revealed. I knew that presently I should hear my name called in a loud voice, as it were an actor summoned by a call-boy. But beyond that point I knew nothing. The actor has had experience; he knows just what he will see when he goes on the stage, and what he will say. I had had no previous experience of a court-room, nor had I the slightest idea of the questions I should be asked. Doubtless questions would be put for the purpose of trapping me, and if I wished to avoid being trapped I must remain clear-headed. Panic seized me for a little while when I found that I could not remember several dates that had been burned on my brain by constant repetition.

New impressions gained ascendancy. The power of the law

became something tangible, shaping, like an octopus. Within that great stone building lived an octopus whose many tentacles had reached as far away as the Murchison, and farther still, to New Zealand.

A tentacle had come out writhing, feeling for and fastening about a young man whose gameness and sunny nature had made him ever a welcome guest. And with terrible quickness the tentacle had been withdrawn, wrapped about Snowy Rowles, who never again would laughingly chase us on his motor-cycle, and make and accept outrageous bets. And other tentacles of this great octopus called the Law came outward from Perth, dexterously searching for some fifty of us, until one by one we had been found, examined, drawn from as far away as New Zealand, to testify against Snowy Rowles.

I may state, in parenthesis, that without doubt a great majority of the Crown witnesses wanted to believe that Rowley was innocent of the charge laid against him, and would have welcomed with joy the production of proof that he was not guilty. Had it been established that he was innocent, his return to the Murchison would have been a triumphal progress.

We witnesses knew more than those city people who had carefully read our evidence given at the inquest. We had been moving behind the scenes, as it were. We were conversant with bush conditions and the psychology of the bush people. We had been able to compare notes, which had given us a clearer understanding than the newspapers could possibly have given their readers. Rowles had said one thing to one and something else to another, and yet a different version to a third, on one particular point. He had told so many lies. In my own experience he had told three different stories of how he acquired Ryan's truck.

We knew that men could disappear in the bush and their skeletons not be found for years afterwards, if ever. We knew that sometimes a member of the great floating population of Central Australia might have sound reasons for a voluntary disappearance. We knew that it would be possible – nay, probable – for Carron, Ryan, or Lloyd, to disappear voluntarily for some reason or other; but improbable, if not impossible, that three men about the same time should voluntarily disappear, and two of them give their property to "Snowy" Rowles.

For me, as for those others, it was impossible to disassociate the disappearance of Carron from that of Ryan and Lloyd. There came the rumour that Carron had been seen at work on a station after May, 1930; but I could not give this story credence. There was no rumour that Ryan or Lloyd had been seen after they went to Challi Bore, on Narndee Station, with Rowles.

Whilst the acorns dropped about me, whilst semi-consciously I wondered why some one did not gather them in to feed to a pig, I tried to imagine what Rowles's defence would be. What defence could he possibly put forward? How was he going to explain his possession of those two watches? How account for the shirts of a kind not sold in Australia? How explain the strange fact that the rifle Carron look away from Wydgee Station was found in his hut on Hill View Station? How was he going to account for two full days, May 18 and 19, 1930, which he said he had spent at Windimurra homestead, and which three witnesses had said, in effect, he had not?

If he left Carron trapping at the Windimurra homestead when he went to Paynesville to cash Carron's cheque, why did he go direct to Youanmi from Paynesville? Why in the, name of common sense did he not reply to Lemon's telegram of inquiry when it was given to him and he knew it was a reply-paid telegram?

That Carron was dead, who could doubt after having seen the relics found in the ashes of a fire on a Government Reserve, relics that had been identified at the inquest by Carron's wife, by Carron's jeweller, and by Carron's dentist?

Candidly, it appeared incredible. It was so difficult to believe that the Snowy Rowles we knew was in the dock of a criminal court. It was equally difficult to believe that the Snowy Rowles we knew had, one day in March, 1926, snatched a bag containing £300 from a shop girl in Perth; and that in 1928 he had robbed several country stores on the eastern wheat-belt.

An acorn fell with painful effect on the back of my hand which rested on the bench. Summer was nearly over.

And for you, Snowy, alas, the winter has come!

The Bones

After months of preparation, the Crown had at length declared its case against John Thomas Smith, known as "Snowy" Rowles. To the Court it introduced Constable Hearn, who detailed his finding of the fire at the 183 Government Reserve, and the items he discovered among the ashes. Detective-Sergeant Manning clearly described the course of his investigation, by which he had built up a wonderful case from the very sands of the Murchison.

Dr. William McGillivray, the Government Pathologist, now gave evidence regarding the human bones submitted to him for examination. One of the packages given him contained fragments of a human skull. Small bones in a tobacco-tin, he said, might be those of human fingers or toes, or animal paws or toes – he was doubtful which. The contents of a matchbox were burned human teeth, one of which was a molar tooth. Other teeth shown to him he declared to be artificial teeth. He would not say if the pieces of skull bones were those belonging to the skull of a white man or an aboriginal. He thought no one could tell that.

Dr. McKenzie, who sat on the witness stand with plaster casts of human skulls on the table before him, stated that he thought that pieces of bone when built into larger pieces indicated that they did belong to the skull of a white man.

The Book Plot

Arthur William Upfield deposed how he searched for a method of destroying a human body; how he found it; the details of it.

When Lancelot Bowen Maddison, the boundary-rider north of my former section was called, he was asked if he knew Rowles. He replied:

"I know him well. I first met him on the fence just north of the Camel Station, soon after I commenced work there. He was then riding a motor-cycle in the course of his duties as an employee of Narndee Station. I saw him frequently after that. I was at the Camel Station one night with Arthur Upfield, David Coleman, George Ritchie, and Rowles. We all joined in a discussion of Upfield's projected book, The Sands of Windee. We particularly referred to the disposal of a murdered man's remains."

Carron's Dentist

Arthur William Sims, dentist, of Hamilton, N.Z., said he had attended a patient named Leslie George Brown, and he identified the photographs of Louis John Carron as Brown. On August 1, 1929, he made a complete lower denture for Brown, and also filled several upper teeth. On August 20 he placed a small amalgam filling in the biting surface of one of Brown's upper molars.

Mr. Gibson, Crown Prosecutor, handing witness teeth found in the fire ashes near the bore at the 183-mile, asked:

"Do you find there four upper inciser pin teeth and a number of diatoric teeth, making a complete lower denture save for one incisor?"

Witness: "That is so."

After carefully examining the molar tooth found in one of the ash heaps near the bore, witness said:

"It has a drill hole in it in exactly the same place as the hole I drilled in Brown's molar tooth. The filling has gone from this tooth. The amalgam filling I placed in Brown's tooth would not stand up to great heat."

Carron's Jeweller

Thomas Andrew Long said that he was up to March, 1927, a jeweller trading in Queen Street, Auckland, N.Z. After examining the gold ring found with other relics in the camp fire-site, witness said it appeared to be one of his own faceted wedding rings. It was marked "18 ct., Red. 1286, M.C." He had a letter in his possession from the wholesale jewellers saying that rings marked in that fashion were made only in New Zealand.

Mr. Curran, defending Rowles: "I suppose that in the course of a year a good many wedding rings marked like that one would be sold throughout New Zealand?"

Witness: "Yes, that would be so."

Mr. Curran: "How can you be so sure that you cut and rejoined that particular ring for Mrs. Brown (Carron's wife)?"

Witness: "At the time Mrs. Brown wanted the ring altered I was very busy and my chief assistant was away. I gave the ring to an assistant who was not an expert goldsmith. He botched the job, and had I not been so busy I would have dropped the ring into the melting pot and cut another. This ring is of 18 carat gold, and my assistant re-joined the cut ends with a 9 carat gold solder. The lighter shade of the solder against the ring itself has not been destroyed by the fire."

The ring was handed to the jurymen, each of whom examined it intently. After the trial it came out that the ring with its 9 carat gold solder was the deciding factor in their verdict.

In his statement made to Detective-Sergeant Manning, the accused said that he picked up Carron at an outcamp named Condon on Wydgee Station, and that he brought him on to The Fountain outcamp where John Lemon then was camped in the employ of Narndee Station. The next day they went on to Watson's Well, on the Vermin Fence, then northward along the Fence to the 206-mile gate where the road between Youanmi and Mount Magnet passes through the fence. From there they went on and camped at the old deserted homestead of Windimurra Station.

The statement continues: "The next day I went to Paynesville, about 15 miles away, in my truck. Carron agreed to cut in the money for the goods we wanted, and gave me the Wydgee cheque for £25/0/7 to cash for him. I waited until sundown for the licensee to return from a mine he was working. I stayed the night at the hotel. The next day I returned to our camp, and gave Carron £4/8/- and the publican's own cheque for £16. The following night we went to Mount Magnet together, arriving between nine and ten o'clock. We had supper together at Joe Slavin's shop. Carron, who was a teetotaller, objected to my having a few drinks that night, and said he could do better alone. He took his gear off the truck. I went back to the hotel, and Carron came after me and reckoned he might be unable to cash Moses's cheque (the Paynesville publican) as it was made out in my name. So I gave him £16 for it. When I cashed Carron's cheque I endorsed Carron's name on the back. After giving Carron the cash I walked back into Mr. Rodan's bar. When the hotel closed at eleven o'clock I returned to the truck and drove five or six miles along the Youanmi road, where I went to sleep till morning, when I continued the journey to Jones' hotel at Youanmi. I only heard that Carron was missing last Monday when I saw something in a Murchison paper. Carron went on to Geraldton. He wrote me from there -"

Rebuttals

The manager, the overseer, and various stockmen swore that Rowles and Carron never camped at the old deserted homestead through which they passed. Just before leaving the Paynesville Hotel the accused told the licensee that he was going to Wiluna on a prospecting trip.

It was definitely proved that instead of returning to the old Windimurra homestead, and Carron, Rowles went direct to Youanmi, a distance of about 70 miles. He left Paynesville at about ten o'clock, and he arrived at Youanmi at 12:30 the same morning.

That was on May 21. The records of the Youanmi Post Office, and the evidence of the Post Master, showed that that afternoon Rowles took the Post Master to a station homestead in his truck to deliver a telegram.

When on the witness stand Rowles, being confronted with this, amended his statement, and said that he had forgotten that trip to Youanmi. He still maintained, however, that he returned to Carron after leaving Paynesville. He was neatly trapped into saying that he was not in Youanmi on May 22, and at a carefully calculated moment the astute Crown Prosecutor produced evidence to prove his lie. He produced the Youanmi storekeeper's docket book containing the carbon copies of the sales he had made on May 21 and 22. The first entry for May 22 was "S. Rowles, pair overalls, 11/6."

The Summing-Up

Mr. Justice Draper in his summing up said:

"Some of the statements made by Rowles in this case were hard to reconcile with those to be expected from a man who had committed no crime. It is for you, gentlemen of the jury, to decide. You are the ones to decide, but perhaps you will find it difficult to reconcile the statements made by Rowles as to his movements with Carron, with the evidence given in this court. The Crown case was that Carron had been murdered and the bones broken up into very small pieces, and distributed in heaps of ashes.

"There is a curious thing in this case, and I mention it for what it is worth. Upfield gave evidence that he was in the neighbourhood for some time. He says he remembers a discussion one night in a small room when the accused was among others present on October 6th, 1929. I suppose they want something to do in the bush," observed his Honor dryly. "Anyway, the interesting subject of discussion was how a human body could be destroyed without leaving any trace. The indications are that the method then dismissed was carried out in this case, but whether Rowles did it is a matter for you to decide."

Discussing the question of whether the skull bones were from the head of a European or aborigine, his Honor said they might ask themselves, remembering the articles found in the ashes with them, was it usual for natives to wear shoes with eyelets, was it usual for them to wear artificial teeth in the upper and lower jaws, and did they wear gold wedding rings.

"It would be a strange coincidence," observed his Honor, "seeing that Carron possessed things identical to all these articles, if those found in the fire did not belong to him."

The Verdict

The jury retired at five minutes to four on Saturday afternoon, and returned to give their verdict at six o'clock that same day. Rowles was brought up. Whilst waiting for Mr. Justice Draper to take his seat, whilst standing on the steps of the dock, he craned his head to see if he could read his fate on the faces of the jurymen. Failing that he turned to look at the massed witnesses. When the judge did take his seat, the accused mounted quickly into the dock, to stare hard at the jury. He was seen to shake his head, as if he knew that he was doomed.

"Guilty."

The dread word sounded like two strokes of a bell in the hushed court.

Asked if he had anything to say, Rowles replied in a steady voice:

"I have been found guilty of a crime that has never been committed."

"Is that all? Is that all you have to say?" asked the judge.

Rowles remained silent.

The hush was broken by the judge's voice pronouncing the sentence of death.

Appeal Fails

Rowles through his counsel, Mr. Fred Curran, appealed to the Supreme Court of Western Australia on the grounds that:—

(a) Evidence relating to the disappearance of two men named James Ryan and George Lloyd and to my association with them was wrongfully admitted. (At the hearing it came out that it was Rowles's own counsel who first brought in the matter of Ryan and Lloyd.)

(b) That the trial judge wrongfully admitted evidence by one, Arthur William Upfield, a novelist, to the effect that during October, 1929, I was present and took part in a discussion relating to the disappearance of human bodies. And that I had been arrested on another charge and had escaped from legal custody.

(c) That there was no evidence that Louis Carron was dead.

(d) That the learned trial judge misdirected the jury on the evidence.

(e) The trial resulted in a miscarriage of justice.

The State Full Court unanimously dismissed the appeal.

Counsel for Rowles then appealed to the High Court, of Australia, sitting in Melbourne, and this court rejected the application tor the appeal to he heard by it, by a two to one majority.

A public petition was organized by the Groper Brotherhood and Housewives Association, and finally presented to the Attorney General. A public meeting was held at a theatre to urge Rowles's reprieve. Letters appeared in the papers appealing for clemency for the sake or his mother.

The Curtain Falls

But Rowles was hanged on the morning of June 13, without making confession; although the relatives of George Lloyd wrote urging the condemned man to say something regarding the fate of Lloyd.

Some few days before the end Snowy Rowles made a dramatic statement from the condemned cell. He said that on his return from Paynesville to his camp he found that Carron had accidentally poisoned himself with poisoned butter baits used for foxes. That, as he was an escaped prisoner, he feared to inform the police and he burned the body.

It. had no effect but to confirm his guilt, for he could not possibly have gone hack to Windimurra, found his mate, taken the body fifty odd miles and burned it, then travelled to Youanmi, another 67 miles in two hours and a quarter.

Thus passed out a strangely stormy spirit. His life before him, favoured by the gods with a fine physique and good looks, he could have risen high in this country, impelled upward by the personality of his Doctor Jekyll; but the secret devil in all of us, the Mr. Hyde, was too powerful for "Snowy" Rowles.

The Outback Changes

During the second decade of this century there occurred in Australia a profound and significant change, due in minor part to the war, and to a major extent to the internal combustion engine. The year 1914 saw the closing stages of the victory of the petrol engine over the horse; it saw, too, the last generation of men who had lived for and by the horse being displaced by the rising generation who looked to the engine and its higher transport speeds.

To those of us who left Australia in 1914, and remained away until after 1919, the change was clear-cut and astonishing. Encamped at Essendon and Broadmeadows in 1914 we travelled to the city in stuffy coaches drawn by puffing billies. On our return from the war we found the city and suburban railways electrified, smoke and cinders banished from the iron roads, and speed and comfort increased.

In 1912 Cobb and Co.'s horse coaches rumbled across the saltbush plains and through the mulga belts of the Outback. When war broke out they were being displaced by the motor car, and the change-over was completed by 1916. Journeys occupying a day and a night were reduced in time to a few hours.

Men returned from the war with imaginations inflamed by the conquest of the air, and at once they set about planning the ultimate network of airways and aerial medical services. Ministers of religion who had but just become accustomed to drivers, also took to the air. Station managers discarded their buckboards and the services of black boys who drove change horses after them.

The squatters drove fast cars over country where teamsters hesitated to go. They sent men on trucks to repair wells and windmills and fences. On not a few stations the boundary riders were reduced in number, and dare-devil youths on roaring motor-cycles now inspect in one day lines of fencing which formerly occupied many days by horse.

The machine definitely is killing one type of bushman, and it has created another type. The manufacture of stockwhips and plug tobacco has fallen in output. The new generation of bushman takes more pride in tuning a motor engine than in subduing a vicious horse, and it smokes fine-cut tobacco rolled into cigarettes in preference to pipes.

The last generation wore elastic-sided boots and moleskin or dungaree trousers kept in place with kangaroo-hide belts. The new race of bushmen demands smart black or tan shoes, well-cut tweed trousers and coloured braces.

The last generation read Lawson, "Banjo" Paterson and Steele Rudd, while the new generation mentally digests Edgar Wallace, Mulford, and the pseudo-scientific fiction magazines imported into this county from America by the ton.

The pre-war Australian bushmen mostly retired to bag humpies on the banks of outback rivers. They steadfastly refuse to leave the Bush they know and love so well. They visit each other and yarn always of the years before the coming of the motor. They watch the new generation go roaring by on motor-cycles, on old Fords minus mudguards to make them appear to be racing cars, and on trucks. Even the modern blackfellow transports his dogs, his gear, his children and his gin on a truck.

Without doubt, Romance may still he found in the bushlands, but it requires a young and modern mind to unearth it The background is the same, changeless, but the bush people no longer are those described by Lawson and the writers of his time. On the banks of the rivers now live in retirement the Ten-Pot Dicks, the Mulga Dicks, and the Dirty Dicks; the Rainbow Harrys, the Alf the Narks, and the Storm Birds; the Soddy Freds, the Midnight Expresses, and the Starlight Murphys. Dave on the farm runs the wife and kids per car into town every Saturday evening to see the pictures, and no longer does Dad roar and Mum placate. The poor parson drops down in his airplane, where his predecessor dropped in from his buggy.

The chequeman who handed his cheque across a bar with the request to be told when it was cut out has been replaced by the restless station hand who rushes in for a drink and rushes out again to speed on his way behind a steering wheel.

It is a matter of opinion, on which we must agree to differ, whether the change is for the best or otherwise. My own opinion is fixed by intimate experiences gained in the old world of coaches and horse-drivers, bullock teams and station hacks; when life ran more slowly and smoothly; and when men and women had time to think and to plan. The world I favour is that which existed before the engine offered quick transit from the stockyards and the homestead to the city hotel and the crowded streets.

For the pictures and the atmosphere of the Australian bush before the great change swept over it we must now go to the works of Lawson, Paterson and Rudd. These three have for ever preserved a phase of Australian life which, being past, will never recur.

It seems almost safe to prophesy that half a century hence a great proportion of Australian imaginative literature will deal with pre-war Australia and its bush folk in a highly romantic vein. The authors-to-be will create as false a world of old Australia as American writers and picture producers have woven around their Wild West and their Civil War.

The few morbid psychological novels published within recent years will hasten rather than retard the coming distortion of a wholly admirable phase of Australian life and manners. The modern epic novel quite naturally will quickly be forgotten for the one simple reason that the Australian people in the mass are too healthful not quickly to disgorge this mental poison.

No people may stand still, but must go on and on. We can but regret the passing of old Australia and take keen pride in the new. As a nation we can never go wrong if we but continue to practice the virtues universally found among the people of this country up to and including the first decade of the Twentieth Century.

Their outstanding virtues were generosity, sympathy and loyalty – the greatest of the three being loyalty.

Giving to Get

No proverb is more crammed with truth than that which refers to bread thrown upon the waters returning after many days. When a young woman at a street corner rattles a collecting tin under my nose, I find it difficult to refuse parting with at least a penny. When a down and out asks for three-pence to make up a shilling for a bed, I find it harder still to refuse.

When a swagman calls at the back door, I never refuse him a meal. I am far from being naturally generous. When giving I do not feel a glow of pleasure. I give simply because life has taught me that to give is an excellent insurance against adversity, and that, no matter how secure one may feel today, tomorrow winter may come.

Winter came to Henry Marshall when, with his savings, his wife and he bought the goodwill and licence of a wayside hotel on the Darling. The licencee before him had let the business down, and when Marshall started he waited long and vainly for customers.

Not a motor car, or a buckboard, or even a swagman ever stopped before the door, save the mail car, whose passengers never alighted there. His bar was stocked with the best of liquors; his wife, a splendid cook, was limited in her art to the satisfaction of her husband and herself. To occupy his time, Marshall dug up the garden or went fishing on the river.

One hot morning, when sitting on the front verandah, he watched the slow approach of a swagman. He noted the listless manner in which the man walked, the shabby clothes, the cigarette swag; and when the traveller was about to pass by, he called him in for a drink.

Within the bar, the swagman told his tale; how he had left his family in Melbourne to go on tramp in search of employment, and of his hopes of securing a job on one of the stations.

At this time, long before the grant of sustenance, it was almost as difficult to get station work as it was to find a job in the cities, and frankly Marshall pointed out the hopelessness of an inexperienced man obtaining bush employment.

When dinner was announced, the swagman was invited to

dine. After dinner, he was urged to stay the night.

The next morning he left for the lock building near Wentworth with a letter of introduction to a foreman whom Marshall knew. In his swag were two of Mrs Marshall's blankets, and on his feet were Marshall's best boots.

The summer wore on – and the traffic continued to pass Marshall's without stopping. Later, by the mail car, Marshall received an expensive pair of boots, and, later still his wife was sent two new blankets.

One week before Easter the swagman wrote to say that he had been promoted foreman, and that he was bringing his wife and a few friends to stay for the holidays. He urged the Marshalls to be sure to have a large stock of provisions.

On the Thursday before Good Friday the swagman and his family arrived in a hired car; and before ten o'clock that night, the swagman's friends arrived in cars of all descriptions, cars loaded to the axles with 111 lock workers. The swagman's wife acted as offsider to Mrs Marshall, while two of the men were put on as waiters at £1 a day.

When I stayed at Marshall's hotel for a three weeks' fishing and shooting holiday, not one car, not a buckboard, not a swagman passed the door. The garden had gone wild – Marshall could not spare the time to cultivate it.

With camels once I camped near a boundary gate on the Wanaaring-Wilcannia road. That track is long and hot and dry, and that day had been long and hot, too. The bush was hushed to sleep by the balmy night, and the only sounds reaching me were the camel bells, when, abruptly into the firelight, stepped a swagman.

He was worn out. His tucker bags were empty. He ate my tucker and smoked my tobacco.

In the morning he filled his bags from my supplies. Because I was short of tobacco, and because he would reach a homestead that day when I would not reach one for another week, I gave him a ten-shilling note. He was most grateful. I certainly was grateful to him for his racy talk which illuminated what otherwise would have been a dull evening.

Quite a lot of water flowed down the Darling, and even a local flood crept down part of the Paroo, before I arrived at Bourke to put up at the Railway Hotel.

In the bar a man said to me:

"Travellin', mate?"

I said I was.

"Have a drink and put this in your kip," he said, when sliding along the counter toward me two £10 notes.

Regarding the philanthropist with astonishment, not knowing him, I declined the money. Good naturedly he reminded me of the camp near the boundary gate, and of our chance meeting three years previously.

I still refused his money, because it so happened I had a little of my own, but, he being now a boss drover owning his own plant, I went to work for him at £1 a day on an 18 months trip.

Then there was Spud Wilson, whose generosity was well rewarded.

He took a cheque for £300 off a South Australian station and, when on his way to Broken Hill to spend it, he reached one afternoon a selector's house. Out from the house ran a white-faced woman to beseech him to take a rifle away from her husband who was bent on suicide.

Within the house Wilson found the selector barred into the bedroom. When he knocked on the door and demanded admittance, the gun went off.

With an axe he smashed his way into the bedroom to find the selector stretched on the floor, and blood dripping from a long, bullet-made scratch on the side of his head.

Having revived the selector, Wilson demanded an explanation, the gist of which was that the mortgagee threatened to close on the property because of the non-payment of a paltry £100.

The following day Wilson and the would-be suicide drove to Broken Hill in the latter's ancient truck, and there Wilson paid the mortgagee and sent the selector home with £50 worth of stores and clothing.

He always said that he had a remarkably fine bender on the balance of the cheque.

In the course of time the selector repaid Wilson double his loan. A few years later he purchased a large station, and eventually repaid all the money borrowed to purchase it. Then he died – quite naturally – leaving the estate to be divided between widow and Wilson, who then was camped in a hovel suffering from Paroo Rot.

Wilson's share amounted to £15,000.

Incidents such as these may be multiplied. The bush folk give and forget; but they seldom take and forget. To give is good insurance, for in this unstable life, many of us are up today and down tomorrow.

It is surprising how bread thrown upon the waters will return with increase.

Chefs of the Outback

It has been said that the chef of the Savoy Hotel, London, draws a higher salary than that of a British Cabinet Minister. I myself have worked under a chef in Australia who drew £30 a week, and having cooked for a State Governor at a station homestead, as well as for bushmen in a lamb-markers' camp, so I claim to write with authority on cooking and bush cooks.

A £7-a-week city chef is quite an ordinary kind of cook! The £30-a-week cook was one who had spent three years with a pastry cook, eighteen months with a butcher and poulterer, one year with a fishmonger, and ten years under a famous Paris chef – which proves that a first-class chef must serve a long and varied apprenticeship.

The Savoy Hotel chef, indeed, has to be a linguist, an artist, and an inventor. On his private stove, when inspiration rides his genius, he concocts new sauces, syrups and condiments, the recipes of which are guarded as strictly as next year's dress fashions.

If the ordinary chef cannot turn out a tasty meal, he is more fitted to use a pick and shovel. The culinary artist in charge of the kitchen of any big hotel has everything possible to aid him, or rather, his chief assistants have; for the important chef is really an architect who plans a menu and watches his assistants build it for the dining tables.

In my impish moments, when I would like to see the Prime Minister building a house, and Mr. Blamire Young painting a fence, I would like to observe the chef of any famous hotel deposited at the foot of a gum tree together with a bag of plain flour, a carcase of mutton, potatoes, and a quantity of rice, some tea and sugar, and a billy can and one frying pan; and to tell him to cook a meal for a party of hungry drovers. To watch him would be a source of intense joy.

Of a certainty, your good bush cook is a fellow blessed with abnormal intelligence. He is almost akin to the Savoy chef in imagination, while in several respects he is superior. He has to create a variety of meals out of nothing, as it were, and with ingredients seldom containing eggs and butter and milk. He is lucky if he has a stove on which to cook, and ice chambers are not for him.

If the Duke of Gloucester could have found time to visit the station where Rainbow Harry was cooking – just where it is difficult to ascertain because Rainbow Harry never stays more than two months in one kitchen – His Royal Highness would have returned to England with vivid and delightful memories of a visit to the bush. For breakfast, Rainbow Harry would serve porridge, grilled chops, the like of which I defy anyone to buy in a city, bread such as no city baker can turn out, and coffee.

His dinner would comprise sheep's head soup, if possible to get, baked Murray Cod garnished with river-mussel sauce, roast lamb – real lamb and not a small ten-years-old ewe foisted on us down here as lamb – with baked potatoes and wild spinach if no garden greens were available, and a sultana pudding that melts and does not go soggy in the mouth.

All good bush cooks are born inventors. There was Alf the Nark – no cook turned out better yeast bread. He once was cooking for a gang of musterers in a kitchen fitted with a stove. It was not a large stove. Yet he found no difficulty at all in making it serve to cook meals for eleven hungry men, as well as for the cooking of his famous yeast bread.

The month was August, and one evening the returning musterers brought in seventeen emu eggs, the sight of which made the cook's eyes gleam. Alf the Nark made us scrambled eggs for breakfast the following morning, and we demanded scrambled eggs for dinner that night when we brought back to camp a further fourteen emu eggs.

Yes, all good cooks are inventors. With the emu eggs, Alf decided to experiment. He judged that the contents of one emu egg were equal to twelve hen eggs, and one morning, before rolling flour into his bread batter, he stirred into it the contents of two emu eggs. In due time he made the dough, permitted it to rise, punched it down and portioned it into the baking tins, and, when it had risen again, he put it into the oven – after having tested it by keeping his bare arm in it, while successfully counting ten.

Eighty minutes did he always give his bread to bake. Once it was placed in the oven, nothing would induce him to look at it until fifty minutes had elapsed. On this occasion, when the fifty minutes had passed, he found some difficulty in opening the oven door.

Then he discovered the batch of bread filling every particle of the oven's interior and glued to its five sides so firmly that he was obliged to use a spade to scrape it out. He told us that if he had not opened the oven door when he did, that bread would have exploded the stove and wrecked the kitchen!

Then there was the writer who decided that if he did not teach himself to make yeast bread, the soda in the dampers would give him incurable dyspepsia. After several efforts, he made a yeast with a kick in it. Into a pail went about seven pounds of good flour, and into that went about a pint of yeast.

The next morning the batter was working beautifully. He made it up into a dough and set it beside the fire to rise. It rose all right, and, following telephoned instructions, he kneaded it down and waited for it to rise the second time.

It did not rise the second time, however. Thinking that the heat of cooking would make it rise, he buried it in the ashes according to the age-old formula of cooking dampers. The cracking ash-cover proved that the cooking bread was rising; but when the cracks in the ash-cover disappeared, it proved too that the bread had fallen again. A round cannon ball was dragged out of the hot ashes, and when in desperation and disgust, this cook took it out and threw it away, it happened to fall on an iron-hard clay-pan, which it starred as though the clay-pan was of ice.

Your bush cook who can create a meal out of next to nothing, and your station cook who can, with limited materials, produce an amazing variety of dishes, are real culinary artists. Your city chef who nonchalantly sends in a thirteen-course dinner from unlimited supplies, is a mere tradesman compared with the bushmen. The bushmen can offer you a dish of braised mountain duck, which you would never guess was a fifty-years-old cockatoo, or a crow of unguessable age; he can make a cake in which one would swear he had put half a dozen eggs when, in fact, he had neither eggs nor butter; he can make a tough steak so tender that anyone without teeth could masticate it; while, given just a bare sporting chance with a few extras, he can turn out a ten-course dinner that several State Governors and at least one Governor-General, touring the outback, will remember.

Lords of the Track

The professional Australian sundowner is distinctly a different type from the American hobo, who is largely criminal, and from the British tramp, who is dirty in his habits and person. Not all sundowners are "won't works" – not all, by a long shot, are always penniless.

In my notebook of character sketches are many jolly fellows who proved to be excellent travelling companions, and whose lives are worthy of the attention of any famous biographer. How some of them earned their curious nicknames is puzzling, even to themselves.

Among the many is "The Flying Dutchman," who owned property in Brisbane, and whose only vice was writing poetry. That the the poetry was good was no excuse.

"Organ Face" was a morphia maniac, and his most persistent fad was to shave morning and evening with the regularity of the tides, no matter how his poor hands trembled. His philosophy was perfect. He maintained that the man who never worked was as well off as the man who worked all the year round.

Supreme among them all is "The Jail King." His hobby was to be incarcerated in every Australian jail, and, at the time I met him, he had been an every South Australian jail, was contemplating the New South Wales jails, and hoped soon to start on the Victorian jails.

"Wonky" carried a cigarette swag consisting of two shirts rolled in a piece of calico. He never was known to wear boots or hat, and he believed in fairies. Described them, too, and repeated what they said to him, and what he said to them.

Of importance among the gallery is "The American Ball Tosser." A diminutive man of jockey weight, his bete noire was policemen. Not that he hated policemen as might you or I, for he regarded them from the lofty height of a World's Lightweight Champion. His greatest performance was given in Oxide Street, Broken Hill, when his arrest for insulting language was effected only by the combination of seven policemen and a wheel-barrow.

"Rainbow Harry" was famous on two counts: the colouring in his cooking, and his liberality to tramps. It seemed almost impossible for him to turn out a white blanc-mange. It had to be blue, or red, or red and blue in layers. As a station hands' cook he had no equal, and, when on the track, could make splendid cake with a couple of handfuls of flour and three sultanas. Asked for meat or flour by a professional hiker he would shout loudly that he had none of one or the other, loudly enough for the boss to hear; then silently take the man's ration bags and fill them to the brim.

Here, on page sixty-three, is "Sparrow-up-the Spout." Recently I heard he had died. His hiking ground extended from Wentworth to Burke, New South Wales – 500 miles by road and 1,500 miles by river bank. He followed the river always. He knew every bend, every sand-spit, every hollow log. Not once in many years did he sleep outside a hollow log, and it was in a hollow log that they found him dead.

Under my hand there turns up "Sailor Lad," who tramped with me to Cunnamulla, Queensland. If there is a port in the world he had not visited, it must be right on the South Pole. Name any shipping port from Liverpool to some African river port, and he could tell you the number of hotels there were in it. A brave man, he could be depended on in a crisis, and sometimes I think that Conrad put him into his novel "Typhoon," as the captain of the ship.

It looked like rain before morning when we decided to camp off the creek flats on a high sandhill. After the usual yarning over the fire, we turned in. Over and under my blanket was a tent-fly, and presently, on the fly, I distinctly heard a "cleet-cleet-cleet!" On striking a match I beheld seven or eight-size scorpions running vigorously over the fly whilst round the glowing embers of the fire there were a hundred others. With a yell, I rolled out of my comfortable bed and rushed down to the hard, grey flats; trailing a blanket behind me which I violently shook.

"Come out of it, Sailor! That sandhill is one scorpion nest," I yelled. He grunted, yawned, then mumbled sleepily: "Oh! they're all right if you don't roll on 'em." He slept there till morning. I slept on an iron-hard clay-pan.

The Blankets That Wouldn't "Stay Put"

There used to be a hut in the vicinity of a well, west of Wilcannia, on the Darling, that almost certainly seemed to be haunted. Somewhere back in its history, a camel rider hurried to the place to gain shelter from a thunderstorm, and just as he was alighting from his mount a flash of lightning killed both man and animal.

Afterwards several men swore that they had seen the ghost of a man on the back of the ghost of a camel arrive, and halt near the well. The human ghost then walked swiftly to the hut, and disappeared within it!

Twelve years after the tragedy I reached the place just before night fell one evening in June, when the ground was soggy with water and the south wind blew with icy temperature across a cloudless sky. Ghost or no ghost, I determined to camp for the night in that hut.

Beside the well I "hooshed" down the three camels, and unloaded them. They hated to kneel there, and only after leading them away some 200 yards was I able to hobble them. Then, when the noselines had been removed, they incontinently bolted, their hobbled fore-legs making great lunging strides. Without doubt they were badly frightened by the locality.

An excellent beginning!

Having carried the gear into the hut, I made a fire and placed the filled billy over the flame, and then gathered a supply of wood from the encircling scrub, as the full moon rose whitely from the eastern timber. Half an hour later the iron chimney showed blotches of red heat, and the family was dining on damper, cold mutton chops, and milkless, but well sugared, tea.

There I sat on the tucker box, pleasurably warmed by the fire, with Hool-em-up on one side and Tum-tum, the cat, on the other. Both the cat and the dog should have been enjoying the shelter and the warmth, for the dog had run at least 200 miles that day, and the cat had ridden for nearly ten hours in her especial pack-bag. But they were obviously uneasy, like the camels, who were frightened by their surroundings.

The south wind whistled and moaned, whispered and shrieked.

When the cooking damper was rising in its bed of ashes, I made up my bunk so that I could read by the firelight, as the supply of fat was becoming short; and when the damper had been removed from the ashes and was cooling on its edge, I lay on the bunk reading a particularly thrilling thriller.

I was just at that part of the book where the madman was on the point of cutting the heroine's throat when the hut rocked beneath a terrific blow. In a split second I was on my feet facing the door, Hool-em-up was crouched hard against my legs, hackles stiff with fright, and Tum-tum was standing with stiffened legs on one of the cross beams supporting the roof. From outside came a low hissing noise. A dull thud came from beyond the door.

Then with dreadful slowness the door began to open inwards.

I looked for a window through which to escape. There was none. The only egress was through the slowly opening door beyond which – ! With a howl Hool-em-up dashed forward. He howled again as he disappeared through the doorway. He yelped as he fled to the scrub. The cat hissed and spat. No longer was it possible for me to remain inactive.

With a flaming wooden billet from the fire held aloft, I charged wildly as the dog had done, the door by this time being wide open. Beyond it the well and the dark scrub lay revealed in the brilliant moonlight. I leaped outside, the torch presented like a sword. I trod on something which yielded and gave a moan of anguish . . .

A hundred yards separated me from the haunted hut when I stopped at last and returned, pride spurring my deadened feet. I saw nothing, could hear nothing but the wind. But outside the door lay the body of a heavy black duck which, mistaking the iron roof, reflecting the moonlight, for water, had crashed to its death on it! Hool-em-up did not appear until morning, and the three camels were then as far away as they could get – in a paddock corner nine miles distant.

But, all the same, I never camped at that hut again.

Then there was the Haunted Fence – and here originality is claimed for the locality of a haunting.

With two dogs and a galah I was camped beside a dog-proof fence. At that moment before falling to sleep, when the mind is in its most receptive state, the dogs began to whimper, and, on sitting up to look in the direction they indicated, I saw, approaching along the fence, a great white Thing, rising and sinking alternately.

In the presence of a ghost, inactivity spells defeat.

The Thing was now quite close. The dogs were emphatically scared. So was I, but I managed to point the shot gun and press both triggers at the same moment. From the fence something white dashed away – and at the foot of the fence something white lay still.

Poor thing! It was only a goat, which had been engaged in friendly argument with another goat on the other side of the fence. It was quite a young goat, and we profited by the fright!

And now having broached the subject of ghosts in an easy, anecdotal fashion, the subject will be treated with more respect; for, after all, there may be real ghosts which are not the creation of imagination or of indigestion, ghosts whose presence a man can feel and animals can see. Consequently the following experience can be supplied with no adequate explanation.

At the close of a brilliant day in late August I selected a patch of clean sandy ground, beside a billabong off the Warrego, on which to camp for the night. I was alone, my dog having picked up a poison bait four days previously. After supper, having cooked a damper and some meat for the morrow, I gathered my bushman's mattress composed of leaves, laid upon it a strip of waterproof sheeting and one blanket, and dropped off to sleep with three blankets over me and a roaring leaping fire beside me.

I woke to find that the fire had subsided into a mound of red coals, and that three blankets lay in a heap about a yard beyond my feet.

Puzzled to account for this, and too sleepy to bother about it, I replenished the fire, re-arranged the blankets, and slept again. And again I awoke to find myself very cold, the fire low, and my blankets in a pile about a yard beyond my feet.

It was then just after ten o'clock, the night being dark and silent. For two hours I sat before a leaping fire and pondered over this strange series of incidents. At length, wearied by unanswerable questions, I composed myself for the third time and slept.

And for the third time did I awake to feel the cold of death, and to find the blankets in that singular pile beyond my feet.

In a kind of numbed frenzy I gathered wood and threw it on the fire until a tall column of flame was shooting skywards and driving back the encroaching shadows. Without real justification I was mastered by fear – fear which directed my feet to carry my body at top speed through blanketed darkness; fear braked only by the knowledge that surrender to panic would result in possible fatal injury through collision against a tree or a fall into a cliff-sided billabong. And until day broke I walked round and round the fire, feeling that something was watching me, wrestling with the demon which rode me.

For two hours I searched diligently for tracks in the vicinity of the camp, to find none of man or beast or bird save my own. I could understand a man throwing his blankets to one side or the other; I could understand getting up and tossing the blankets into a pile in the unlikely position, and returning to bed without remembering the act. But I could not understand the exact triplication of those acts. There was, and is, no explanation!

From an old aboriginal I learned afterwards that on that camp site a lubra and her paramour had been killed by the woman's tribal owner. Was it she who had teased me that night? Does a ghost have the power to lift blankets?

If so, she most certainly must have enjoyed the spectacle presented by a white man walking round and round his camp fire with every single hair on his head on end.

The minx!

Influenza

What beats me is why the doctors have not long ago wiped out the influenza plague. Tens of thousands of pounds have been spent in controlling, if not wiping out, the plagues of cholera, smallpox and malaria, but influenza continues to ravage humanity and levy a toll of millions of hours of wastage every year. When I went to the war my body was marked and scarred by the hypodermic needle and various juices were squirted into me which really did save me from all the plagues known to man – bar influenza.

There was that brilliant doctor once stationed at Parkhouse, England, around whom is wrapped mystery for he was as great as Lister and yet remains unknown. He had further claim to fame in that he did not regard every soldier as a malingerer. I complained of a succession of colds, and after an examination we agreed that it was quite unnecessary for the human race to be bothered with colds.

"I can give you an injection which might innoculate you against the common cold which is often the forerunner of influenza," he said dubiously.

"Is the alternative – death?" I asked dramatically.

"No, no! Of course not."

"Very well, then, shove it in, sir," was my eager plea. "I'm sick and tired of this snivelling nose."

When giving me the shot he asked me to report without fail when the next cold attacked me, but when I had to report the next attack three years later the war was over.

Before the war influenza was never as prevalent as it has been since. It never placed me *hors de combat* before 1916, and after that wonderful doctor's inoculation wore out of my system I have been laid low every year.

Medical advice to get into the fresh air, avoid theatres and crowds, and do the daily dozen undoubtedly is good advice, and is conducive to general good health, but in warding off influenza it cuts no ice.

When I was riding the South Australian Border Fence I did not go to theatres or become one of a crowd. I did not live in a house in the corners of which are supposed to lurk countless germs. I did sleep in a tent when it rained about three times in the year. I had not come in contact with a human being for twenty-two days, and therefore the influenza germ, which put me down for the full count, could not have hopped on to me like a flea from a dog.

To be candid, I did not enjoy that particular attack. The nearest abode was a station homestead eighteen miles distant; the nearest water supply four miles. I had about a gallon of water, and for three days I lay on a stretcher under a mulga and strained my ears listening for camel bells.

As for fresh air, I had as much of it as the birds, and I am quite sure that no influenza germs were hopping around in a shade temperature of 114 degrees. Perhaps the little fellow who got me had been hiding in the water-bag.

An attack which produced some humour was one which laid seven of us low. We were mustering sheep for shearing, and our head-quarters was a large hut, twelve miles out on the run. A rainfall of a few points in conjunction with a week-end gave us three days' holiday, and the running of the flocks to and from the shed was not interrupted.

The morning of the first day two men complained of pains in the head and back and they did not get up. The cook was ladling porridge into the breakfast plates when he dropped the pot, staggered to his bunk and collapsed. We removed his boots and covered him up, and I took on the cooking when another promised to do my accumulated washing.

The next morning two others failed to rise, and when that day closed all hands bar the cook were out of action. One romantic young fellow possessed a revolver, and he spent his enforced leisure shooting holes through the iron roof until it so got on my nerves that I had to take the weapon from him.

The third morning I was telephoning the boss to send out more men, when a sword was driven through my kidneys and I just managed to reach my bed. The boss, being a wise man, sent out to cook a man so filled with whisky that not all the germs in creation could weaken him, and five days later we were back at work although still suffering from undoubted influenza.

Every year the influenza microbes attack in a different manner. During the severe 1916-17 winter which laid over Northern Europe an unbroken frost for six months, despite the theory that frost keeps germs dormant, I went down before a most determined attack when in charge of a large camp post office. Had I reported sick, I would have been bundled off to hospital and lost a wonderful cushy job. It was the seventh evening when one of my orderlies got windy and went for the doctor.

As the doctor was about to leave he whispered to my first assistant, and only after I had threatened send the latter back to the horse-lines did he confess that the doctor thought I had meningitis.

"Go along and ask Theo to come here," I ordered.

"Theo," I said to the Officers' Mess barman. "I've got meningitis. A bottle of whisky will cure it. How much?"

He brought the medicine and I directed him to pour it into a tin kettle, add sugar and watch carefully that it did not explode when heating on the red-hot stove. I drank three parts of a pint pannikin of undiluted whisky, and the next morning I was sorting letters when the doctor came in.

It is about time something was done to curb the activities of this plague. It has cost me six weeks loss of time within the last two months, and during these years of depression one cannot afford to go to the distilleries for medicine.

There is a multiple fortune awaiting the doctor who can produce an anti-influenza serum to sell cheaper per shot than a half bottle of whisky.

Poison

Once on my way to Ivanhoe, N.S.W., with half a ton of rabbit skins, I called on a selector friend to offer to bring anything he required back from the town.

"Thanks," he said. "Go to Blank and bring me two stones of spuds, three pounds of butter, and half a case each of jam and milk. Oh! and half a pound of strych, and a seven pound tin of cyanide. White strych, remember. Might as well give them foxes strawberry jam as coloured strych."

Having dispatched the skins to the Sydney market, I called at the general store and collected my friend's parcel. It was dark when I reached his house, and he then had the table set for a meal, and a billy simmering over the fire. Being short of sugar, he opened the parcel on the table, and from among the four bottles of strychnine and the tin of cyanide, produced the sugar he required. Later, when he wanted to illustrate a yarn, he used the poison receptacles, his knife and fork, and the salt tin to mark various positions on an imaginary map. We swapped stories that night, with sufficient poison on the table to kill 10,000 rabbits and 8,987 human beings – about.

As with many laws in this country, those governing the sale of poisons are worthy of the attention of a Wodehouse. If I wish to buy from a chemist sufficient poison with which to kill a sick cat, I have to sign a book and have with me a witness to add his name to mine; but from the bush I can obtain from a country store-keeper, or a wholesale house, poison by the pound weight.

Yet despite the easy accessibility to poisons, there are remarkably few accidents among bush people with whom it is of almost daily use. When employed on State Government vermin fences, and when engaged in trapping, I always had an open bottle of strychnine in the tucker box. The strychnine issued by Government Departments invariably is coloured; it used to be black, now it is coloured pink. For a reason which I could never ascertain, coloured strychnine is twenty per cent. as efficient as the white crystals. No bush trapper will use coloured strychnine, save to poison the jaws of a dog trap. As my selector friend said, one might as well offer foxes and wild dogs strawberry jam as baits poisoned with coloured strychnine.

Personal observation has convinced me that if there is a death more dreadful than that caused by strychnine poisoning, I do not wish to hear of it. Were I some chimerical person, invested with unlimited power, I would prohibit the manufacture of strychnine. Of course, vermin must be destroyed. Rabbits and eagles may be destroyed by cyanide, which is quick and almost painless, but I have yet to hear of foxes and wild dogs being destroyed with cyanide solution.

"Take a load of rations out to old Bluenose Harry," the manager of a Queensland station instructed me one morning long before the war.

Bluenose Harry was an old and cunning dodger, and I found him camped beside a water hole fifteen miles from the homestead. It was a cold night, and after a meal we lounged in the warmth of a leaping camp fire, when I listened to tales of adventure, one of which has remained in mind. Bluenose told it in language I am unable to produce here.

"I got a stiffener of strych once when I was a pimply-faced young feller," he said. "Me and another lad was was helpin' to drove sheep down from Wanaaring to the Hill. The boss was an easy kind of bloke, but the cook! His dampers was sods, and his plum duffs was cannon balls. Me and the other lad was always at him about 'is sods, and several times he threatened to give a proper sod wot would make us sick. And one morning he did sure enough.

"We'd camped at a Gov-ment dam, and after breakfast we rode off right away to some station sheep yards where we had camped the woollies, having saddled up before breakfast, and we was letting the sheep out of the yards when the boss fell down."

"I was looking at him, surprised like, when he seemed to get bigger and bigger. I looks up and everything I seen looked bigger than it oughter. Me eyes went wonkey. Me mouth began to taste worse than a recovery. I wanted to be sick, and I was sick. And the pain! I sweat, and then I froze. Sometimes the light was so fierce that it hurt me eyes, and then it was so dim I could 'ardly see anythink. I see me mate crawling off to the dam, and I after him. 'An the boss coming on behind us, and calling to us not to drink if we wanted to live. As though I wouldn't have rather died with water in me mouth than live as I felt then.

"But he needn't have worried. None of us reached the water till sundown, and by that time we had got rid of most of the strych we had eaten in the breakfast sod. The cook? How did we get on?"

Bluenose Harry leered like a devil. "We got over it all right, bar the shakes every year in that month for years after. The cook only gave us enough to make us sick – as he said he would, but he was dead. He took enough strych to kill twenty men."

Again the old dogger leered. From his tucker-box, against which he leaned, he took a two-ounce bottle of white strychnine crystals, and, with the point of his knife, abstracted sufficient to well cover a threepenny piece. I saw him lay the poison on his tongue and wash it down his throat with a draft of black tea.

In those days inexperienced, I harnessed the horse to the dray and drove back to the homestead, where I aroused the manager at four o'clock in the morning, frantically summoning assistance.

"You new-chum ass!" he growled sleepily. "Old Bluenose Harry is a strychnine eater. When you see a man's hands and his face twitch you can bet on it."

As far as I know, Bluenose Harry lived for ever; but one trapper, Combo William, was really too bad in the manner he handled poisons. He used to carry strychnine loose in a waistcoat pocket, the more easily to secure a pinch with which to bait the remains of a calf killed by wild dogs. When I knew him there never was a button to the waistcoat, which seemed always to flap violently when he walked or rode.

It must have been flapping about one day when he grilled mutton chops over an open camp fire, and either he absentmindedly mistook his poison pocket for the salt tin, or some of the crystals fell from it to the meat. Anyway, Combo William expired.

In the bush, we are wickedly careless with poisons, but many of us die only of old age.

Christmas Memories

Christmas again! At no other period of the year does one's mind enjoy such vivid introspection of the years that have gone, each marked by its Christmas. It is far easier for us to recall what we did, whom we met, where we were, during the many Christmases than it is to recall how we spent our birthdays or Easter holidays.

Conditions with every one of us have changed, either for the better or the worse; but certainly no Christmases were so filled with joy as were those of our childhood. They stand out boldly on the photographic plate of the mind: a marvelous engine, a wonderful doll, an illuminated Christmas tree – dreams come true as they never have done since.

My father owned a general store in the south of England. In one show window, on a pedestal, was once displayed a large steam railway engine made of brass. I wanted that engine, as never have I wanted anything. I was told that if the engine was not sold it would be given me Christmas morning, and my days and evenings were spent with my face glued to the window, suffering an agony of dread every time an assistant entered the window room to remove an article of purchase. I did not know that the engine really was not for sale. I remember walking in the dark, searching the bedroom table, finding the blessed engine. I remember how I loaded it with water and lit the spirit lamp beneath the boiler, thence to watch the engine run on the rails, my face on a level with the line so that the oncoming engine appeared so real.

There was a Mr. Brown who was a kindly chemist, the husband of a huge, kindly woman and the father of two boys of my own age. One Christmas Eve he brought drums and bugles and took me home with him, and there in a room behind the shop he led the youthful band whilst Mrs. Brown stopped here ears with her fingers, and the customers were obliged to wait.

The old English custom of the family reunion at Yuletide is, perhaps, not so general in this land of wide spaces. I see an old woman in bed, slowly dying, and beside the bed an illuminated fir-tree standing in a tub. Despite the tree and the great canopied bed there was room enough for her seven children and her eleven grandchildren. They propped her up with pillows, and the years have not dimmed memory of her marble face, the white lace cap, the bright bird-like eyes which vied with the hanging copper bed-warmers reflecting the light of the fire.

The Christmas gathering still takes place, but one is not of it. There was the Christmas spent on the great dog-proof fence dividing South Australia from New South Wales. Two weeks previously I had obtained from Broken Hill a hamper and several bottles of beer, knowing that the day would be spent in solitude with my camels, the dog and the cat. As they went by I counted the days, often tempted to drink the beer when the temperature was around 120 degrees in the shade. The day arrived, finding me camped beside water and fair camel feed. I decided I would defer dining till the sun went down and the flies were banished, and then, by extraordinary fortuity, a stockman came along. He was welcomed and urged to camp the night, the hamper contents used as a bait. That made him chuckle and explain that Christmas was past a full week.

I remember the Christmas spent among the German pineapple growers of south Queensland, hospitable people whose houses are built on piles. Everyone in the district was invited to spend the Christmas night at the home of one of the wealthiest settlers, where, on the broad verandahs, there was dancing, and beneath the house, amidst the carts and the packing gear, huge barrels of beer were on tap. They drank heartily those Germans, and they were not alone. All were welcome. An uproariously happy Christmas night – and eight months later, when I wanted to au-revoir some Australian friends, I dared not do so in uniform.

An outstanding Christmas was that spent at Maadi, Egypt, with the 1st Light Horse Brigade. Beneath the rush-work shed roofs, we had our table messes. Each mess appointed a treasurer to collect spare piastres with which to purchase poultry and Pilsner, the cooks willing to roast the former in return for a bottle or two of the latter. My friend, William Snell, as wide as he was tall, persuaded us to leave the poultry to him. He awoke me at two o'clock Christmas morning, gave me two sacks, and led me to the houses comprising Maadi, each house guarded by a night-watchman sitting in a sentry-box beside the garden gate. William led the way – over a back wall – to a poultry shed. Opening the door a fraction he inserted a bamboo rod, having at its end a rag saturated with chloroform borrowed from the doctor's tent.

To me he passed out the fowls and the ducks. I dropped them into the bags, and later, when we had to negotiate the wall, I sat astride it to receive from William the two bags, and to drop them on the further side, William was never tired of reminding me of the fool I was for not having wrung the birds' necks before putting them into the bags, because when dropped to the ground the ducks regained consciousness and their quacking aroused fifty native watchmen.

It was half a mile to the camp, quite a long way for a man carrying twenty head of game. William had to tarry to delay the pursuit, and by morning there was not a feather above ground as evidence.

A clock-work motor-boat! That is what a young fellow wants. I tell him that times are hard, and can promise him nothing. But I will buy him the motor-boat, because I cannot forget the gleaming steam engine. In England, now cold and dreary, a steam-engine; in Australia, warm and sun-lit, a motor-boat. How aptly these toys typify the two countries? But to us all Christmas means the same thing, unexplained by the philosopher – LOVE.

At School

Recently it fell to my lot to introduce my young son to a West Australian State School, and whilst on the way my mind reverted to a National School in the south of England, which took the place of the preparatory school in my poor education.

Sonny, aged seven, has come from a country school in Victoria, where the discipline was lax and the enthusiasm for teaching not intense. In the East, Western Australia is not only renowned for its opportunities on the land but its educational benefits are equally well known, thoughtful parents being attracted, as are thoughtful farmers. Hand in hand we walked a tree-shaded pavement and came to a big single-storied building, surrounded by vast playing grounds, upon which was not a single piece of paper or rubbish. Beyond the highly polished open windows, the interior looked invitingly cool and restful, and had I been led there blindfolded I never would have guessed, so quiet was it, that I stood before a school.

From the lofty central hall opened numerous classrooms, and through the glass doors the children were seen sitting at neat, clean and comfortable desks. The whole effect was light and sunny, a wonderful contrast to that National School which I attended forty years ago, a place reached down a narrow alleyway – a gaunt grey structure, over a chapel in the days when Nonconformity was young and regarded with disfavour by the boisterous public of the period following the Puritan Era. There were no classrooms or even light partitions dividing the classes, of which there were six, each class being huddled against the next, so that after a little practice, if one became bored with say, a geography lesson, one could easily follow the more interesting history lesson being given the senior boys, several classes removed. This practice must be stressed because the art was not easy to acquire.

From nine till twelve and from one till four o'clock this National School was cacophonous uproar, which, during any one period of twenty seconds, was something like this:

"Meat is a noun, but meet is a verb – William the Conqueror, ten sixty-six – Blake, come out here – sixteen plus ten divided by thirteen is how many? You, Parkins, how many?"

Slick – slick – slick! as Blake is caned on the palm of his shrinking hand.

"How many times have I told you that Q is not written like that?" Smack – smack, as an iron hand meets a tender ear. "Go on, go on. A-N-X-I-E-T-Y spells, what?" A thud, guffaws of laughter, when a long form seating a dozen boys is pushed over. More ear and head smacking – much more.

"Now, we'll have that verse again. Smith, you are not singing – How much is five per centum of twenty-three pounds? – What are you chewing, Bradley? Ten sixty-six, sir – Come out here! – I didn't do it, sir. – I'll give you something to chew – I didn't 'it 'im on the 'ead, sir." – Slick – slick – slick.

The shouts and the orders of the male teachers, each armed with a cane and full authority to use it, the upsetting of a blackboard or a long form, the smacking of ears and the yelps of the caned, the piping voices answering questions, and the softer hum of those lads risking punishment, in preference to quite unnatural silence, created such uproar that the wonder was, on our leaving, being able even to read and write. They were hard days yet glorious days. The scholar required a hide like a steer, while the teachers had to be made of cast-iron to survive long the conditions of teaching in a National School. Dirt was everywhere. The long desks were never painted and seldom scrubbed. The little windows, high up in the walls, I do not remember being able to see through. In summer the place was unbearably hot. During the winter the atmosphere was foetid from damp clothes and unwashed bodies.

Now the contrast. At half-past three I awaited my son outside the Modern (W.A.) School. Every window was open; yet there reached me only the modulated voices of the teachers. A bell was rung for school dismissal, and, with fortitude, I prepared my nerves to meet the shock of pandemonium. But the children emerged quietly and orderly. Naturally, voices were raised in happy release. Every child, without exception, was well dressed and clean. Not one dull vacant face did I see, and not one fight.

Again my mind went back to the National School. There would have been something of extraordinary general interest if, after school, there had not been at least three fights proceeding simultaneously. The majority of the boys were without collars; many of them garbed in rags and tatters; some had never known the comfort of boots, and some the comfort of a bath. Two of them stand out vividly in my mind. He was just a loose-limbed, red-headed, bull-necked young giant who once said: "Me ole man 'ad bacon for breakfus and I "ad the rind." Later he joined the Royal Navy – 90 per cent of those boys did – and he died off the Falkland Islands. The other was fat and quiet. He was shunned by many because his clothes were verminous, but his handwriting was utterly beautiful, and, through scholarships, he reached the London University. To-day he designs warships at a particularly high salary.

But I am glad – very glad – my son has not to attend an English National School of forty years ago.

Writing a Novel

Quite a number of people think a novelist is a sort of superman; whilst others believe that writing a novel is the sort of task they could toss off with ease, given time or a quiet room in which to write.

The secret of success is not difficult to write. A study of the careers of the successful will reveal it in the one word, practice. Most established authors wrote for years before anything they wrote was honoured with printer's ink. The same study will disclose the further significant fact that remarkably few famous novelists wrote a brilliant first novel. Their progress was sure if slow, which proves that if you do not go up as a rocket you are unlikely to come down as the stick. Hard work, many disappointments, and more determination, made up the cement-hard foundations on which rest the achievement of the lords of fiction.

The joys and trials of the writer of this article are ancient signposts beside the road which it seems every literary aspirant has to travel. The first story of novel length was written at the age of fourteen. Nothing done since gave as much pleasure as the writing of that novel. To read the manuscript twenty-six years after writing it brings a smile of derision, of the youthful fire and unrestrained imagination. The days of its writing are still vivid in memory, but their golden glow has faded for ever.

Since then a dozen novels have been written, but none in the comfortable leisure of the best. One was written when boundary riding the border fence between South Australia and New South Wales, two when cooking for Queensland station hands, another when prospecting in the Flinders Range, part of yet another at the close of days spent looking for work in Adelaide, three in the south of Western Australia. They were written on work benches and tucker boxes, when the flies were a pest, or mosquitoes bit or when sandstorms raged, and when the mercury in the shade stood as high as 120 degrees. They were written because the pleasure the writing gave was transcendent. As a saint loved the martyrdom of the stake, so did I love the martyrdom of the pen.

The joy of creating banished all discomforts, and was a threefold spur to determination.

It was not, however, till twenty years of endeavour had elapsed, that a story was written of promise enough to induce a publisher to back it with his money. By this time it was beginning to be understood that, no matter how facile one's pen and how vivid one's imagination, there are as many inflexible rules covering this branch of art as there are covering all other branches of art. It matters not how gifted and determined one may be, the rules of the game must be mastered.

As someone has said, it is not what you put into a novel, but what you leave out that counts. Ambiguity is fatal, brevity the greatest of virtues. Human character must not be portrayed too closely. Real men and women are angels today and devils tomorrow; yet allow your hero to commit an evil act, or to allow your villain to perform a good deed would be to let them do something "out of character" – than which no fault of fiction is more heinous. Balance, too, is important. Chapters should end on a note of suspense, and the book must end with the climax of the story, not an anticlimax.

My tenth manuscript of a novel was the first to be sent to a publisher. Being presented in my non-copperplate script, it was returned unread. The eleventh was unlucky, being burned with the rest of my effects in a camp fire near the Queensland border fence. The twelfth effort struck oil, and the first milestone on the long road was passed when the six presentation copies of my first novel came to hand. When handling the copies in their colourful wrappers and smelling the fresh printer's ink my mind went back to early 1920, when I stood before the bookstall on Waterloo Station, London.

There I saw novels of England, Canada, Africa and America. Adventurous Canada was vividly represented by Ralph Connor, mysterious Africa by Rider Haggard, romantic America by Zane Grey, England by a dozen famous men and women. Millions have read these authors' work and through them have become familiar with the countries they represent. Australia, however, remains comparatively unknown; for, although this country has produced writers of renown, many of them have written stories of any part of the world other than their own country. It is almost the fashion that, having gained a footing on the literary ladder, the ambitious must rush to Europe.

Why? Why, indeed, when there is to be found a vast, almost virgin mine of local colour, in which adventure and romance are to be met with every day. Surely it would be a not unworthy ambition for an Australian to try to occupy a position equal to that of, say, Mr. Zane Grey. The field is open. To win such recognition should not be difficult, since there are extremely few competitors. Perseverance, plus talent, would eventually overcome the almost general indifference to novels by Australians. In this country the fact that an Australian novel has been found worthy to be published in London cuts no ice. The fact that the book has been written by an Australian automatically damns it unless the scene of the book lies outside of Australia. It is a benighted outlook that will one day fade away, and we shall come to be as proud of our writers as we are of our athletes.

The Call of the Wild

Mary – her surname does not matter – was, and is, one of those women known by every fortunate man, no matter what his station in life, no matter the kind of life he has led. This particular Mary was tall, straight, and gaunt. I saw pictures of her dressed in the fashions of long ago, and in them she was beautiful. When I first knew her she was tall and gaunt.

Her husband was killed by bolting buggy horses, and he left her with a small station and two little children. Did she rush home to mother? She did not. She carried on, nature working her face with the plastic surgery of hard labour into those fixed lines of gauntness. But she was able to make her son a doctor, and her daughter a second edition of what she once was. And what once she was, a man glimpsed when he looked into her grey eyes and felt the urge to wind his fingers among the tresses of her snow-white hair.

I blame Mary for making me incapable of drawing a wicked woman character in my novels. Try hard as I may, I never can muster sufficient hate and loathing to draw a proper villainess. Memory of Mary always intrudes.

The greatest want that your young immigrant experiences is the influence of a good woman, and he sustains that want when at the most impressionable age of his life. Which is why the Big Brother movement should be maintained and extended at all cost when the stream of immigration begins again to flow.

I had been in Australia three years when I met Mary. I worked and saved money – to spend recklessly in town or city. I lived hard both ways, and Mary tried to show me that I was getting nowhere, and would never get anywhere, along the path I was treading. When I told her of my lost dreams of a farm and a house, when I confessed to my backbonelessness, and pictured two young people fooled so superbly by immigration literature, she came to understand how it was I lived only for the day; how it was I had no ambition but to keep moving on like Jules Verne's Captain Hatteras.

I could myself see that this constant rushing about, this demanding my cheque and walking hundreds of miles before accepting the next job, certainly would not take me anywhere worthwhile; and on Mary's advice I went to Sydney with about £40, determined to get a city job, stick to it, and become a captain of industry.

Whereas, on a former visit, I had spent £198 in three weeks, this time I rigidly kept expenditure down to £4 a week. Discovering no possible hope of taking up my profession, I went to work as a warehouse clerk, and occupied my leisure with writing a novel which no publisher could be expected to accept, and paragraphs which "The Bulletin" failed to find of literary merit.

But – it was of no use. A gardener burning gum leaves in the park, Sunday visits to the Zoo to see the camels, the horse bell summoning us to meals at the boarding house in combination were too strong for me. I had tasted freedom: I craved and craved for more. The boss caught me reading Lawson's collected verse under the title of "While the Billy Boils," and began to roar. I told him with great pleasure to keep the job, walked out and caught the next train to Bourke.

From a drover's camp beside the Diamentina, I wrote to Mary and admitted my lack of staying power. I sent her the manuscript of the novel, and she replied in a ten-page letter urging me to save my money and stick to my writing. Later on she wrote again to say that she had burned the manuscript and advised me to surrender all honors to the Russians who long had raised the lurid sex novel to a fine art.

Came the war. I wrote a war book in 1916; was advised to submit it to a Sydney daily, as all war stuff was cornered by writers who foretold the end of the war to fall on the next day. I was but a common digger, and could not see the war ending the next day. In time I inquired of the Post Office about the manuscript and was curtly informed that it had been "Sunk by Enemy Action." The Germans evidently did not like the adventures of a bachelor in Cairo.

After the war, I wrote short stories for the Novel Magazine, and 300-word articles for the Daily Mail. I became confidential secretary to the head of a big ordinance depot in the south of

England – but I still heard the tinkle of horse bells; could still smell the scent of burning gum leaves; could still see the track winding across the limitless saltbush plains.

Returning to Australia, I went bush with the eagerness of a man going to his bride. During the long absence I had suffered, joyed, loved and sorrowed, but I had not lived. I know I had not lived.

I found One-Spur Dick living in a bag humpy on the river bank near Wilcannia. He was going blind. I was broke but happy. He stoked the fire as he once used to do, and I read to him paper-backed novels until I could read no longer, and he then recounted the stories in detail which I had read to him ten years previously.

Strike-a-Light George had died at Bullecourt. I bet he groused that last morning about the tucker, and I bet that he died game. In 1924 I met Jake the Hangman, and he shortened my drop by eleven inches, sorrowing at my loss of weight. I never saw Pompey George again, but I heard he rose to be a major in the Camel Corps Transport in Egypt.

The only person of the many I had known before the war, who did not welcome me back to the bush, was Mary. Mary cried – which was no welcome. Mary fed me with fresh scones and cream and jam, which was better than crying. Then she lectured me, which was not so nice. I remember her lecture because of its down-right common sense.

"This is what you have done," she said in tones both soft and kind, but which hurt me much more than had she screamed at me. "You have thrown away a profession. You have thrown away chance after chance. You are no better off today than you were sixteen years ago. In fact, you are worse off, because you are sixteen years older. You are nothing but a waster; a failure; and if you are not careful you will throw away the one talent you have left. As you are so mad about the bush, why don't you tell people outside the bush all about it? To my knowledge you have written seven worthless books. Write about the bush; write about the bush people; write about me, if you like."

So it was that I came to see I could still cling to the real Australia, and regain ambition to make something of my life.

Mary was my Big, Big Sister. Seventy-two she will be this year, and still running her station.

Just before writing this article I sat on my verandah watching the giant shadow of Mt. Dandenong creeping across the valley to Little Joe and Mt. Donna Buang. Watched the shadow reach Warburton and engulf it; watched it creep up the timbered slopes of Mt. Donna Buang. Above that mountain all day long had hung a great cloud which appeared undecided whether to evaporate or turn into an active water-dog.

The valley sank deeper and deeper into the blue shadow. Donna Buang shed its warm, purple cloak, and raised over itself the bed quilt of deep blue night. Above it, seeming to be beyond it, the cloud became a leaping flame as though the very world around Neerim South was burning as Hell is alleged to be.

And like the day which is past, life is so short and there is yet so much to see and to do. With the passage of the years, each year slips by faster. I have never done any good for myself or for anyone else, but I have learned the art of living in a hard school. It was no university education, and the syllabus does not contain the study of dead languages and dead literature. I am less interested in the travels of Ulysses than in the travels of Jake the Hangman, and much less interested in Latin than in the more modern language so easily spoken by One-Spur Dick to his mules and bullocks. Dick's language could shift ten tons across hundreds of miles of virgin country. What classical language could do that? And again, what were the achievements of Ulysses – a fool who did not know a good poker hand when he held it – compared to the achievements of Mary, aye, and of the hundreds of other Marys and Johns whose faith in the real Australia never waned, whose love for this land remained ever true?

Their great university of the wild has been my university. I thank that English doctor who caused a fool to be sent out here, and I thank God that I figuratively kicked my profession in the seat of its pants. A fine house, a beautiful car, a million or two in the bank are less than nothing when weighed in the scales against content with little things and life in the world of One-Spur Dicks, and Marys, and Irish Muldoon.

I thank God that the living personality of the bush has got its fingers dug into the roots of my soul.

The Spirit of the Bush

There is an old saying which runs: "Once you have lived beside the Darling River, to the Darling you will come back to die." We are apt to think of the past with delightful retrospection and, as our fathers did, to talk of "the good old days" – yet almost always with the sincere desire to live them again.

Our literature often mentions the spirit of the bush, but seldom with understanding, and, therefore, without appreciation of the actual fact that the Spirit of the Bush is indeed a tangible entity, swaying men and animals enslaved of its allure of greater power than that of the sea over the sailor, or of a country over an exile, a power which has to be obeyed by men, white and black, by kangaroos and emus, even the rabbit.

Why will a blackfellow, camped amid plenty, suddenly go off on a walk-about? Why will a white man abruptly demand his cheque, to carry his swag instead of spending his money on a city holiday? Why is it that kangaroos and emus will vanish in a night, fleeing from lush lands? Why do bushmen living in cities, weighted with responsibilities, sometime experience actual pain akin to nostalgia, in their ears the elfin call tugging them back to the bush?

And that, too, a parched bush, flat and hot, treeless, or supporting but stunted trees, rimmed by the mirage or dimmed by wind-driven sand.

In Melbourne one is surrounded by every physical comfort, with places of entertainment offering and money to spend. The roar of a city's traffic reminds one of childhood days. One realises the ambition of years – and yet the bush will persist in calling, calling – night and day.

The Darling . . . The sun has gone down beyond the nigh 2,000 miles long avenue of giant red gums, the western sky a scarlet sheet. On a clean sand-spit away from the ants a shallow hole has been scooped and the "nap" has been laid over the hole.

From the top of a stick thrust into the moist ground at the edge of the water a white line slants downwards to a rippleless river.

Already that line has hooked a three pound perch.

In and out of the silver edged shadows, on the water ducks paddle – large hefty black ducks heavier than Indian Runners. The light is going. A fox "quoke-quokes" while coming off the plain for a drink. Soft, distinct, musical, a horse bell methodically clangs!

Wheeler's Well . . . The burning sun has dropped behind the distant mulga. The iron of the ancient hut cracks and creaks with relief. Solitude – the nearest neighbour twenty-six miles away. The hens are going to roost. The last of the galahs are leaving the water troughs they have visited in their hundreds.

A short walk over the red-brown sand before the darkness completes the isolation.

And accompanying me, a dog and her two romping pups, the pet sheep and three tame galahs.

A station homestead . . . Daybreak, saddling a black gelding which serves as a night horse. The morning still crystal clear and cold. Jimmy roots and half bucks to warm himself before gently cantering over the river flats to the sandhill country, where some thirty working hacks expect us.

There they are! A pair of grey buggy-horses hiding behind a currant bush hoping to be missed. And Tiger, the outlaw whom only one half-caste can ride – and that not long. He shakes his head and stamps his hoofs. The moment has arrived for which he has waited all night.

Squealing and bucking he sets off for the homestead, the others following. At first a procession, then a wild race – with Jimmy the night horse, ex-stock horse, savagely pulling at the bit to get in front of Tiger. A thudding of hoofs – quicker, quicker! The air like ice pressing against blue flesh. The dust cloud hiding the leader, blurring the outlines of the field.

Direct to the stockyards does Tiger lead his following, and sometimes Jimmy and his rider are among the ruck.

The dead monotony of the bush! The soul-crushing sameness. "No thrills to be got outside a cinema or off a racecourse."

Twenty-two camels drawing a loaded table-top waggon across the flat, treeless saltbush plain, north of Broken Hill. Twenty-two camels facing a rust-coloured wall rising from horizon to zenith with incredible swiftness. Unyoke! Unharness! Quick – jump to it!

Rattling trace chains, bellows of protest at the unusual haste. Rough fingers working at buckles, lifting and dropping harness.

Chances taken with wicked, foot-striking camels to hobble all, before the wall falls on everything.

It is done. The wall is solid and fearful, its surface here sucked inwards, there puffed outwards, swaying, advancing, menacingly eating up the world. The camels swing their rumps round to meet the storm, thump to the ground, and begin placidly to chew their cud. A freshening wind, blowing towards the wall, seems to undermine its base, to make it topple forward on camels, waggon and men.

A hissing "Woof." Daylight dies, gives place to blackness of the tomb. Twenty, thirty minutes pass before the light begins to come back – the sun appearing like a dead planet, then like Australian gold. The storm passes on, is gone. No thrills?

I wonder if old Tom, and Bill the Bikeman, and Rainbow Harry are still alive and living in their petrol-tin-bag humpies on the bank of the river near Menindie. And all those other old age pensioners who lived on other river banks near other towns, near enough to fetch supplies, far enough to be in the grand old bush.

No need for them to live out there, did they not wish. And yet – where else would they live, calm and serene in old age, happy in their colourful lives, and happy, too, in the knowledge that they will die beside the old "Gutter"? Members all of the great secret society which obeys the grand master – the Spirit of the Bush.

Well, one cannot eat his cake and have it. One will undertake responsibilities, will be driven by ambition.

But how wonderful to be able to cast off the chains of the city, to be able gladly to savour that soft, alluring, plaintive call.

Sources

Going Bush: "My Life Outback Starts," *The Herald*, Melbourne, 12 January 1934, p12; "My Life Outback No 1: A Dream and the Sad Awakening," *The Advertiser*, Adelaide, 13 January 1934, p15; "Up and Down Australia No 1: Going Bush," *The West Australian*, Perth, 26 January 1934, p3.

One-Spur Dick: "My Life Outback No 2: One Spur Dick," *The Herald*, Melbourne, 13 January 1934, p24; "My Life Outback No 2: On the Road with a Mule Team," *The Advertiser*, Adelaide, 20 January 1934, p20; "Up and Down Australia No 2: Mule Driver's Offsider," *The West Australian*, Perth, 2 February 1934, p16.

Opal Gouging: "My Life Outback No 3: Opal Gouging with Big Jack – and his Cat," *The Herald*, Melbourne, 15 January 1934, p19; "My Life Outback No 3: Opal – Empress of Precious Stones," *The Advertiser*, Adelaide, 27 January 1934, p9; "Up and Down Australia No 3: Opal, Empress of Stones," *The West Australian*, Perth, 7 February 1934, p18.

Camels and a Fence: "My Life Outback No 4: Dire Tale of Goanna and Two Camels," *The Herald*, Melbourne, 16 January 1934, p17; "My Life Outback No 4: The Dog, a Goanna and Two Camels," *The Advertiser*, Adelaide, 3 February 1934, p11; "Up and Down Australia No 4: Camels and a Fence," *The West Australian,* Perth, 9 February 1934, p4.

Camels and a Scorpion: "My Old Pal, Buller," *The Herald*, Melbourne, 10 March 1934, p33; "The Real Australia (8): A Scorpion and Two Camels," *The West Australian*, Perth, 28 March 1934, p20.

The Man Who Lost Count: "Lonely Terrors of the Bush: The Man Who Lost Count!" *The Herald*, Melbourne, 25 November 1933.

The Ration Sheep: "The Sheep They Couldn't Kill," *The Herald*, Melbourne, 17 March 1934, p14; "The Real Australia (5): Lombroso and a Ration Sheep," *The West Australian*, Perth, 21 March 1934, p13.

Tramping by the Darling: "My Life Outback No 5: On the Tramp by the Darling," *The Herald*, Melbourne, 17 January 1934, p16; "My Life Outback No 5: Tramping by the Darling," *The Advertiser*, Adelaide, 10 February 1934, p11; "Up and Down Australia No 5: Tramping by the Darling," *The West Australian*, Perth, 10 February 1934, p14.

The River Pirate: "The Real Australia (9): The River Pirate," *The West Australian*, Perth, 2 April 1934, p4; "The Pirate of the Darling," *The Herald*, Melbourne, 14 April 1934, p33.

The Gentle Grafter: "The Real Australia (2): The Gentle Grafter," *The West Australian*, Perth, 6 March 1934, p20.

Kissing the Capitalists: "Kissing the Capitalists," *The Bulletin*, Sydney, 8 August 1934, pp48-49.

Wells and Water Troughs: "My Life Outback No 6: Fighting the Thirst-mad Mob," *The Herald*, Melbourne, 18 January 1934, p31; "Up and Down Australia No 6: Wells and Water Troughs," *The West Australian*, Perth, 12 February 1934, p13; "My Life Outback No 6: Frenzied Rush to Drink," *The Advertiser*, Adelaide, 17 February 1934, p11.

Crabby Tom: "My Life Outback No 7: When Crabby Tom Ran Amok," *The Herald*, Melbourne, 19 January 1934, p20; "Up and Down Australia No 7: Cooks and their Habits," *The West Australian*, Perth, 13 February 1934, p18; "My Life Outback No 7: Crabby Tom and his DTs," *The Advertiser*, 24 February 1934.

Broke in the City: "The Real Australia (1): Broke in the City," *The West Australian*, Perth, 5 March 1934, p16; "Broke in a City," *The Herald*, Melbourne, 28 April 1934, p32; "The Real Australia: Broke in a City," *The Adelaide Chronicle*, 6 June 1935, p49.

A Cure for Snakebite: "The Real Australia (4): The Antidote," *The West Australian*, Perth, 19 March 1934, p18; "A Cure for Snakebite," *The Herald*, Melbourne, 24 March 1934, p32; "The Real Australia," *The Adelaide Chronicle*, 6 June 1935, p47; "A Cure for Snakebite," *The Bony Bulletin*, No 32, May 1990, pp3-5.

Waiting for Rain: "The Real Australia (7): Trials of a Squatter," *The West Australian*, Perth, 26 March 1934, p18; "The Real Australia: How They Waited for the Rain: The Courage of One Woman," *The Herald*, Melbourne, 31 March 1934, p15; "How They Waited for the Rain," *The Bony Bulletin*, No 16, February 1986, pp7-8.

The Musical Hut: "The Melody Hut," *The Herald*, Melbourne, 3 March 1934; "The Real Australia (3): The Musical Hut," *The West Australian*, Perth, 12 March 1934, p16; "The Real Australia," *The Adelaide Chronicle*, 6 June 1935, p47; "The Melody Hut," *The Bony Bulletin*, No 18, September 1986, pp7-8,

Whitewashing a Police Station: "The Real Australia (6): Whitewashing a Police Station," *The West Australian*, Perth, 23 March 1934, p26; "Whitewashing a Police Station," *The Herald*, Melbourne, 7 April 1934, p32.

Chasing the Rainbow: "The Real Australia (12): Chasing the Rainbow," *The West Australian*, Perth, 16 April 1934, p12.

Boys into Camp: "One Digger's War No 1: How the Boys Went into Camp," *The Herald*, Melbourne, 19 April 1934, p22.

All Aboard: "One Digger's War No 2: All Aboard – and Columbo Invaded," *The Herald*, Melbourne, 20 April 1934, p22.

Ducks for Christmas Dinner: "One Digger's War: Ducks for Christmas Dinner," *The Herald*, Melbourne, 21 April 1934, p32.

Laughter and Death at Gallipoli: "One Digger's War No 4: Laughter and Death at Gallipoli," *The Herald*, Melbourne, 23 April 1934, p17.

Hammer and Tongs in the Somme: "One Digger's War No 5: When the Germans Nearly Won," *The Herald*, Melbourne, 24 April 1934, p20.

The Man Who Thought He Was Dead: "The Hummer," *The West Australian*, 30 January 1932, p2; "The Man Who Thought He Was Dead," *The Herald*, Melbourne, 28 October 1933, p32.

Pimple's Elixir: "Pimple's Elixir," The Bulletin, Sydney, 12 September 1934, pp49-50.

A Dog-proof Fence Job: "My Life Outback No 8: Sand-storm Terror in Sturt's Country," *The Herald*, Melbourne, 20 January 1934, p32; "Up and Down Australia No 8: A Dog-proof Fence Job," *The West Australian*, Perth, 14 February 1934, p6; "My Life Outback No 8: Guarding a Border Fence," *The Advertiser*, Adelaide, 3 March 1934, p9.

Fun for the Afternoon: "Fun for the Afternoon: A Tale of an Intelligent Bull in the Outback," *The Herald*, Melbourne, 28 July 1934, p33.

The Yandama Dragon: "The Yandama Dragon," *The Herald*, Melbourne, 28 December 1935, p26.

A Real Life Drama: "The Real Australia (11): Ever Backwards," *The West Australian*, Perth, 7 April 1934, p20.

The Strike Leader: "The Real Australia (10): The Strike Leader", *The West Australian*, Perth, 3 April 1934, p14.

The Man Who Laughed Last: "The Man Who Laughed Last: Old Man Angus and the Kangaroo Steak!" *The Herald*, Melbourne, 25 August 1934, p33.

Fur Fever: "My Life Outback No 9: Mad Fever of the Skin Game," *The Herald*, Melbourne, 22 January 1934, p10; "Up and Down Australia No 9: Fur Fever," *The West Australian, Perth*, 17 February 1934, p5; "My Life Outback No 9: Fever of the Skin Game," *The Advertiser*, Adelaide, 10 March 1934, p9.

THE MURCHISON MURDERS: *The Murchison Murders,* Sydney: Midget Masterpiece Publishing Co, 1934; Miami Beach, Florida: Dennis McMillan, 1987.

The Outback Changes: "The Outback Changes: What Mechanised Age Has Done," *The Herald*, Melbourne, 29 September 1934, p6.

Giving to Get: "Giving to Get: A Centenary Moral," *The Herald*, Melbourne, 18 August 1934, p6.

Chefs of the Outback: "Chefs of the Outback: The Real Test of Good Cooking," *The Herald*, Melbourne, 22 December 1934, p29.

Lords of the Track: "Lords of the Track: Sundowners I Have Met: Nicknames and Fads," *The Daily News*, Perth, 30 July 1932, p10.

The Blankets That Wouldn't 'Stay Put': "Some Outback Ghosts: The Blankets That Wouldn't 'Stay Put'," *The Herald*, Melbourne, 7 July 1934, p33.

Influenza: "When Influenza Comes to Stay: Vagaries of a Germ in Flanders Mud and Outback," *The Herald*, Melbourne, 28 May 1934, p6; *The Advertiser*, 26 May 1934; "Why This Influenza?" *The West Australian*, 23 June 1934, p5; "Please Banish Influenza," *The Adelaide Chronicle*, 31 May 1934.

Poison: "Tales of the Nonchalant Bush: Poison!" *The West Australian*, 14 April 1932; "Poison!" *The Herald*, Melbourne, 13 January 1934, p33.

Christmas Memories: "Christmas Memories," *The Daily News*, Perth, 24 December 1932.

At School: "At School," *The West Australian*, c1932.

Writing a Novel: "Writing a Novel," *The West Australian*, 26 July 1930, p6.

The Call of the Wild: "My Life Outback No 12: The Irresistible Call of the Wild," *The Herald*, Melbourne, 25 January 1934, p22; "Up and Down Australia No 12: Call of the Wild," *The West Australian*, Perth, 22 February 1934, p18.

The Spirit of the Bush: "The Lure of the Bush: Where Nature Has Her Way," *The Herald*, Melbourne, 28 October 1933, p6.

CPSIA information can be obtained
at www.ICGtesting.com
Printed in the USA
LVHW01s0020080518
576390LV00003B/282/P